**Desktop Publishing**

**for Librarians**

**on the Apple Macintosh**

# Desktop Publishing for Librarians on the Apple Macintosh

Peter Stubley

Gower

Aldershot • Brookfield USA • Hong Kong • Singapore • Sydney

© Peter Stubley 1989

All rights reserved. No part of this publication may be reproduced, stored in a retrieval system, or transmitted in any form or by any means, electronic, mechanical, photocopying, recording, or otherwise without the prior permission of Gower Publishing Company Limited.

Published by
Gower Publishing Company Limited
Gower House
Croft Road
Aldershot
Hants GU11 3HR
England

Gower Publishing Company Limited
Old Post Road
Brookfield
Vermont 05036
USA

Apple, Mac, and Macintosh are trademarks of Apple Computer Inc.

ISBN 0 566 03622 3

Printed by Watkiss Studios Ltd., Biggleswade, Beds. 7/89

For Lucy

# Contents

Figures and tables ix
Preface xi
Acknowledgements xiii

## Section 1: Background information

### 1 An introduction to DTP 3

DTP: is it really desktop publishing? – the beginnings of DTP – the alternative approaches to DTP – the drawbacks to DTP – finally – references

### 2 Hardware 13

Introduction – the Apple Macintosh range – WIMPS interface – printers – ancillary equipment – references

## Section 2: The software of DTP

It can't all be useful. Can it? 33

### 3 DTP-specific packages 35

PageMaker – Ready, Set, Go! – XPress – references

### 4 Word processing software for DTP 67

MacAuthor – FullWrite Professional – references

### 5 Graphics software — 89

Types of graphics software – graphics file formats – paint and draw programs – graphs – clip art – scanned images – references

### 6 Ancillary programs — 113

Do we have to purchase more software still? – spelling checkers – outliners – text finders – keyboard enhancers – references

## Section 3: DTP in the library

The gathering tide – references — 129

### 7 The library guide: a DTP example — 131

The library guide as the subject of DTP – format – layout – text entry – graphics – final adjustments

### 8 Library applications — 147

Current awareness bulletins – writing of books – library notices – library newsletters – CD-ROM – the right software for the job – references

### 9 The management of DTP — 171

Why DTP is different from IT – staffing considerations – costings – training – security aspects – good computer practice – good operational practice – references

## Section 4: Appendices

Appendix A  Glossary — 189
Appendix B  Software directory — 193

Index — 199

# Figures and tables

| | | |
|---|---|---|
| Figure 2.1 | The Apple Macintosh | 15 |
| Figure 2.2 | The Apple Macintosh II | 16 |
| Figure 2.3 | The WIMPS interface of the Apple Macintosh | 19 |
| Figure 2.4 | Desk accessories on the Apple Macintosh | 21 |
| Figure 2.5 | The Apple LaserWriter II | 24 |
| Figure 3.1 | Basic user interface of PageMaker | 37 |
| Figure 3.2 | Editing a style sheet in PageMaker | 42 |
| Figure 3.3 | Application of a style in PageMaker | 42 |
| Figure 3.4 | User interface of Ready, Set, Go! | 46 |
| Figure 3.5 | Treatment of A5 page in Ready, Set, Go! | 47 |
| Figure 3.6 | Built-in grids in Ready, Set, Go! | 49 |
| Figure 3.7 | Design grids in Ready, Set, Go! | 49 |
| Figure 3.8 | Style sheets in Ready, Set, Go! | 53 |
| Figure 3.9 | User interface of XPress | 56 |
| Figure 3.10 | The Text Specifications box in XPress | 59 |
| Figure 3.11 | Links displayed in XPress | 60 |
| Figure 3.12 | Character specifications in XPress | 63 |
| Figure 3.13 | Style sheet creation in XPress | 63 |
| Figure 4.1 | Page setup in MacAuthor | 69 |
| Figure 4.2 | Style sheet in MacAuthor | 71 |
| Figure 4.3 | Creation of a frame in MacAuthor | 74 |
| Figure 4.4 | Insertion of a graphic in MacAuthor | 74 |
| Figure 4.5 | Icon bar display in FullWrite | 79 |
| Figure 4.6 | Layout dialogue box in FullWrite | 80 |
| Figure 4.7 | Insert citation in FullWrite | 83 |
| Figure 4.8 | Posted note in FullWrite | 84 |
| Figure 4.9 | Drawing facility and Picture menu in FullWrite | 86 |
| Figure 5.1 | Effect of scaling on MacPaint, PICT and PostScript graphics | 93 |
| Figure 5.2 | Creation of a simple drawing in SuperPaint | 96 |

| | | |
|---|---|---|
| Figure 5.3 | Plug-in paint tools in SuperPaint 2.0 | 98 |
| Figure 5.4 | User interface of FreeHand | 99 |
| Figure 5.5 | Drawing of library counter produced in FreeHand | 101 |
| Figure 5.6 | Library notice produced in FreeHand | 102 |
| Figure 5.7 | Bar chart drawn in Cricket Graph | 103 |
| Figure 5.8 | Clip art from 'The Visual Arts' Sets One and Two | 105 |
| Figure 5.9 | Scanned image in Digital Darkroom | 108 |
| Figure 5.10 | TIFF image saved from scanner software | 109 |
| Figure 5.11 | Second TIFF image saved from scanner software | 110 |
| Figure 5.12 | Composite image created in Digital Darkroom | 110 |
| | | |
| Table 5.1 | File sizes of scanned image in different formats | 95 |
| | | |
| Figure 6.1 | Analysis window in Spelling Coach | 115 |
| Figure 6.2 | Spelling replacement in Spelling Coach and MacAuthor | 115 |
| Figure 6.3 | Outline created in Acta | 118 |
| Figure 6.4 | Start of text search using Gofer | 121 |
| Figure 6.5 | Results of text search using Gofer | 121 |
| Figure 6.6 | QuicKeys window showing 'mousies' options | 123 |
| Figure 6.7 | Macro sequence created in QuicKeys | 123 |
| | | |
| Figure 7.1 | Variations of page size available with PageMaker | 133 |
| Figure 7.2 | The creation of columns in PageMaker | 135 |
| Figure 7.3 | The selection of type styles in PageMaker | 136 |
| Figure 7.4 | Page view and the toolbox in PageMaker | 137 |
| Figure 7.5 | Completed master pages in PageMaker | 138 |
| Figure 7.6 | Place command in PageMaker | 140 |
| Figure 7.7 | Text wrap around graphic in PageMaker | 142 |
| Figure 7.8 | Imported text and graphic before final adjustment | 143 |
| Figure 7.9 | Separation of library guide text into two stories | 144 |
| Figure 7.10 | Library guide created in PageMaker | 145/6 |
| | | |
| Figure 8.1 | Publishing a folder using TOPS | 149 |
| Figure 8.2 | Copying a WordStar file to a Macintosh using TOPS | 151 |
| Figure 8.3 | Translating WordStar to MacWrite using TOPS | 151 |
| Figure 8.4 | Librarianship current awareness bulletin in WordStar | 152 |
| Figure 8.5 | Librarianship current awareness bulletin in PageMaker | 153 |
| Figure 8.6 | Current awareness outline in Acta | 155 |
| Figure 8.7 | Application of MacAuthor II styles to Acta outline | 156 |
| Figure 8.8 | Bibliography note in FullWrite | 161 |
| Figure 8.9 | Notice of meeting created in MacAuthor | 163 |
| Figure 8.10 | Help screen from MacSpirs | 165 |
| Figure 8.11 | Display of record from ERIC search on CD-ROM | 167 |
| Figure 8.12 | Control over citation elements in ERIC on CD-ROM | 167 |
| | | |
| Table 8.1 | Matching software to library applications | 169 |
| | | |
| Table 9.1 | Cost per page of output from a laser printer | 178 |

# Preface

This book was conceived as a practical guide to desktop publishing (DTP) for librarians. It was the intention to provide, above all, a critical and moderately unbiased guide to the software together with suggestions for its use in libraries. In doing this the bias of the book is different from many of the many texts already published on DTP which concentrate on the background to the technology and simple outlines of packages.

DTP has expanded rapidly in a short time. From the amateurish connotations at its beginnings, it is now used extensively, if the literature is to be believed, in numerous businesses, and parts of the technology are even considered seriously by some newspapers. This book concentrates on 'non-professional' DTP – high quality single colour (i.e. black on white) documents of all types output to a laser printer – for the simple reason that most libraries will be unable to afford much else. The main area of exclusion is that of colour, for though the display technology is with us and most software can now handle colour, economic colour laser printing via DTP is still some years away.

One or two other areas have also been intentionally excluded. As explained in chapter 1, DTP is more than committing words to paper and sending them to a laser printer. It also involves layout and typographical know-how, and graphics skills. In at least two of these areas others are more qualified to write than the present author and a number of excellent cited works will provide good background reading for anyone needing jumping off points. As far as graphics skills are concerned, it is emphasised throughout that these cannot be picked up like a book from a shelf, and most librarians will find that this aspect is better left to qualified designers and artists.

It will be seen from the title that the book concentrates on DTP on the Apple Macintosh. DTP software is, of course, now available for most types of personal computer but for many users the Macintosh implementations remain the most sophisticated, consistent, and easy to use. They also provide an excellent antidote for those librarians allergic to unhelpful DOS commands. As a result, and coupled with the relative ease of transferring files, there are already a number of Macintosh DTP installations in libraries that were formally hotbeds of MS-DOS.

In accordance with the aims of the book, after a brief introduction to DTP and a description of the hardware on which it runs, the rest of the work comprises two substantial sections that concentrate on a description of specific software packages and the use of DTP in libraries. Section 2 on software covers not only DTP-specific packages, but in addition, word processors that incorporate some DTP features, graphics packages and ancillary programs. The number of software packages is now so great that no attempt has been made to provide a comprehensive coverage, although the three main DTP packages that run on the Macintosh form the whole of chapter 3. The latest versions of all the software packages have been discussed at the time of writing, but as new revisions appear with amazing regularity some parts of the book will be quickly outdated. In spite of this, and as most revisions are closely based on previous versions, it is hoped that the book will have value in introducing librarians to this varied software. Information on revisions can be obtained from the Macintosh literature or directly from the companies listed in Appendix A.

Section 3 deals with DTP in the library. Beginning with chapter 7 a very specific and detailed example of the technology is presented in the production of a two page library guide. Chapter 8 describes a range of other examples including two ways of producing a current awareness bulletin. Finally, it must be recognised that while DTP can cause a significant improvement in the appearance of all library publications, the full benefits will only be seen if the technology is managed correctly. Chapter 9 deals with this aspect in some detail.

It is hoped that the book will be of use to all librarians whether or not they have previous experience of operating microcomputers. The output from DTP tends to attract even those librarians who have had no previous interest in information technology and for this reason it is an application that will see much growth in libraries over the next few years. If the book encourages more librarians to be attracted to DTP and to gain pleasure from it, then it will have done its job.

Peter Stubley, March 1989.

# Acknowledgements

This book arose out of an enthusiasm for using DTP and associated software on the Apple Macintosh and its writing has been helped by others with similar enthusiasm. Most particularly, Keith Cox of Apple Centre (West Midlands) has provided access to software suppliers who would otherwise have presented me with closed doors. (In spite of Keith's help some still did.) He has also provided advice and assistance at various crucial times throughout the whole project and did more than your average friendly Apple dealer was ever supposed to do.

A book that devotes half of its length to a description of software has to rely to a large extent on manufacturers, distributors and suppliers for access to the packages. So it was in this case and assistance was provided by: Lesley Affrossman, formerly of TMC; Keith Fraser, formerly of Letraset UK; Elliot Kahan of Heyden and Son; Brian Liddle of Aldus UK; and Paddy McManus of Ashton-Tate UK. Mike Glover of Icon Technology and Mark Lewis of MacLine deserve special mention for being founts (not fonts) of Macintosh knowledge whatever the time of day.

Four friends – Mary Auckland, Malcolm Kendall, Steve Smith and Bill Tuck – laboured over typescripts and offered constructive advice on layout and content. It cannot be said that this was always taken. Bill was in on discussions at an early stage and at various points it looked as if we would be collaborating on a different kind of DTP book. In the event, this was not to be. Sue McNaughton of Gower was, as usual, generally in the right place at the right time.

Special mention must go to Margaret who yet again had to forego lots of potentially interesting things but still provided the love and the excellent cups of tea.

As the book is about DTP I will end with the obligatory few lines in the hope that someone might be interested in how it was done. The whole book was written and simultaneously laid out in MacAuthor, on a Macintosh Plus, with the exception of pages 109–110 and 145–146. The first two of these contain scanned images which cannot be imported into MacAuthor and so they were created in PageMaker. Pages 145–146 were intended to show the hypothetical library guide as output by PageMaker and this is what they do – inclusive of crop marks and deliberately excluding page numbers. Furthermore, the pages have been output on an Apple LaserWriter IINT. Camera ready copy was printed on a Linotronic 300 in the Department of Visual Communications at Birmingham Institute of Art and Design (Birmingham Polytechnic) with excellent support from David Murray.

Peter Stubley, March 1989.

# Section 1

# Background information

# 1     An introduction to DTP

**DTP: Is it really desktop publishing?**

It is sometimes hard to believe that desktop publishing (DTP) has been around for only three-and-a-half years. In that time the technology has been used to sell thousands of computers and software packages, set-up new companies, start new newspapers and magazines, and such has been the marketing drive that it is unlikely that anyone interested in personal computers has not come across the term.

At its simplest level DTP is the preparation of high quality formatted output from a laser printer. The uses that have attracted most attention have been documents with moderate-to-high circulation like newsletters and company brochures but there is no reason why smaller publications should not come under the DTP banner. Anything that benefits from a better appearance can be produced using the technology but herein lies the ambiguity underlying the name. This equivocation is probably deliberate for it implies a power readily available to anyone with a personal computer and the relevant software: that of publishing and spreading ideas around to as many people as possible and to whoever will listen. As Seybold says (page xii): 'Publishing is, after all, the very heart and soul of civilization itself. One needn't belabor this point: without the publishing process we would still be living in the dark ages'. Who would not want to take advantage of this opportunity? (certainly not the present author).

But the direct output from a DTP system constitutes only publishable, not published, material. It may be 'near-typeset quality' and combine text with pretty or persuasive illustrations but, in the majority of cases, there still remains a great deal of work to be done before it is released to the public. Considerations will include the type of binding; the type and design of cover; the methods of production of double-sided sheets; what style and what degree of marketing is to be used; the length of the print run and how to achieve this; and the method of distribution. For these reasons various commentators have coined their own alternative term. Tuck, for example, states that: 'As currently practised, it is not really about publishing, or even desktops, but about using microcomputers to improve the quality and lower the costs of printing ... DIY printing is therefore closer to the mark'.

For long runs of material aimed at a wide audience DTP is not yet, if it ever becomes, anything like a viable alternative to the methods offered by traditional publishing houses. But what it can do, even in this context, is shift some of the onus of publication from the publisher to the individual author by enabling authors to provide high quality camera-ready copy. This should result in a significant improvement in the appearance of academic works in particular, where camera-ready copy had until recently meant something rather different. Whether the author actually wants the extra responsibility that this entails is another thing, although there are obvious advantages in exercising greater control over layout. Time savings over the whole publication cycle are also possible though whether these benefit the author or the publisher will depend on individual circumstances.

Tuck's 'DIY printing' is probably closer to actuality for most companies and for library applications of DTP. The technology gives an easy way of producing the usual range of guides, lists, bibliographies, newsletters, signs, forms, reports, and notices, all at vastly improved quality when compared with the techniques previously to hand. With the exception of small print runs (say up to ten copies for occasional notices) DTP will be used to produce a single master from which multiple copies are run off as required. Generally this will be achieved by the use of a photocopier or enlisting the services of a local reprographic unit.

## The beginnings of DTP

The concept of desktop publishing originated from a convergence of advances in microcomputer and printer technologies and could not have occurred without these simultaneous developments.

*Apple Macintosh*

On the computer side both hardware and software advances were involved. One of the main reasons for Apple being the current market leader in desktop publishing was the introduction of the Macintosh microcomputer in 1984 although it was not until the more powerful Macintosh Plus was introduced in 1986 that the full implications of what was possible was appreciated. However, even at the time of the Macintosh's introduction the foundations for DTP had been laid by the ability to combine text and graphics in a document using the packages MacPaint and MacWrite, something not previously achievable on a personal computer. The Macintosh is described on pages 13–18.

*PageMaker*  In the light of the success of DTP in general and this package in particular it is interesting to return to at least one of the early reviews of the product. Bright, after using a pre-release version of PageMaker wrote: 'It's not often that you receive a piece of software which is totally different from anything you've seen before'. In seeking to point out terms of reference for the reader he went on to state that 'it isn't a spreadsheet, it isn't a database, it isn't even a word processor'. The images of Superman that come to mind from such a description would perhaps not be entirely wrong. This contrasts with the current position when there are at least three mid-priced DTP packages for the Macintosh and many others available to run on different hardware. PageMaker is described in detail on pages 35–44.

*Apple LaserWriter*  In spite of the novelty and sophistication of the software, DTP would not have been a viable and marketable concept without the advent of the laser printer. Until the appearance of this piece of equipment microcomputer users were limited to dot matrix printers with their admittedly ever-improving 'near-letter quality' output and the far more expensive but electric-typewriter quality daisy-wheel printers. With Apple's ImageWriter, dot matrix printers were for the first time able to represent any screen mixture of different type styles and graphics but the output in some cases was rough to say the least. The Apple LaserWriter went a number of stages further with its ability to produce what at the time of its introduction appeared to many people to be near-typeset quality. At a printing resolution of 300 dots per inch the quality is far in excess of that obtainable with other printer types but close inspection shows some poorly formed characters, certainly when compared with the output from imagesetters such as the Linotronic 300 which operates up to a maximum resolution of 2540 dots per inch. In spite of this the laser printer is suitable for a wide range of jobs and once one has been used it is difficult to go back to working with more conventional output. The main drawback to their more widespread use is their cost and when the Apple machine was introduced in 1985 at a price of £6,995 its generalised application appeared out of the question. Progress with the technology since then, together with the greater volume of sales and increased competition, has led to continually falling prices until machines with a better specification than the original are now available for less than half the price.

## The alternative approaches to DTP

What DTP offers the user is the ability to organise a document in a visual way, by adjusting dimensions here and there and by changing the relative position of objects until a satisfactory layout is achieved. Once the screen version is acceptable it can be output to a page printer for the production of masters or for proofing. Before these easy-to-use packages were available, the minicomputer systems used to prepare text for typesetters utilised embedded codes to denote formatting characteristics to be applied throughout a document. The codes – collectively known as the markup language – act as instructions for the typesetting program and some of these languages have now been transferred for operation on personal computers. The most widely known is probably T<sub>E</sub>X for which there are two implementations on the Macintosh, but others include JustText, also for the Macintosh (see Lin), and the UNIX-based nroff and troff (see Richey). A good introduction to the capabilities of type encoding programs is provided by Brown.

Type encoding programs have their supporters, particularly among users with long familiarity of typesetting equipment, and they apparently provide greater control over typographical effects than is presently possible with DTP software. However, by their very nature they will remain the province of the enthusiast. It appears unlikely that they will ever find widespread use in a library where staff just do not have the time to spend learning a new programming language that offers only minor benefits. It remains to be seen whether DTP packages will approach the close control permitted with embedded code programs but, for the most part, librarians will live with the easy-to-use alternatives. Lu (1988, page 209) hits the nail firmly on the head when he says: '... although these markup languages work, they are the antithesis of the Macintosh. Why live with embedded commands when you can create completed pages on the Mac and send them directly to a PostScript typesetter'. For this reason, type encoding programs form no further part of this book.

In terms of 'real' DTP, the early idea of a page make-up program was that graphics and text were created independently and then brought together to produce a document in the required final layout. Although this concept still persists, and most people using desktop publishing software will first compose large chunks of text on a word processor, there has been a move to incorporate a number of the better attributes of word processors into some of the packages. The best example of this so far is to be found in Quark XPress discussed on pages 55–65. An alternative move has come from the other direction, from the producers of word processors who are including several of the features of page layout programs into their products. The package that pioneered the use of sophisticated layout features in a word processor was MacAuthor from Icon Technology and this is discussed on pages 67–76.

There is some feeling that integrated packages combining word processing and DTP offer the worst of both worlds but the weight of evidence to support this view is not great and, in any case, is based on current technology. In a few years time, when powerful processors are more generally available and the software has been re-written to take full advantage of the increases in speed, there will be no reason for not incorporating full DTP facilities into word processors. It should be possible to do this in such a way that DTP does not interfere with basic word processing operations but can still be called up and overlaid on the text by those users who require the facility. When this happens DTP might disappear as a separate entity and simply become subsumed into the umbrella term of word processing.

**The Drawbacks to DTP or why it's not all plain sailing**

Each of the chapters on the library applications of DTP – chapters 7 and 8 – not only details the way the technology is used but also points out the advantages of the new approach and, particularly, the potential drawbacks. This latter is considered to be especially important in an area that has been subject to such intense marketing hyperbole. Anyone who has used DTP software knows that it is not as straightforward as the advertising men suggest and that the promised pot of gold at the end of the rainbow rarely materialises. Certainly it doesn't appear without a fair degree of serious training, serious swearing and, possibly, even the serious studying of manuals.

There are two factors in particular that are unconnected with the software and independent of the application but that are vitally important for anyone undertaking serious DTP work: graphics and layout. Neither of these are given sufficient emphasis by the software suppliers and it seems to be assumed either that talents in both these directions are innate or that they are easy enough to be picked up as you go along. It should never be forgotten that both areas require professional expertise, skill and talent.

*Graphics*

Graphics is one of those areas that nowadays seems to be easily available to anyone with the money to purchase the packages described in chapter 5. The prevailing view appears to be that we can all become artists and illustrate our publications and documents to professional standards. While there is a grain of truth in this we must be aware of our limitations in this area and be willing to bring in outside help as necessary. We train ourselves and our staff to be aware of our limitations in our own profession – when dealing with library users – and we should follow this through into unfamiliar territory, especially if the going gets rough. Library publications are too important to be damaged by the amateurish illustrations that some users produce with graphics software.

*Layout*  Layout is treated a little more seriously by some companies who supply booklets on page design with their software package or even a set of prepared templates. However, layout is a little bit like dancing; it is alright in theory to read books on the subject and obtain a reasonable idea of what is required but it is much better working closely with someone with experience to ensure you don't put a foot (or at least too many feet) wrong. The booklets supplied with PageMaker and Ready, Set, Go! both provide sound advice, and anyone following this intelligently will make a good stab at page layout. However, anyone planning a serious involvement in newsletter or book design should discuss alternatives with professionals before going too far, and at the very least they should consult the excellent books by Miles, and Pyle and Harrington.

*Typographical points*  A fundamental part of any printed communication is the typographic style and this is a further factor which is unlikely to be fully appreciated from 'reading around the subject'. Typography is one of those aspects that is assimilated unconsciously but that otherwise passes by largely unnoticed, even though it forms so much of our daily lives. Even people who have a great deal of word processing experience have little awareness of different type faces, largely because with the technology up to the advent of DTP there was little or no choice. DTP, and especially the Macintosh, changed all that by offering as many different typefaces as users could afford and had the disc space to store.

Unfortunately, with this great power, as in so many cases, came abuse. In an effort to impress the reader by using as many typefaces and type styles as possible some publications lost all sense of cohesion. One of the worst examples was the way numerous notices incorporated shadow style, probably because it had been used so rarely (through good taste?) up to that point. A telling paragraph from Lu (1985, page 235) is worth repeating:

'Please use fonts with care. Don't make all your correspondence look like kidnapper's ransom notes; don't commit crimes against typography. Look at well-designed books and magazines and note how few fonts and typestyles they use.

**The only use for the San Francisco font is as an example of bad taste.**'

This is all very well, but how does the librarian coming to DTP for the first time decide which of the multitude of type faces and sizes to use? One obvious way is to consult a range of books and follow the most appropriate examples, but for the unpracticed eye it is not easy to identify the faces. In most cases the old standbys such as Times and Helvetica will be adequate but if the publication is being prepared for external consumption – such as a book – seek advice from the publisher. As more users get to grips with DTP so it is becoming common to indicate the type specifications used and it will accordingly become easier to choose the correct ones for the job.

*Font or fount?*

It is not only in the area of typefaces that the newcomer to DTP can experience problems for familiarity has to be gained, to at least a small extent, with the special terminology of printing. Furthermore, there are minor but important differences between British and American usage and spelling. The main spelling difference lies between the American 'font' and the British 'fount', both strictly meaning a complete set of type of one style and size. As much of the literature of DTP has originated from the US and most British users have become used to the American spelling, it is this that has been used throughout this book. However, it is worth pointing out that 'font' is still loosely used as a reference to a typeface which further complicates the matter.

*Dashes and rules*

Other typographical difficulties can occur with the different types of dash available to printers – the hyphen, the en rule, and the em rule. For text produced on a typewriter it is common for the hyphen to be used irrespective of context and in some cases for two hyphens to be used to designate the longer en rule. In British practice the en rule is particularly important for it is used to designate parenthetical phrases and ranges and, especially, the pagination of bibliographical entries. For details on the precise usage reference should be made to Butcher, pages 106–107. Again, US practice differs for they refer to dashes rather than rules, and also favour the even longer em dash for parentheses and ranges. A browse through the Desktop Publishing Bible by the Waite Group and the book by Seybold will indicate the American uses of the em dash.

*Spaces*

Similarly, a range of spaces is available on typesetting systems. The em space in particular can be used to create a standard indent for the first line of paragraphs. In addition, adjustments can be made to inter-letter spacing so that the whole is easier to read and more aesthetically pleasing, particularly where large type sizes are being used. Where this occurs between specific letter pairs it is known as kerning and is useful in reducing space between two characters, by fractionally overlapping them. A variant, tracking, permits the overall white space to be uniformly adjusted throughout a selected section of a document. For further information on kerning see McCunn and for examples of tracking refer to Seybold (page 88).

It is also important that white space is used to good effect throughout any library publication – the margins surrounding text should help to relax rather than irritate the reader, and the space separating text and illustrations, and titles from their illustrations, should be large enough to ensure that one does not merge into the other. Careful attention to these factors can immeasurably improve the appearance of a document and will ensure that the DTP system is used to its full potential.

The final typographical point is the point. This is the commonly used printers unit of measure with 72 points to the inch. Whether newcomers steadfastly refuse to work in this unit or not they will still come into contact with points for all packages specify their type sizes in this way. A related unit, the pica, is equal to 12 points.

**Finally**

It may be that DTP is, if not in the descendancy then at least yesterday's hype, for the next technological miracle to make businesses part with money is said to be desktop presentations. It is unfair to describe this wonder in a sentence but it basically comprises the preparation of slides and overhead transparencies on a personal computer. In an excellent piece of debunking (of media terminology, corporate man and probably one or two other things as well) Bywater provides all that most people would want to know on the subject, in addition to cheekily pointing out that it uses the same abbreviation as DTP. For the purposes of this book DTP always means desktop publishing. In these circumstances the sooner DTP loses its hype status and is recognised as important (essential?) as spreadsheets and word processing the better it will be for all serious users.

**References**

Bright, P. PageMaker and LaserWriter. *Personal Computer World*, vol. 8, no. 10, October 1985, pp. 166–171.

Brown, M. About type encoding programs. **In**: The Waite Group. *Desktop publishing Bible*. Sams, Indianapolis, 1987. ISBN 0 672 22524 7, pp. 321–339.

Butcher, J. *Copy-editing: the Cambridge handbook*, Second edition. Cambridge University Press, 1981. ISBN 0 521 25638 0.

Bywater, M. Shut down. *MacUser*, no. 32, February 1989, pp. 130.

Lin, P. JustText. **In** The Waite Group. *Desktop publishing Bible*. Sams, Indianapolis, 1987. ISBN 0 672 22524 7, pp. 369–380.

Lu, C. *The Apple Macintosh book*, 2nd edition. Microsoft Press, Bellvue, Washington, 1985. ISBN 0 914845 66 7.

Lu, C. *The Apple Macintosh book*, 3rd edition. Microsoft Press, Redmond, Washington, 1988. ISBN 1 55615 110 1.

McCunn, D. Features of conventional typesetting systems. **In** The Waite Group. *Desktop publishing Bible*. Sams, Indianapolis, 1987. ISBN 0 672 22524 7, pp. 31–51.

Miles, J. *Design for desktop publishing: a guide to layout and typography on the personal computer*. London, Gordon Fraser, 1987. ISBN 0 86092 097 6.

Pyle, J. and Harrington, S. *Making leaflets work: the librarian's guide to effective publicity*. Sheffield, Publicity and Public Relations Group of the Library Association, 1988. ISBN 095140430X.

Richey, S. UNIX and its text processing tools. **In** The Waite Group. *Desktop publishing Bible*. Sams, Indianapolis, 1987. ISBN 0 672 22524 7, pp. 225–238.

Seybold, J. and Dressler, F. *Publishing from the desktop*. London, Bantam Books, 1987. ISBN 0 533 34401 3.

Tuck, W. Desktop publishing: what is it and what it can do for you. *Aslib Proceedings*, vol. 41, no. 1, January, 1989, pp. 29–37.

The Waite Group. *Desktop publishing Bible*. Sams, Indianapolis, 1987. ISBN 0 672 22524 7.

# 2    Hardware

**Introduction**

The hardware for DTP falls into three categories: the microcomputer on which the software runs; printers; and any ancillary equipment, which may not be absolutely necessary but which makes life easier. In this chapter the various models that have appeared in the Apple Macintosh range over the years are described in broad terms together with an outline of the Macintosh user interface. The use of laser printers and the importance of PostScript are covered in the following section and the chapter concludes with a discussion of ancillaries including such things as hard discs, big screens and scanners.

Numerous books have already appeared on the operation of the various Macintosh models and for this reason the descriptions here are restricted to a minimum. Anyone requiring more detailed information than appears below or in the Apple manuals is advised to consult in particular the excellent books by Coleman and Naiman, and Lu.

It is also not the job of the present work to make comparisons, in either direction, between the Apple Macintosh and the IBM PC or PS/2. Again, several of these already exist in other sources. In one such comparison, Margolis included the following comment which is particularly relevant in the present circumstances: 'The Macintosh's user environment can be compared to the quiet structure of a library, while the PC's is more like the frenetic interaction of a commodities exchange pit'. This is not of course to say that Macintoshes should be used beyond question in libraries; only to hint at it.

**The Apple Macintosh range**

The Apple Macintosh appeared in January 1984 to a mix of generally favourable to ecstatic reviews. It was so different from virtually anything else on the market, and it offered technology similar to that available on Apple's former Lisa machine at a more affordable price, that its success seemed assured. In retrospect it is apparent that some of the hyperbole and enthusiasm (see, for example, Scales, and Meakin) was a little misplaced although maybe this machine really has changed the face of personal computing.

The first machine to become available was simply called the Macintosh – figure 2.1, without keyboard[1] – and comprised a 16-bit Motorola 68000 processor, 128k (kilobytes) of RAM (random access memory) and 64k of ROM (read only memory) all enclosed in a single small box with small screen and single 400k floppy disc drive. A full preview of this machine was provided by Williams. At a time when most computer manufacturers have moved over to 3.5 inch floppy discs it should be remembered that in 1984, of the major computers, only the Hewlett-Packard HP 150 and the Macintosh used this size of drive. As Williams pointed out (page 54): 'the Macintosh will secure the place of the Sony 3.5-inch disk as the magnetic medium of choice for the next generation of personal computers'.

Many of the complaints about the early Macintosh centred around it being a closed system, allowing no expansion through the use of the add-on cards that had been common in the Apple II series. However, any owner of infinitely expandable computers having limited means (i.e. librarians) will know the frustrations of hardware incompatibility and the inability to run all available software packages. By making the Macintosh a closed box, Apple forced software developers to conform, by and large, to the new interface instead of going away and developing something of their own. The result is that most Macintosh programs have a similar look and feel and users can swiftly get to grips with new software with only a short learning curve and with no additional expense (although some cynics would say that Apple charges a high enough price for its basic machines anyway). The other advantage is that there is great compatibility between applications and consequently data can be interchanged readily.

In spite of its initial enthusiastic reception, the Macintosh was for a long time considered a toy by much of the 'serious' computing and business community, partly because of its small size and the size of its screen, and partly because of its lack of power. Also, as with any new computer it took time before software companies began writing serious applications for the machine and this was the basis of further criticism. An attempt

---

[1]Figures 2.1, 2.2 and 2.5 are all images taken from 'The Visual Arts' – see Chapter 5, page 104.

**Figure 2.1 The Apple Macintosh**

was made to remove some of these limitations by increasing memory to 512k, but neither this so called 'Fat Mac' or the earlier machine would have been suitable for DTP if it had existed at the time. It was not until the arrival of the Macintosh Plus that the machine began to be taken seriously.

The Macintosh Plus came with three major advantages over its predecessors: 1 megabyte of RAM as standard (with ROM increased to 128k), one 800k disc drive (twice the size of the earlier models), and a SCSI (Small Computer Systems Interface) port. This latter for the first time made it easy to add on hard discs with acceptable transfer rates and other peripherals such as scanners. The machine also appeared at the time when Aldus began to seriously market PageMaker, and much of the initial advertising impressed on businessmen the importance of DTP through the combined efforts of PageMaker and the Macintosh Plus. A typical review on the appearance of the Macintosh Plus was that written by Walker.

One of the main reasons for the Macintosh proving so suitable for DTP was the bit-mapped high-resolution screen which granted relief from the tyranny of the 80 column display for the first time in a home computer. However, the bit-mapped screen did more than this; it permitted the facility of representing characters in any font and type style and the ability to intersperse graphics and text anywhere on the screen page. Coupled with the extremely easy to use interface and using a limited combination of software packages that by today's standards look rather primitive it was possible for the first time to produce a text document featuring diagrams without the familiar manual cut and paste routines.

Following months, if not years, of speculation Apple unveiled their new upgraded Macintosh, the Macintosh II, early in 1987. At the same time the 'expandable Plus' – the Macintosh SE was announced. This showed a further increase, if not in power then in storage, by being available in a version with an integral 20 megabyte hard disc as well as the 800k floppy drive. Towards the end of 1988 the SE was upgraded to 2 megabytes of RAM with a 40 megabyte hard disc, and both this and the original SE became virtually the standard Macintosh computers for small DTP installations.

But it was the Macintosh II – figure 2.2 – that caused the most interest when it appeared, for here was a full 32-bit microcomputer (Motorola 68020 chip with a 68881 floating point co-processor), admittedly with price to match, that supported colour and was expandable with six slots and up to 8 megabytes of memory. The full specification and description of the computer appeared from Williams and Thompson. The six NuBus slots, by allowing the addition of coprocessor, local area network and video cards, enabled users to produce hardware configurations to suit their own requirements and in this way the Macintosh II has gradually established itself in a wide variety of serious professional applications such as computer-aided design. As far as 'basic' DTP is concerned the Macintosh II offers, above all, an increase in speed over earlier models. When DTP requirements start to expand to incorporate scanned images the Macintosh II becomes virtually essential with its ability to connect grey scale monitors, larger capacity hard discs, and take RAM up to 8 megabytes.

**Figure 2.2 The Apple Macintosh II**

The most recent hardware from Apple has increased the power of the Macintosh still further by introducing the Motorola 68030 processor into both the Macintosh II range (to produce the IIx) and, perhaps more importantly, into the 'traditional' desktop design. The Macintosh SE/30 appeared in January 1989 to favourable reviews. As Swarbrick explains, the 68030 integrates the functions previously carried out by a combination of the 68020 used in the Macintosh II and the 68851 Paged Memory Management Unit. As such the 68030 chip should provide a sounder base from which to provide true multi-tasking in the Macintosh. The machine comes in two configurations with 2 or 4 megabytes of RAM, both with 40 megabyte internal hard discs. Perhaps most important of all is the inclusion of a floppy disc drive (in this machine and the IIx) that will read 720k and 1.44 megabyte MS-DOS discs in addition to standard Macintosh floppies. A similar configuration appeared two months later with the announcement of the IIcx, a slimmed down version of the Macintosh II with a smaller footprint and just three NuBus expansion slots. For the next generation of DTP software (and other applications) that will require greater power to run effectively these are likely to prove the machines to go for.

*Use of fonts*

The Macintosh uses two types of font: one for screen display and the other for printing. All the screen fonts are held in a 'System folder' on the hard disc and from here they are readily accessible to the majority of Macintosh software packages: separate fonts do not have to be loaded for use in specific programs. The screen fonts are generated using QuickDraw, the internal drawing routines of the Macintosh and for most purposes they are a good representation of the fonts actually printed. However, as the resolution of the screen is approximately a quarter of that of the LaserWriter, some definition of characters is lost. More importantly, styles such as italic are machine-generated and decidedly do not represent their printed counterparts, making it difficult to decipher the spaces between italic and non-italic words. As the Apple dot matrix printer, the ImageWriter, prints a representation from the screen it duplicates this idiosyncrasy and accordingly is not suitable for preparing copy for proof reading. To overcome the drawback of the limited screen display PostScript versions of screen fonts are available but are not widely used.

All PostScript printers come with a number of typeface families built into the printer ROM. These are stored as outlines – with separate outlines for regular, bold, italic, and bold italic styles – from which bit maps are created whenever the fonts are to be used by the printer. Fonts not built into the printer can be purchased from third party suppliers, stored on hard disc, and downloaded at the time of printing. Where a screen font has been used in a document and a downloadable PostScript font is not available, a bit map is created from the screen font and used by the printer.

*MultiFinder*

At the time of writing true multitasking is not available on the Macintosh although definite steps are being taken in that direction. What is around is a pseudo multitasking system known as MultiFinder which lets more than one program co-exist in memory and a limited number of background tasks to be undertaken. For some DTP operations MultiFinder is ideal for it permits the immediate swapping between programs that is a boon when incorporating or modifying graphics. Its main disadvantage is that it requires at least 2 megabytes of memory to run two medium sized applications and so users of older Macintoshes are either left out in the cold or have no option but to purchase more, expensive, memory. Furthermore, some commentators, while being smitten with this technique when it first appeared, have since become disenchanted and have resorted to other means to get the job done. For example, Hewson uses a combination of QuicKeys and other programs to move between software packages.

*RAM considerations*

Throughout 1988 the demand for add-on memory for Macintoshes increased greatly, fuelled largely by the potential of MultiFinder. Though this is likely to continue for owners of older machines, the trend on the part of Apple seems to be to ship computers with RAM greater than the 1 megabyte of the original Plus and SE. While it is difficult to see the potential of a machine when moving into a new area of endeavour, librarians should purchase the Macintosh with the largest RAM they can afford, within reason. In a year or two 2 megabytes will be considered standard (a pretty low standard) and 4 megabytes or more will required to handle the increased demands on the system.

**WIMPS interface**

One of the most impressive, infuriating or interesting features of the early Macintoshes (depending on your point of view) was the now familiar visual interface consisting of mouse and pull down menus. Though the WIMPS interface – Windows, Icons, Mouse, Pull down menus – was not developed by Apple it is now virtually synonymous with the Macintosh, in spite of other well publicised attempts to reproduce it. The basic system probably needs little introduction, being familiar to most computer users, but an outline of its operation is provided below for those who may be coming to the Macintosh and DTP for the first time. Figure 2.3 indicates some aspects of the WIMPS interface on the Macintosh.

The screen obtained on switching on the Macintosh and to which one returns between programs is known as the desktop,

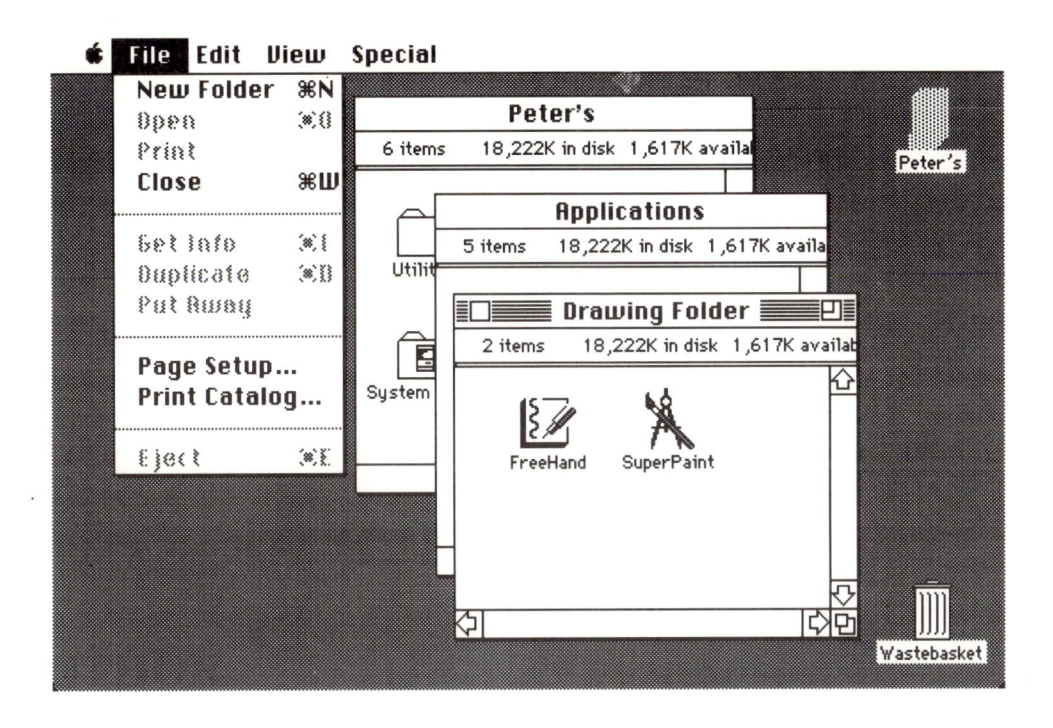

**Figure 2.3 The WIMPS interface of the Apple Macintosh**

no doubt because it is dull, grey and boring and can easily become cluttered with rubbish like most wooden ones. Files and programs appear on the desktop in **windows**, areas that are shaded white in contrast to the desktop and which can be manipulated in a number of ways: they can be moved to any position on screen; adjusted in size – to fill the entire screen if required; made to overlap other windows; and closed so that their contents are not immediately visible.

The contents of windows can be viewed in a variety of ways: by name; by date; and by **icon**. The icon is a small pictorial representation of a file, program or disc, those for programs having been created by the program developers and those for files or representing discs being part of the standard Macintosh visual interface. The Macintosh uses a file maintenance system known as HFS – hierarchical file system – which enables folders to be built up and nested one inside another so that like files can be kept with like – a bit like a classification scheme. Using icons for these folders it is easy to transfer files and maintain a good visual impression of where they are.

Much of the manipulation of windows is achieved through the use of a pointer which is moved about the screen by moving a plastic **mouse** on the work surface in the same general direction. The mouse has a single button and pressing this and dragging the mouse, or clicking the button once or twice have similar (if not identical) effects across all Macintosh software. For example, by dragging with the mouse button depressed, windows can be moved around the opening screen but this same action is also used for moving objects in draw programs. The pointer changes shape depending on how it is being used and again, many of the shapes are common across programs. Thus, the 'I-beam' pointer indicates the text insertion point in most word processors but it is also used when text is being changed or added at the desktop level.

The mouse is further used to activate **pull down menus**. The majority of commands used in Macintosh software are gathered under a limited number of broad headings (File, Edit, etc.) spread across a 'menu bar' at the top of the screen. The commands within each menu item are displayed on pointing to the item and pressing the mouse button, and a specific command is selected by moving the pointer to it until it is highlighted. The pointer to a large extent thus replaces what on other machines would be achieved by keyboard commands and in fact many of the commands have keyboard equivalents that can be used as shortcuts. In the same way that mouse actions are identical across most Macintosh software, so is the concept of pull down menus and though the content of the menus changes from program to program, once the idea is mastered it is easy to adapt the knowledge to any application. For this reason, Macintosh users are traditionally the worst readers of manuals, the only stumbling block coming when an unusual icon or menu option is encountered.

A variant of pull down menus that has appeared in an increasing number of programs in the last twelve months is pop-up menus. These generally occur in dialogue boxes where a fixed number of alternatives are permitted by the software and these all appear when the mouse button is depressed. The difference is that pop-up menus emanate from the dialogue box rather than from the menu bar at the top of the screen, and as such they are more immediate and should save time. A further variant is available from some Macintosh desk accessories which permit menus to appear anywhere on screen whenever, for example, the command and option keys are pressed at the same time as the mouse button. Again, the advantage is that when these are installed there is no need to move to the top of the screen to select commands.

One of the most useful series of commands available from the pull down menus is for editing documents. Four options are generally provided: **cut, copy, paste** and **clear** and the beauty of these is that they are similarly universal, being included in most programs and permitting the transfer of data (including graphics) between applications. The Macintosh uses the idea of a Clipboard for storing information prior to transfer to another document or to another place in the same document, and the

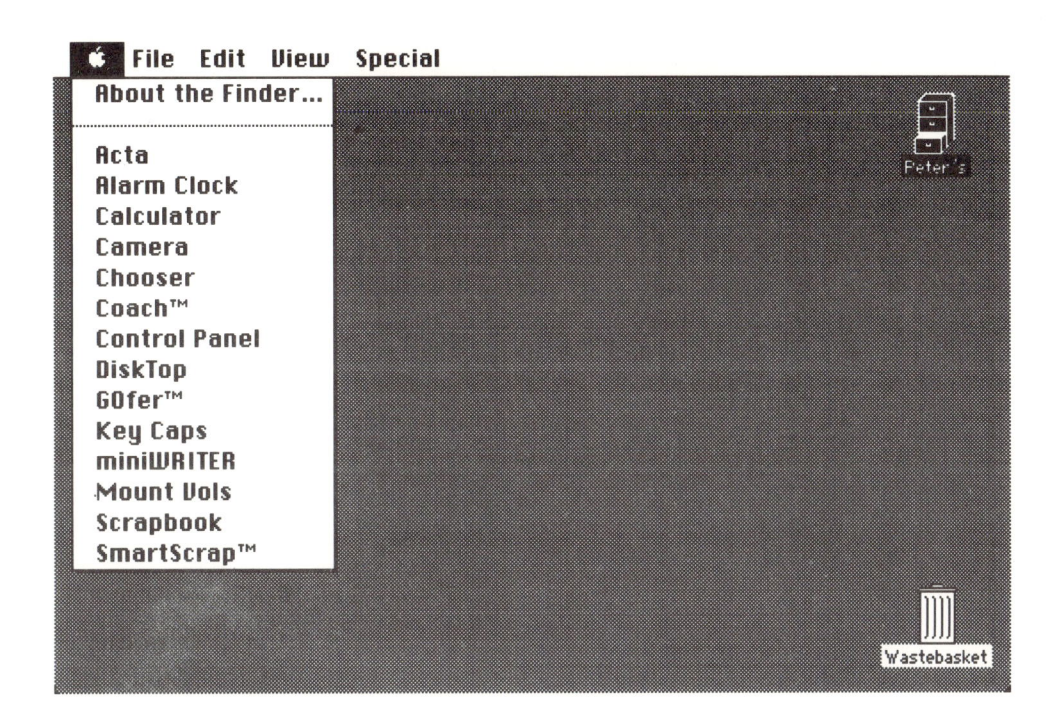

**Figure 2.4 Desk accessories on the Apple Macintosh**

commands cut and copy place data on the Clipboard. Paste subsequently transfers the information that is on the Clipboard into the document at the cursor position. If text or graphics is to be removed from a document but not stored on the Clipboard the clear command can be used. This is particularly useful if the existing content of the Clipboard is to be retained for future use.

A final but important aspect of the Macintosh interface, and one that gives rise to discussions of fervour amongst Macintosh devotees, is that of **desk accessories**. These are programs that can be accessed at any time to help out with specific jobs – e.g. a quick calculation – and literally sit on top of the current application. Hundreds of desk accessories have been written for the Macintosh and some of these are discussed in detail in chapter 6. They are accessed via a pull down menu from the 'Apple' in the top left-hand corner of the screen as shown in figure 2.4. Variants that do the same type of job are INITs (INITial programs) that become effective when the Macintosh is started and CDEVs (Control DEVices) that exist in the Control Panel, itself a desk accessory. QuicKeys, described in chapter 6 is a CDEV.

While desk accessories are undoubtedly useful they can give rise to problems through mutual incompatibility and interference. For example, bringing up Gofer with Spelling Coach brings MacAuthor to a halt in MultiFinder. Unfortunately there is no way of predicting this before the programs have been purchased and added to the system. The only positive in this is that many of the developers of desk accessories are aware of the uses to which their product is put and do attempt to solve incompatibility problems in future software releases.

**Printers**

Serious DTP work is not possible without some sort of laser printer. As reported by Carson (page 18), at least one public library in the UK uses a dot-matrix printer for DTP-related work, but to capitalise on the high quality typography and graphics possible with the software, a laser printer should be considered a minimum requirement. For some jobs the use of an imagesetter will be a pre-requisite. A good introduction to the use of printers generally for DTP can be found in Lang's book (pages 96–116).

*PostScript or not?*

When the Apple LaserWriter appeared to general acclaim in 1985 there was little else on the market for potential users and newcomers to DTP to consider. With the explosion in growth of the market place so purchasers have not only to choose a unit from the variety available, but also to consider another quandary: should the laser printer have PostScript or not?

In some circles laser printers are known as page printers, for the obvious reason that they set up and print one whole page at a time. This is in contrast to dot-matrix and daisy-wheel printers which receive printing instructions from the computer one line at a time. Page printers consist of two main parts: an engine and a controller, and the key component of the controller is the page description language (PDL). This is used to convert the output from the printer driver into a form that can be understood and accurately interpreted by the printer. The advantages of this stem from the fact that once a page has been set up, many of its characteristics will be repeated (headers and footers, and the typeface/s) across the whole document so that the processing time for subsequent pages can be reduced.

The main advantage of a good PDL is that it is device independent so that a document set up on one machine can be transferred to another without modification or loss of quality as long as the PDL on both is the same. The primary characteristics of an ability to define accurately all aspects of a page – type, line graphics, scanned images in any combination – are obvious. Though a number of PDLs have been developed (see for example, Wilson-Davies page 23) the most common utilised by the current crop of DTP systems is PostScript by Adobe Systems Incorporated. Seybold (page 183) quotes the president of Adobe Systems describing PostScript as 'a strategy to connect composition programs and output devices'.

PostScript is to all intents and purposes a computer programming language like any other and for most jobs it will be transparent to the user, being generated by the printer driver on the Macintosh. In fact an increasing number of programs are using the abilities of PostScript directly to allow sophisticated or unusual effects to be sent to the printer. Thus, the graphics programs Illustrator, FreeHand, and Cricket Draw produce their best results when connected to a PostScript printer, and MacAuthor utilises graphics outlines that are written in PostScript.

It is also possible to write executable PostScript programs manually. The main reason specified for doing this is usually that special effects not available from existing software can be produced, but before one becomes carried away, thinking of all this latent power close at hand, one basic question should be asked: are you prepared to program? Most librarians will utilise DTP because the software is powerful and easy to use and because there is no programming involved – almost in spite of the fact that the technology is computer driven. PostScript may be logical but like all computer programs it uses a terminology all its own and in spite of encouragement from various quarters such as journal articles and books it is not easy to come to grips with. For those wishing to persist the introductions provided by Kleper and Phillips will be of interest but the real detail will be found in the books produced by Adobe itself and the chapter by Waite.

There are two main disadvantages with PostScript and both are being addressed in different ways. The first of these is the fact that while a PostScript program can be created and displayed on screen, the results of it – the special graphic effect – cannot. For example, the integral graphics of MacAuthor are totally written in PostScript and when used to enhance a page are just not visible on the screen. One way round this is to use Display PostScript but some recent reports suggest that this will not be utilised by Apple at least for some considerable time. Display PostScript is to be used in the Next computer. The other disadvantage is cost and one of the reasons for the additional cost of PostScript printers is the licensing fee paid by the printer manufacturers to Adobe. One of the ways around this is to use a different PDL and a number of 'PostScript clones' have recently appeared on the market (Meng), but again, none of these look as if they are going to upset Adobe in the near future.

*Laser printer models*

The printer choice for the majority of Apple-based DTP systems is generally made from the Apple LaserWriter II range. At the time of writing this consists of three models with the same Canon LBP-SX print engine and body size but with different controller cards for different performances – figure 2.5. The IISC is the bottom-of-the-range model which, significantly, is

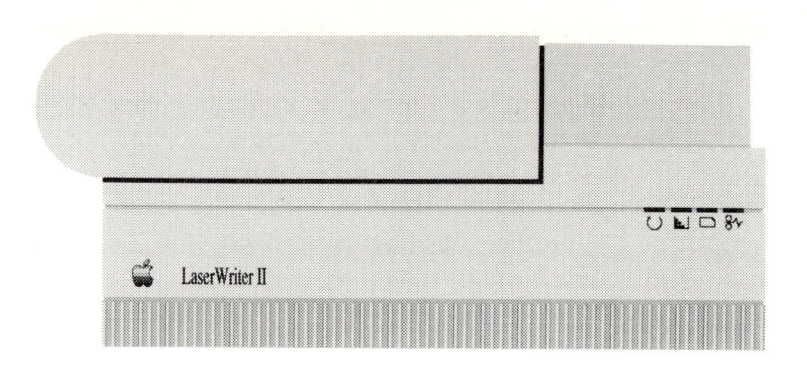

**Figure 2.5 The Apple LaserWriter II**

not supplied with PostScript. It prints directly from the QuickDraw commands generated by the Macintosh and because of this is primarily suitable for printing text-only documents: it is largely unable to reproduce the special effects possible with some of the more sophisticated graphics packages. Of the early Apple PostScript printers the LaserWriter Plus became the favourite, largely because of the increased number of built in fonts. The IINT is in effect the replacement for the LaserWriter Plus and will be considered by most users to be the best buy, especially as it is cheaper than its forebears. The IINTX is the top-of-the-range model with expansion possibilities such as an external hard disc port and the ability to take RAM up to 12 megabytes.

As indicated by Heid, a wide range of non-Apple laser printers can also be connected to the Macintosh and have proved popular in some circumstances. Thus, the General Computer Personal Laser Printer has received good reviews as a lower cost alternative to the LaserWriter IISC. Like the Apple printer this is a QuickDraw rather than a PostScript device. For some operations the standard laser printers may be considered inadequate, not because of the limited printer resolution but for other considerations such as engine life. The life of the Canon LBP-CX engine on the original Apple LaserWriters was 100,000 copies, or five years at 20,000 copies per year. As a general office printer this would be sufficient, but for a library print unit wishing to produce all its own *copies* rather than just masters, it is clearly inadequate. By comparison the LaserWriter II range released in January 1988 has a duty cycle of 300,000 copies but some institutions would likewise judge this as insufficient to stand up to the rigours of continuous printing. By comparison, the Dataproducts LZR-2665 laser printer has a rated engine life of 3,000,000 pages.

*Imagesetters*

For high quality work, output from a laser printer at a resolution of 300 dots per inch may be inadequate and the trump card of connecting up to a phototypesetter must come into play.

Whether this is really DTP is questionable – you may, after all, have an extremely large desk top – but is also somewhat beside the point. If the quality is required then whatever means are used would appear to be acceptable and in any case the original would have been created using the techniques of DTP.

As pointed out above if a standard page description language such as PostScript is used then files can be printed on a phototypesetter without modification. In addition, proofing can take place on the output from a PostScript laser printer in the knowledge that the phototypeset output will be identical in all respects but for print resolution. This is not true if dot matrix printers are connected up to the same DTP software.

The phototypesetters in most general use for connecting to Macintosh DTP systems are the Linotronic 100 and 300 machines. The complete range includes the Linotronic 500 for large-format documents, and the recently-introduced 200P aimed at bureaux. In the Linotronic literature the point is made that the term typesetter has now given way to imagesetter as a more accurate representation of the transformation of digitised information (both graphics and text) into traditional form. With the Linotronic 100 final print resolution is a maximum of 1270 dots per inch while the Linotronic 300 is capable of 2540 dots per inch. As both machines are key components of professional typesetting systems, they were in use well before the recent interest in PostScript as a machine-independent PDL. Accordingly, when a Macintosh is connected to either machine a translator is required to convert the PostScript emanating from the printer driver into the native language of the imagesetter. This is achieved through a PostScript Raster Image Processor (RIP) which is integral to the Linotronic 100P machine but is a separate unit connected to the Linotronic 300. This latter unit, in addition to providing the translation capabilities, also incorporates an 80 megabyte hard disc for storing fonts and user files.

The other major difference between imagesetters and laser printers is in their treatment of output. Whereas the laser printer is a no-nonsense device, the finished document being propelled from its rollers into the user's waiting and eager hands, the output from the imagesetter requires photographic processing. Thus, the output, made onto photosensitive paper, film or even printing plates, has to be developed in a separate unit before the results can be viewed. Although this two-stage process sounds laborious it need not unduly concern the librarian as few libraries (if any) are likely to be able to afford an imagesetter for their own publications. If the use of an imagesetter is considered essential for special publications, there are sufficient high-street bureaux touting for business to enable a good price to be obtained. Some larger institutions may even have purchased an imagesetter that can be used by the library, no doubt at a cost.

**Ancillary equipment**

*Hard discs*

As time goes on and the software places greater demands on the hardware, so the need for hard discs has moved from the 'it would be nice to have' to the essential. Any librarian moving into the DTP field in a serious way should not consider the purchase of a Macintosh without a hard disc. PageMaker version 3.0, for example, occupies 900k of disc space and as, at the time of writing, the standard Macintosh disc drive reads floppies of 800k maximum, a hard disc is vital to run the program. Also, as more users become involved in graphics applications so the demand for hard discs of greater capacity than the standard 20 megabytes is increasing.

As the demands have grown so the computer companies have started to supply integral hard discs in their machines compared to the position a few years ago when these were almost the sole province of third party suppliers. The need for *separate* hard discs for the Macintosh would therefore appear to be on the decline. While this may be the case for the Macintosh Plus/SE, anyone with a Macintosh II may still need an external hard disc to ensure the portability of their large files between different machines and between their workplace and an imagesetting bureau.

*Big screens*

The other verging-on-the-essential piece of ancillary equipment is the big screen. What is not essential is the price of these units though in the two or so years since their introduction prices have fallen relatively quickly and the variety increased so that they can no longer just be considered the province of the enthusiastic equipment-mad Macintosh fanatic with oodles of money.

It is not just the small size of the Macintosh Plus/SE display that necessitated the use of big screens but the serious take-up by many companies of DTP. In Britain and Europe the most common paper size is A4 and when even simple pages are being laid out it is an advantage to view the complete design on screen. When complex mixes of text and graphics are being prepared the whole view is essential and, furthermore, it reduces the need for constant proofing on the laser printer. But DTP is not just viewing a single page in isolation. It is, amongst other things, ensuring that a two page spread is balanced and carries the right impact and to be able to achieve this on screen obviously requires something approaching an A3 display.

What is purchased in practice will depend on a number of factors such as compatibility with software; compatibility with other hardware, either existing or proposed; available workspace

– most big screens have equally big footprints; and not least price. The screens do not operate in isolation and require software to ensure automatic recognition by the Macintosh and compatibility with a range of software. Accordingly, screens should be purchased from a reputable manufacturer or dealer to ensure that software upgrades are maintained and a long life is obtained from the investment.

The earliest big screens were the Radius Full Page (A4) Display (see, for example, Bobker) and the A3 MegaScreen but since then a wide range has become available. A review of some of those on the market at the end of 1987 can be found in Tyler.

At current prices ranging from £1,000 for black-and-white A4 to around £5,000 for high resolution colour A3, big screens are not cheap. In spite of this, all libraries considering entering DTP in any serious way should consider the purchase of one very carefully. They will save a lot of time and, in particular, an awful lot of frustration and anger being vented on a small defenceless Macintosh.

*Scanners*

In the short-to-medium term, the majority of library DTP jobs will probably be satisfied by the three key pieces of equipment already described: Macintosh with hard disc; printer; and big screen. Coupled with carefully chosen software this should be all that is required to produce most of the library's current publications to a significantly higher standard than at present. That is until some enthusiastic individual who has been poring over the Macintosh literature decides that most of the publications are in fact boring and need sprucing up. The current flavour of the month (and likely to remain so for some time) is scanners, the hardware used to convert photographs and line art into digitised images.

Scanners come in two basic types: sheetfeed and flatbed, although some camera-based systems are also available. Sheetfeed scanners operate in a similar manner to fax machines whereby only single sheets can be handled and these have to physically pass through the equipment. Where images are to be transferred from books and journal articles – and where conservation is important – these are obviously not suitable for library use. Also, if care is not taken, the original can be fed through at an angle giving rise to a distorted image. Flatbed scanners operate like photocopiers, the image to be scanned being placed face down on a glass plate and they are accordingly not only more appropriate for the library but also give better results. Most of the current crop of general purpose scanners available for use with the Macintosh are flatbeds.

A scanner is not a piece of equipment that suddenly leaps into operation when connected to the Macintosh for, as Seybold writes (page 203): 'at the core of every scanning system is a software heart'. Most software enables portions of the original to be selected for scanning, permits enlargements or reductions to be made, and provides options for saving in a range of different file formats. Some manipulation tools may also be provided but as advances occur, the facilities that are currently available in the third-party image manipulation packages may find their way into the software bundled with the scanner.

Librarians with no publishing or scanning experience should carefully consider the move into this area before rushing out and purchasing a scanner. DTP has proved popular so far because the software is substantially easy to use and produces extremely impressive results, even for novice users. Scanning moves DTP into the areas of professional expertise and, while this is not beyond librarians with enthusiasm and ability, it is questionable whether we should be spending our time in this way *at present*. Heid says 'you don't need one to include photos in a publication; you can use the standard graphic artist's technique' and if it takes two months for an informed reviewer (Hewson, page 31) to get to grips with the Agfa scanner, there is little immediate salvation in store for the librarian. By all means find a scanner that can be used or borrowed so that experimentation can begin, but don't rush into a purchase until you are sure what you want to achieve. If the main purpose initially is to digitise your logo or a few local images, arrange this with your local dealer to save time and money. At present scanning is shrouded in unfamiliar terminology and technicalities (for the librarian) but as more hardware is sold there is likely to be a push by the manufacturers and software developers to make the systems far more user-friendly. Prices will also continue to fall and when both these things happen, then will be the time for the less experienced to start scanning.

## References

*Macintosh*

Coleman, D and Naiman, A. *The Macintosh Bible*. Goldstein and Blair, Berkeley, California, 1986. ISBN 0 940235 00 5.

Hewson, D. Power without the struggle. *MacUser*, no. 30, December, 1988, pp. 37–39. Alternatives strategies to MultiFinder. Some of the same software also discussed in: The packages with more Apple appeal. *Guardian*, February 16, 1989, pp. 25.

Lu, C. *The Apple Macintosh book*, 3rd edition. Microsoft Press, Redmond, Washington, 1988. ISBN 1 55615 110 1.

Margolis, A.B. Desktop publishing on the PC. **In** The Waite Group. *Desktop publishing Bible*. Sams, Indianapolis, 1987. ISBN 0 672 22524 7, pp. 112–139 (quote from page 115).

Meakin, D. Enter Macintosh. *Apple User*, vol. 4, no. 2, February 1984, pp. 17–20. (Incorporates article by M. Parrott on 'Inside Macintosh')

Scales, I. Meet the Macintosh. *Personal Computer News*, no. 46, January 28, 1984, pp. 18–20.

Swarbrick, G. Apple Mac SE/30. *Personal Computer World*, vol. 12, no. 2. February 1989, pp. 128–132.

Walker, N. Macintosh Plus. *Personal Computer World*, vol. 9, no. 2, February 1986, pp. 120–123.

Williams, G. The Apple Macintosh computer. *Byte*, vol. 9, no. 2, February 1984, pp. 30–54.

Williams, G. and Thompson, T. The Apple Macintosh II. *Byte*, vol. 12, no. 4, April 1987, pp. 85–106.

*Printers*

Adobe Systems Incorporated. *PostScript language program design*. Reading, Massachusetts, Addison-Wesley, 1988. ISBN 0 201 14396 8.

Adobe Systems Incorporated. *PostScript language reference manual*. Reading, Massachusetts, Addison-Wesley, 1985. ISBN 0 201 10174 2.

Carson, J. *Desktop publishing and libraries*. London, Taylor Graham, 1988. ISBN 0 947568 34 4.

Heid, J. Looking at lasers. *Macworld*, vol. 5, no. 6, June 1988, pp. 119–129.

Kleper, M. L. *The Illustrated handbook of desktop publishing and typesetting*. Blue Ridge Summit, TAB Books, 1987. ISBN 0 8306 2700 6. pp. 378–382.

Lang, K. *The Writer's guide to desktop publishing*. London, Academic Press, 1987. ISBN 0 12 436275 3.

Meng, B. Where are the clones? *Macworld*, vol. 5, no. 8, August, 1988, pp. 103–107.

Phillips, M. Post Modern (PostScript programming). *MacUser* no. 13, July 1987, pp. 52–53.

Seybold, J. and Dressler, F. *Publishing from the desktop*. London, Bantam Books, 1987. ISBN 0 533 34401 3.

Waite, M. Introduction to PostScript. **In** The Waite Group. *Desktop publishing Bible*. Sams, Indianapolis, 1987. ISBN 0 672 22524 7, pp. 341–366.

Wilson-Davies, K., Bate, J.St.J., and Barnard, M. *Desktop publishing*. London, Blueprint Publishing, 1987. ISBN 0 948905 06 9. Publisher's Guide series.

*Big screens*  Bobker, S. The Big picture. *MacUser* (US edition), vol. 1, no. 14, November 1986, pp. 56–59.

Tyler, A. A view to a thrill. *MacUser*, no. 17, November 1987, pp. 69–73.

*Scanners*  Heid, J. Getting started with scanners. *Macworld*, vol. 5, no. 11, November 1988, pp. 235–250.

Hewson, D. Industrial resolution. *MacUser*, no. 26, August 1988, pp. 31–35. A review of the Agfa Focus S800GS scanner.

Seybold, J. and Dressler, F. *Publishing from the desktop*. London, Bantam Books, 1987. ISBN 0 533 34401 3.

though
# Section 2

# The software of DTP

**It can't all be useful. Can it?**

There is a great deal of software available in the DTP area and much of it is less interesting than a packet of cold fish and chips. On the other hand there are a lot of top flight products that are worthy of consideration, that do the jobs they are designed for well, and that are, dare it be said, fun to use. Some of these are DTP programs, some are word processors and others are graphics and ancillary programs.

Even in a book such as this which is devoted to the subject, a comprehensive and detailed review of all the available products is not possible. In selecting the software for consideration emphasis was placed on the major packages available for the Apple Macintosh. It is no coincidence that these are the more expensive packages for they possess a power that can be used gradually as experience grows: in general users will not need to discard these and transfer to something with more facilities when more sophisticated effects are needed. It must also be pointed out that packages of the price of Fleet Street Publisher running on the IBM PC are not available on the Macintosh. The occasional package away from the mainstream has also been included to encourage users to try things for themselves. If readers are interested in a package that has not been covered, it is hoped that they will be able to use the approach taken in the following two chapters as a guide for assessing their suitability.

The first and most obvious group of packages are the DTP programs themselves. These are primarily marketed as specialised products for the purposes of laying out text and graphics imported from other sources. Some are also suitable, to varying degrees, for the direct insertion of text and could be said to compete directly with word processors. Three packages are described in chapter 3 – PageMaker, Ready, Set, Go!, and XPress.

As word processors have become more sophisticated, or at least have included more facilities, so they have begun to incorporate some of the features of DTP programs. For some library operations these packages may be just as suitable – if not more so – than the specialised programs and it is important that all potential users of the software have an understanding of their power. In some quarters these packages have been christened, somewhat pompously, document processors. MacAuthor and FullWrite Professional are the two word processors discussed in chapter 4.

The third category of software covers the graphics packages which are available for creating illustrations for improving the appearance of documents and for emphasising particular points in the text. These include paint and draw programs, the more sophisticated PostScript-based drawing packages, graphing and clip art software, and packages for the manipulation of scanned images. The software discussed includes SuperPaint, FreeHand, Cricket Graph, The Visual Arts, Digital Darkroom and ImageStudio. All are discussed in chapter 5.

In addition to the high end layout and graphics software there are numerous inexpensive packages that can promote a more satisfying, fruitful and active DTP life. Many of these are desk accessories, programs that can be summoned and used on top of an existing application to assist the work that is currently being carried out on screen. Some of these, such as spelling checkers and outliners, are finding their way into major programs but others are, at the moment, more novel and are only available as desk accessories. The ancillary programs covered in chapter 6 are Spelling Coach, a spelling checker, Acta, an outliner, Gofer, a text finder, and QuicKeys, for the creation of keyboard macros.

Information on the use of the packages in various library applications is presented in section 3.

# 3  DTP packages

**The approach**

In what follows three packages are discussed in detail using the same basic approach. Background information is presented on the software and the company who produces it and this is followed by sections on the user interface, format, layout, the handling of text and the handling of graphics. Where appropriate screen dumps have been included to emphasise particular points. A brief concluding view of each package is also provided.

# PAGEMAKER

**Background**

This is the piece of software generally credited with starting the DTP 'revolution' although the word revolution in this context means not a change in society but the stumbling upon a new marketing concept. Whatever, PageMaker has been enormously successful. It is produced by the American company Aldus and first appeared in late 1985; at the time of writing version 3.0 is available for the Macintosh.

As the first one on the block PageMaker has had to suffer both plaudits and criticisms, sometimes, it appears, in equal numbers. While showing the way forward for all the software which followed, it was also relatively easy for competitors to incorporate enhancements for PageMaker's shortcomings until we now have the familiar feature of products leapfrogging one another every few months. By comparison, the agelessness of early versions of microcomputer software such as VisiCalc and WordStar seems a thing of the past.

The practical application of many of the features of PageMaker is described in chapter 7 but to enable a comparison to be made with the other packages in this chapter some of these are repeated below. Accordingly, some features that are not considered pertinent to the sample library guide are described in more detail.

**User interface**

When software has been used for a period and become familiar, even programs that took a lot of heartache and training and that were not exactly intuitive (WordStar?) become difficult to view objectively. So it is with PageMaker, and at times it appears that there is really only one way to lay out a page – that defined by this program. In some cases the very effort that has been put into learning software can be a disincentive to change to new programs, but PageMaker does not fall into this category, being extremely easy to use and get to grips with. Even working without a manual it is relatively easy to find one's way around and the features that one is looking for do tend to be where you would expect to find them in the pull down menus. Users coming to PageMaker from traditional publishing backgrounds may prefer the idea of grids and separate text and graphics frames, but for the uninitiated, as most librarians will be, the program works as people do: by trial and error.

The opening screen for a new document is shown in figure 3.1. PageMaker uses the idea of the pasteboard – the area surrounding the screen page – whereby the elements that go to make up a story can be laid out before and during page make-up. Any piece of text or a graphic can be moved to the pasteboard and held there for as long as necessary while modifications are carried out. This is particularly useful for newcomers for it gives them an easy way to experiment with alternatives before arriving at a final layout. The Toolbox is clearly visible in the top right hand corner of this diagram and provides the means of selecting elements, editing text and graphics, and drawing basic shapes. A full explanation of the use of the tools can be found on page 135.

A fair degree of thought has been given to the ergonomics of the interface so that in general most of the related features that a user needs are provided in close proximity. For example, in the 'Type specifications' box shown in figure 7.3 the required details can be completed easily without constantly reverting to the pull down menus. Having this amount of detail on screen at one time means that it also acts as a prompt for the inexperienced user. A feature introduced in version 3.0 is that of pop-up menus, in addition to the standard pull down type. Pop-up menus come into effect in a dialogue box, for example, 'Type specifications', so that when one of the variables such as font is altered a listing of all those available appears at the insertion point. This probably saves a small amount of time over the

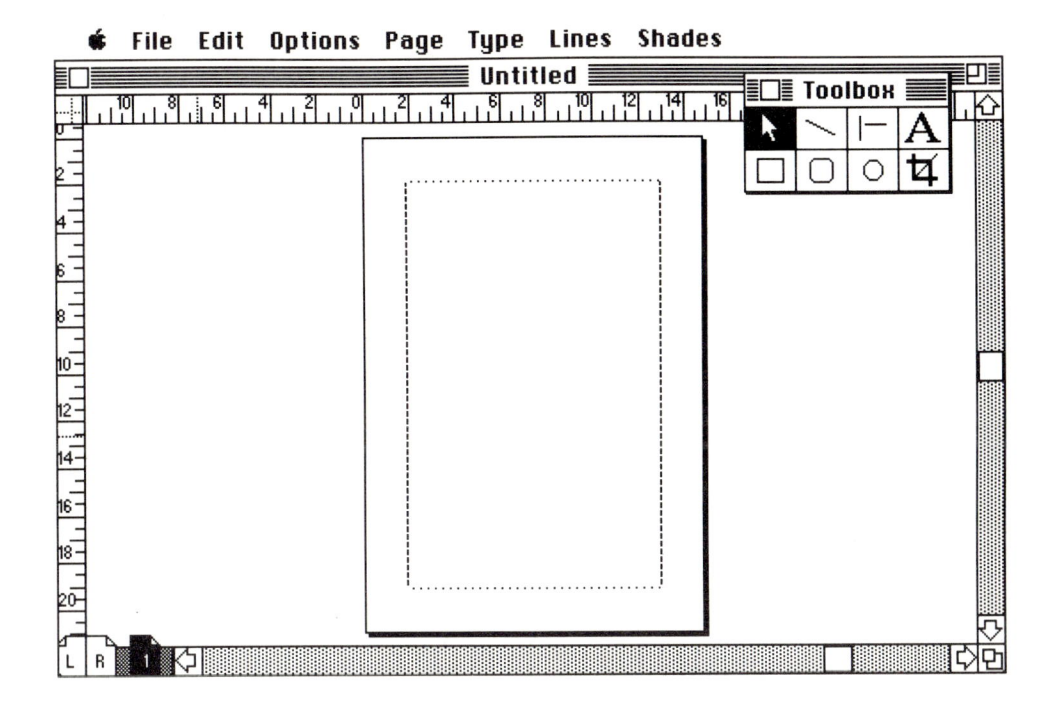

**Figure 3.1 Basic user interface of PageMaker**

previous method of providing scroll bars in selection boxes, but far more importantly, it has a very professional, if not slick, feel to it. Pop-up menus have since appeared in the most recent versions of Ready, Set, Go! and XPress.

**Format**

The working page sizes available as standard within PageMaker are shown in figure 7.1; for British purposes it is good to see A4, A3, and A5 available as direct choices so that reference does not have to be made to another source to check the precise measurement details. It is possible to work with none standard sizes in PageMaker but there seems little point in this if output is restricted to the A4 possible with the majority of laser printers currently on the market. In this respect the ability to open an A5 document direct is particularly important for many publications, particularly library publications, use this size (or does it just seem this way?). PageMaker does something further here, by enabling the page setup to be intelligently linked to the paper size in the connected printer so that, for example, when an A5 document is printed out on A4 paper the output is centred on the page.

PageMaker allows work to be carried out using a range of measurement systems: inches, decimal inches (with the rulers indicating 0.05 inch) picas and ciceros. A pica is a standard typesetting measure of 12 points or one sixth of an inch. A cicero is a French typesetting measure of approximately 4.552 millimetres. The preferred unit is selected from the Preferences section of the Edit menu and thereafter acts as a default for all new documents until changed.

**Layout**

The use of master pages for maintaining continuity of layout throughout a publication, together with the aid of ruler and column guides, is discussed in detail in chapter 7 and reference should be made to page 134 to see how these features work.

Master pages can be modified at any point in the creation of a document but the changes work in different ways depending on whether they relate to columns or text and graphics.

Changes in the number of columns on the master pages are reflected throughout the document but any placed text is not reformatted to the new page layout. For example, a change from two to three columns leaves the already placed text formatted in two columns (with column guides rather oddly representing three columns) but any newly placed stories are run into three columns. This is obviously useful if it is decided to change a layout part way through but it also has its drawbacks.

Users starting from scratch will have no experience to draw upon when making decisions about the number of columns and the space between them. Accordingly, after the placing of text the poor appearance of a few pages may encourage changes to be made to these variables, but as far as PageMaker is concerned the die has been cast. If the column spacing is to be changed there is no simple and automatic way of adjusting the text to the new dimensions and it is almost as easy to start again with new master pages. This obviously results in a waste of time and can be extremely frustrating. It is a disappointment from a program that makes child's play (or relatively so) of most DTP operations.

With text and graphics the master pages are not accommodating in the slightest and any changes are immediately reflected in all pages. Thus, if for some reason a feature that was to appear on every page required a position change on only one or two pages this could not be achieved using the masters but would have to be incorporated as page make-up progressed, or by creating a template for the whole document.

The concept of templates has been implemented well in PageMaker where a complete front-to-back layout, a part layout, or simply master pages, can all be saved as a model for future issues of a document. For example, in the current awareness bulletin described in chapter 8, the first few pages incorporating title page, editorial and the list of subject headings will stay substantially the same from issue to issue and so these are saved as a template. As PageMaker then gives the option of opening a copy rather than the original file work can begin on the next issue without any time consuming editing such as the wholesale deletion of text.

## Handling of text

*Text entry*

For a page make-up program to be extensively used it must be compatible with as many standard word processors as possible and Aldus have obviously worked closely with a wide range of software producers. The Macintosh version of PageMaker 3.0 will import formatted text from MacWrite 4.5, Microsoft Word 1.05 and 3.02, Microsoft Works, and WriteNow, in addition to text files from other Macintosh word processors. The beauty of this procedure lies in its implementation, for PageMaker automatically recognises the different formats from within the Place command and the alternatives do not have to be chosen separately as happens in some applications. A major drawback, at least to the author, is that MacAuthor II file format is not recognised and one cannot help feeling that this has something to do with the fact that MacAuthor is a British product with a correspondingly smaller market than the others. In spite of this Aldus are clearly encouraging developers to review the compatibility of their products with PageMaker for in version 3.0 they have included provision for 'filters' so that other foreign file formats can be translated or recognised.

The Macintosh version of PageMaker 3.0 can also import files from PC PageMaker and a range of other PC word processors such as WordStar 2000, DisplayWrite and WordPerfect. Outside of PageMaker, a number of ways exist of transferring files between IBM PCs and Macintoshes and the practical aspects of one of these, using the TOPS network, is discussed in chapter 8.

The one disadvantage of importing text-only files is that it is not possible to control the typographic variables of the placed text but instead PageMaker default settings are used. Although the default font is Times, PageMaker sometimes gets confused and substitutes another font, particularly if one has been used earlier to input text onto the master pages. This procedure can result in a frustrating amount of unnecessary work reformatting to the required text format.

Whereas previous versions of the program limited page make-up to one page at a time, PageMaker 3.0 permits the automatic flow of a large block of text into a document by adding new pages as appropriate – using the 'Autoflow' command from the Options menu. The flow of text occurs in a sequential fashion, filling each column in turn and for most library purposes this should prove sufficient. If complex layouts are to be used, with stories split between non-sequential columns or pages, these are still possible, although time consuming in PageMaker, whereas both Ready, Set, Go! and XPress offer closer control.

*Exporting files*

The converse of text entry is exporting to word processors, a facility which is particularly useful for maintaining the accuracy and currency of the original files. One *modus operandi* suggests that all writing and editing of text should take place in the word processor before transfer to the make-up program but in practice this is difficult to achieve, except perhaps for authors and journalists who have the self discipline not to change anything once it is in the DTP program. Furthermore, alterations may only become obvious when the final version of the printed page can be viewed and, in fact, may become necessary to fit into the available space. Some people may prefer to keep a version of their original separate from their PageMaker text and others may be happy to overwrite it. PageMaker 3.0 permits both approaches and enables the finished text to be saved in the same formats that it recognises in the Place operation. PageMaker 3.0 does not thus automatically update the text of the original but leaves it to the discretion of the user.

*Text editing*

If changes are to be made to the original text once it has been transferred to PageMaker a number of text editing features would assist preparation of the final version. For example, a spell checker should be available to check the changes; experience has shown this author that relatively more unobserved mistakes are made during the editing of text than in the preparation of the first draft – and at a time when they can cause most embarrassment. PageMaker still does not have a built-in spell checker and one must correspondingly fall back on those available as desk accessories. Similarly, the online thesaurus that is now creeping into the more advanced word processors is also not available directly from PageMaker and neither are even basic search and replace features. It appears that Aldus are firmly of the 'complete your editing before embarking on page make-up' view.

*Style sheets*

In the past few years the realisation has dawned among software developers that word processors used for serious work (and DTP applications) needed more powerful features. In particular, a technique was required for maintaining the continuity of paragraph layout in long documents and, once this had been achieved, a method of rapidly modifying the format of paragraphs throughout the document as a whole. This need led eventually to style sheets, a concept that was first introduced in Macintosh word processors in MacAuthor in 1986. Since then, most top-end word processors have incorporated style sheets of one sort or another and they have subsequently become common in DTP packages.

In PageMaker 3.0 styles can be fully and individually created from the 'Define styles...' section of the Type menu. In the creation of a new style to suit the publication in hand four dialogue boxes are presented for the specification of Type, Paragraph, Tabs, and Colour. These boxes already exist in PageMaker for specification of each of the individual attributes – the Type specifications box is identical to that shown in figure 7.3 – but Aldus have brought these connected features together to enable the full style of particular paragraphs to be defined. An example of a fully defined 'Main paragraph' style is presented in figure 3.2; modifications can easily be made to any of the attributes by pressing the appropriate button.

Application of the styles to the text of the document is achieved from the Style section of the Type menu where a sub-menu of available styles opens up – figure 3.3. The chosen style will then be applied to the paragraph in which the cursor is currently placed, without text having to be initially highlighted, and will apply to all subsequent paragraphs until changed for another style in the pull down menu.

As already pointed out, style sheets are particularly useful in word processors where they can be applied to the text as it is composed. In DTP programs their advantages lie more in ensuring continuity of text throughout the document and it could be argued that they can offer only limited savings in time over manually changing paragraph formats. PageMaker 3.0, however, features two facilities that can speed up the formatting of imported documents. On the one hand, users of Microsoft Word will find that the style sheets of that word processor are supported by PageMaker so that all styles carry over without further effort. For users of other word processors, or where text only files are imported, PageMaker makes use of tags that can be attached to imported text so that the defined styles can be implemented automatically. The use of tags in the preparation of current awareness bulletins is described in detail in chapter 8.

On a less positive note, style sheets can have their disadvantages. For example, if no alternative to the style sheet approach is permitted it means that a separate style has to be established for each minor change in overall layout. For example, when two headings (main paragraph heading and sub-heading) follow each other, each with built in spacing above and below, the space between the headings will be double that required – say two lines instead of the preferred one line. To work round this a separate style would have to be created for one heading or the other (with no line spacing either above or below) to be used on only a limited number of occasions throughout the document. PageMaker works round this disadvantage nicely by providing the standard formatting tools that can be used to override the style sheets where required.

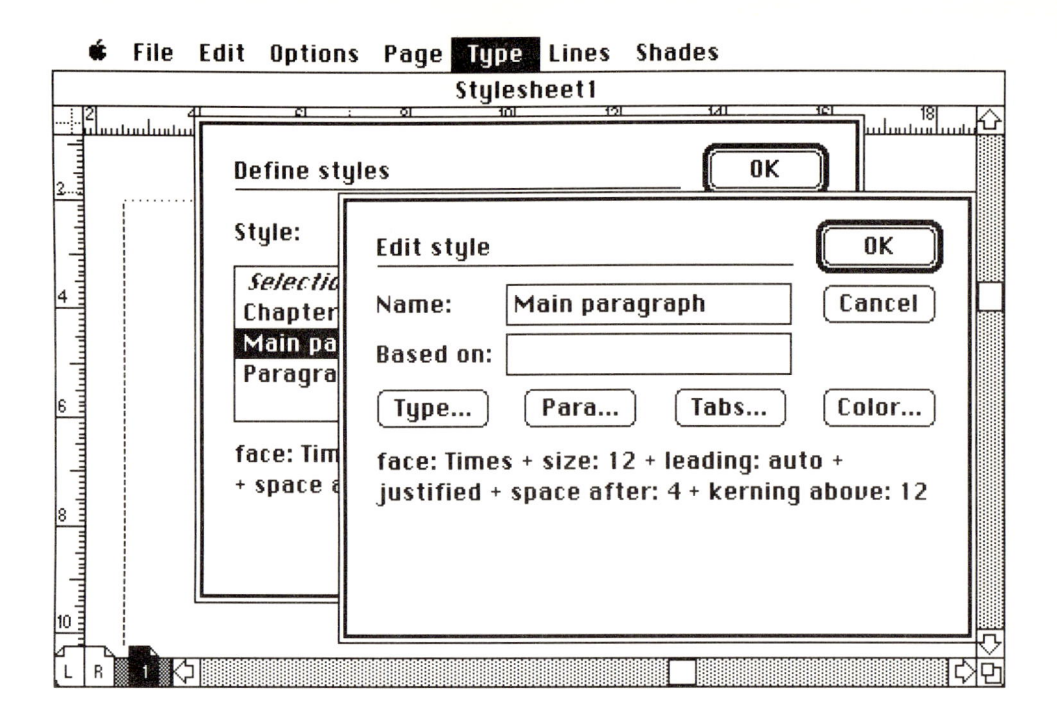

**Figure 3.2 Editing a style sheet in PageMaker**

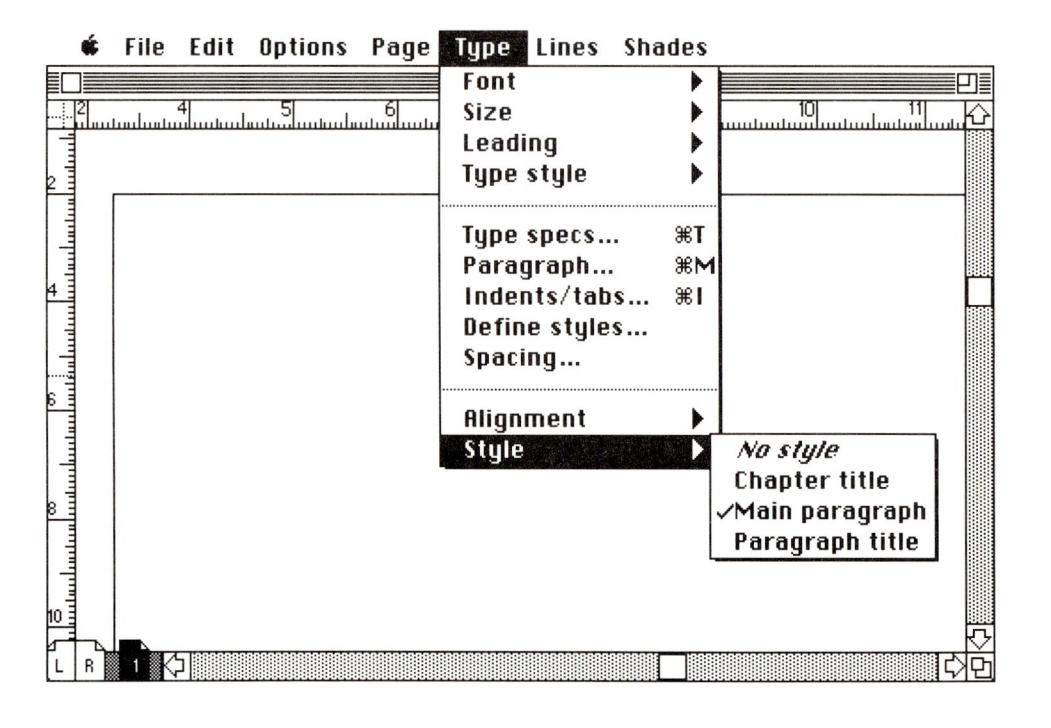

**Figure 3.3 Application of a style in PageMaker**

## Handling of graphics

*Formats*

Graphics are imported into a document using the Place command and, as with text, the major paint, draw and scanned image formats are supported and automatically recognised. Thus, any graphics program that permits the exporting of files in MacPaint format – the standard bit-mapped format on the Macintosh – or PICT – the generally recognised draw format – will be compatible with PageMaker. More recently high resolution graphics applications such as Adobe Illustrator and Aldus FreeHand have become available which permit the exporting of files in the Encapsulated PostScript File Format (EPSF) ; PageMaker also recognises this.

Scanned images can similarly be imported into PageMaker documents as long as the scanner software supports one or other of the generally accepted standard formats. PageMaker's 'favourite' is probably TIFF (Tag Image File Format) which was developed jointly by Aldus, Microsoft and others and has become almost a standard for scanned images, but if the scanner can produce output in any of the other graphics formats these too can be imported. A limited degree of control over the image is provided enabling lightness and contrast to be changed but, as explained in chapter 5, any modifications wrought by the program are impossible to see without a grey scale or colour monitor. Similarly, the application of dot and line screens to provide different printing effects can only be viewed with the correct hardware. Without this, changes made in 'Image control' can only be discerned from printer output and, as scanned images generally take a long time to print, this can be a frustrating business.

*Integral graphics*

The use of the lines and shades menu coupled with the drawing tools from the Toolbox are described in chapter 7 and need no further explanation here.

*Text wrap*

An extremely elegant method of flowing text around graphics is available in PageMaker whereby the 'repel' distance can be set to gain an initial idea of the effect of the runaround. At this point PageMaker creates a 'skin' round the object with handles that can be moved to adjust the text flow. As many handles as required can be added to this skin so that if required the text can follow an outline different from that of the embedded graphic. This process is described in detail in chapter 7.

## Overall view

It is difficult to dislike PageMaker. In its swift and progressive journey to version 3.0 the most surprising thing is that Aldus has managed to retain the easy to use interface and it is this as much as anything that sets the package so much apart from the opposition. As a result the new user can quickly get down to work using the basic capabilities of the program while leaving the more powerful features to be picked up at their relative leisure. For this reason alone PageMaker is suitable for decentralised library use (refer to chapter 9) where a wide range of professional and non-professional staff will have access to the equipment. A relatively small amount of training will go a long way and a significant improvement in quality, if not immediately up to professional standards, will be experienced. On the other hand PageMaker has plenty of power under the bonnet for librarians in dedicated DTP units to be able to produce the quality and range of documents they need.

Having said that, the program is not without its drawbacks. It is irritating to be limited to work on only one document at a time, the method available for the alignment of text in adjacent columns is clumsy and relies on manual adjustment, any change of column width will not automatically adjust text to the new dimensions, and the lack of word processing features is virtually flaunted. In addition the defaults used when placing text only files do not appear to have been consistently applied – occasionally they pick up the last used parameters which is disconcerting when this was a headline in large bold type.

Finally, it is worth pointing out that PageMaker goes out of its way to support a wide range of output hardware, from the different versions of the Apple LaserWriter range to imagesetters: printer drivers for a large number of devices are included as part of the package.

# READY, SET, GO!

**Background**

Ready, Set, Go! has been through more published revisions than any of the other DTP programs discussed in this book. Its transformation has also occurred with so many changes and enhancements that the current version 4.5 bears little resemblance to the original. When it first appeared mid-way through 1985 this was a very simple program capable of handling only one page at a time and permitting no direct importing of text or graphics – see, for example, the review by Tyler (1985). Version 2.0 improved on this by increasing document size to a maximum of 32 pages, and permitting the importing of object-oriented and bit-mapped graphics and ASCII text. The real advance (and reincarnation) came with version 3.0 when the program had for the first time to be taken seriously as DTP software (Tyler, 1987).

Until this time the program was published by Manhattan Graphics but shortly after the appearance of version 3.0 it was taken over by Letraset. This was considered a surprising move for while Letraset had for some time been intending to enter the Macintosh DTP market the company had been known to be working closely with Boston Software on an upgrade of a competing product, MacPublisher. In the event Ready, Set, Go!3 was subsequently distributed by Letraset who have further enhanced the product in two upgrades: version 4.0a that appeared towards the end of 1987 and the latest version, 4.5, which was released at the beginning of 1989.

**User interface**

The opening screen of a new document is shown in figure 3.4. In broad terms this resembles the PageMaker pasteboard – it is referred to in the manual as the Ready, Set, Go! desktop – but there are differences. For one, the newly opened document is positioned at the top left hand corner of the desktop rather than in its centre, and the area of pasteboard to play with is significantly smaller. For many jobs this latter will be of little import.

The other difference is that the Ready, Set, Go! tool bar is fixed and is positioned along the top of the document window. The graphics tools and the pointer are similar to those in PageMaker while the majority of the others relate to the different way in which Ready, Set, Go! lays out a page. Both text and imported graphics must be held in blocks pre-designated by the appropriate tools – T surrounded by a square for text and X in a box for graphics. The graphics cropping tool is this time a set of

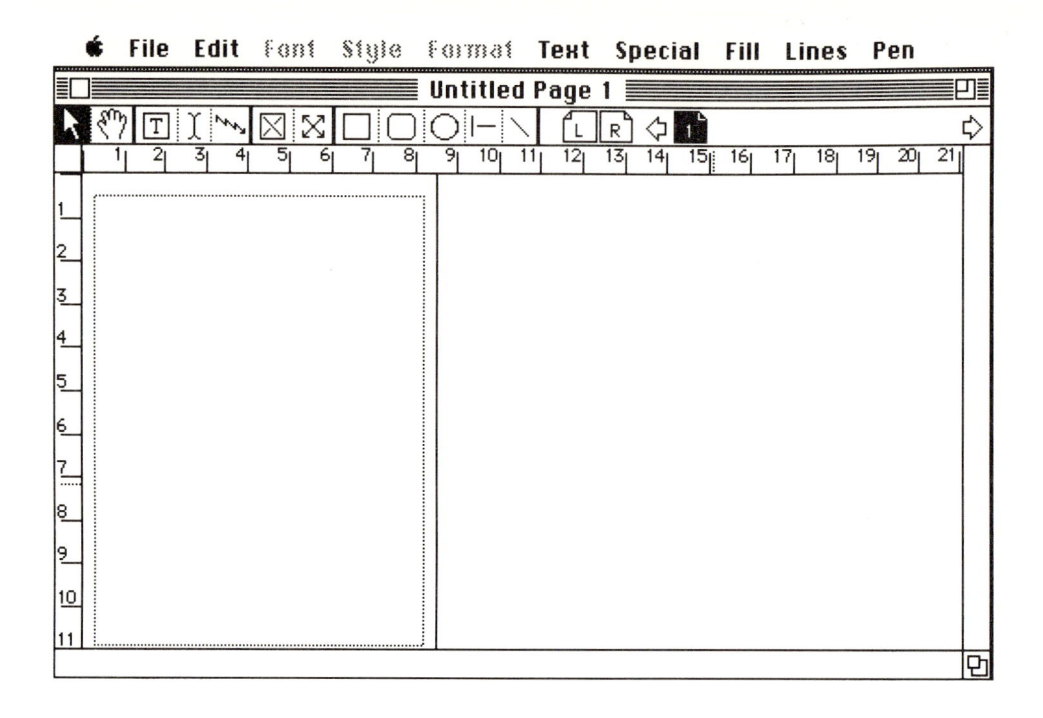

**Figure 3.4 User interface of Ready, Set, Go!**

arrows to all points of the compass, and the lightning bolt is used to link text blocks.

Compared to the single document that can be opened at one time with PageMaker, Ready, Set, Go! permits as many documents to be opened as machine memory will allow. Unfortunately, a pull down command listing all open file names to permit the easy transfer between them has not been included and without this the move becomes tedious. A further interesting feature is that the tool bar appears across the top of each open document window rather than, as might be expected, only once, across the top of the screen.

**Format**

In its Page Setup box Ready, Set, Go! has provision for the following standard sizes: US letter; US legal; tabloid; A4 and B5, but surprisingly, and somewhat disconcertingly, a new document automatically opens at the default page size without giving the user any option. Users also have the ability to work on specific, non-standard, sizes by selecting the 'Other' button and entering the width and depth but some strange things can then start to happen.

For example, A5 is not considered a standard by this program and so the page size has to be to hand to be entered manually.

46

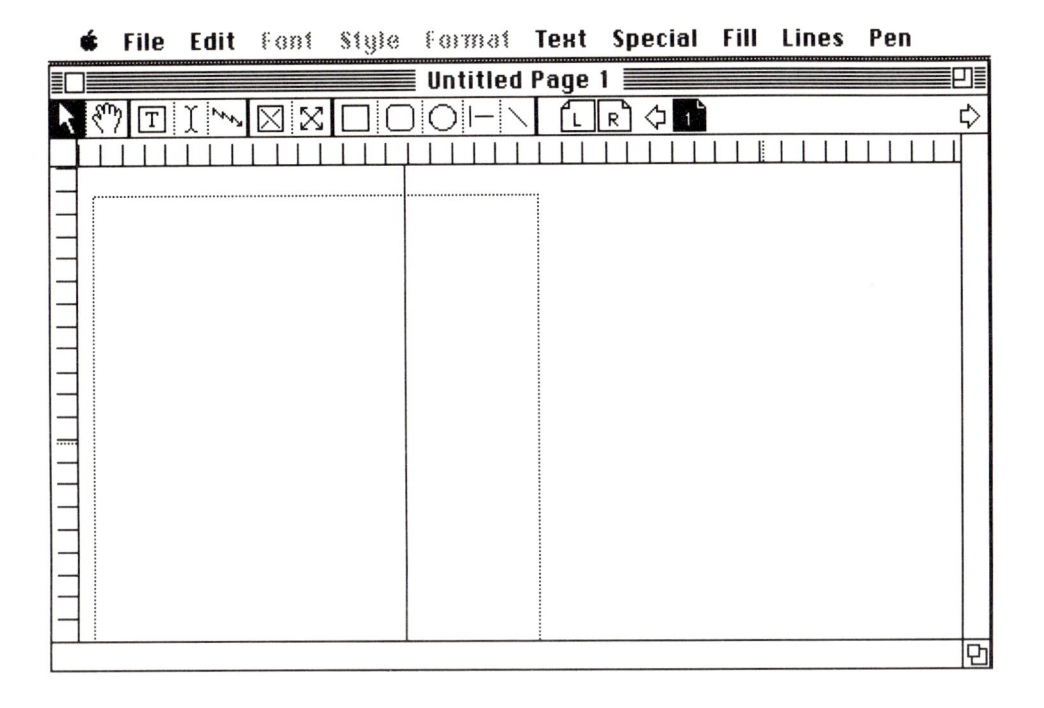

**Figure 3.5 Treatment of A5 page in Ready, Set, Go!**

All very well until the A5 page appears on screen in the top left hand corner with a superimposed dotted line representing the printing area of the page – figure 3.5. This dotted line appears because the LaserWriter will not print to the edges of the paper but it results in the preposterous situation where the full A5 page will not print out on A4 paper. Furthermore, when one of the Ready, Set, Go! custom grids comes to be placed on the page (see the section on layout below) this is aligned with the print area rather than with the A5 dimensions. For non-standard paper sizes the conclusion must be that the Page Setup data does not appear to be linked in any intelligent fashion to the printer output. Work-rounds for utilising non-standard sizes such as A5 are possible but these should not be necessary and lead to a waste of time in what should be a straightforward operation.

The measurement systems available include inches, centimetres and picas/points. The metric alternative suffers from having a half centimetre as its smallest measure compared to the millimetres used in PageMaker. Having control to the nearest five millimetres is not sufficient when working at the high levels of accuracy and typographic control required in quality publications. Admittedly, users needing this level of control can work in picas/points but this is hardly satisfactory for those who prefer to work in metric units.

**Layout**

From studying the manual one gains the distinct impression that page layout in Ready, Set, Go! must be based on a grid which organises the page into columns and rows. The program comes with eight built-in grids – figure 3.6 – with pre-set margins at a rather narrow 0.5 inches all round. For the relative newcomer used to simple columnar text the idea of the grid is not always clear, though a number of books on layout discuss the concept and point out its positive features. In spite of this, one is left wondering if the grid was chosen to offer a different user interface rather than for any pragmatic reason. That Letraset are wedded to the idea is supported by their including a copy of White's 'The grid book' in the software package but it is here, finally, that the careful reader will find salvation. Mixed in with a lot of common sense and good ideas on layout is the statement (page 4): 'If these presized pigeonholes (the built-in grids) can be useful, use them. If not, don't bother. Ignore the rows and just use the columns'. As experience is built up in DTP the grid may become a useful starting point for page design but for many librarians layout in columns will be sufficient for most purposes.

Fortunately, Ready, Set, Go! allows customised layouts to be created easily. Choosing the 'Grid Setup' option from the 'Design Grids' menu displays the dialogue box of figure 3.7 where the margins and the number of columns can be specified. These are then reflected as dotted guide lines on the screen page.

With the release of version 4.5, Letraset appears to have recognised that alternatives should be provided and it is now possible to build up guides on the page instead of just grids. Unfortunately, the implementation of the guides is far from complete and they are there to help position objects than for laying out the basic page. Thus, it is not possible to easily build up a two-column layout with them – because text and graphics blocks cannot 'Snap to' guides as they can to the grids and because all alignment must be done by eye rather than automatically. A combination of grids and guides might do the trick but the program does not permit this heresy.

Master pages are created, and operate, in a similar way to PageMaker. That is, the information on the masters cannot readily be altered on individual pages but it can be removed from any page by de-selecting the 'Use Master' command in the Special menu.

**Handling of text**

*Text entry*

As explained in the section on the user interface, the main difference in this facility between Ready, Set, Go! and PageMaker is that Ready, Set, Go! requires all text to be confined within text boxes or blocks. These are created using the

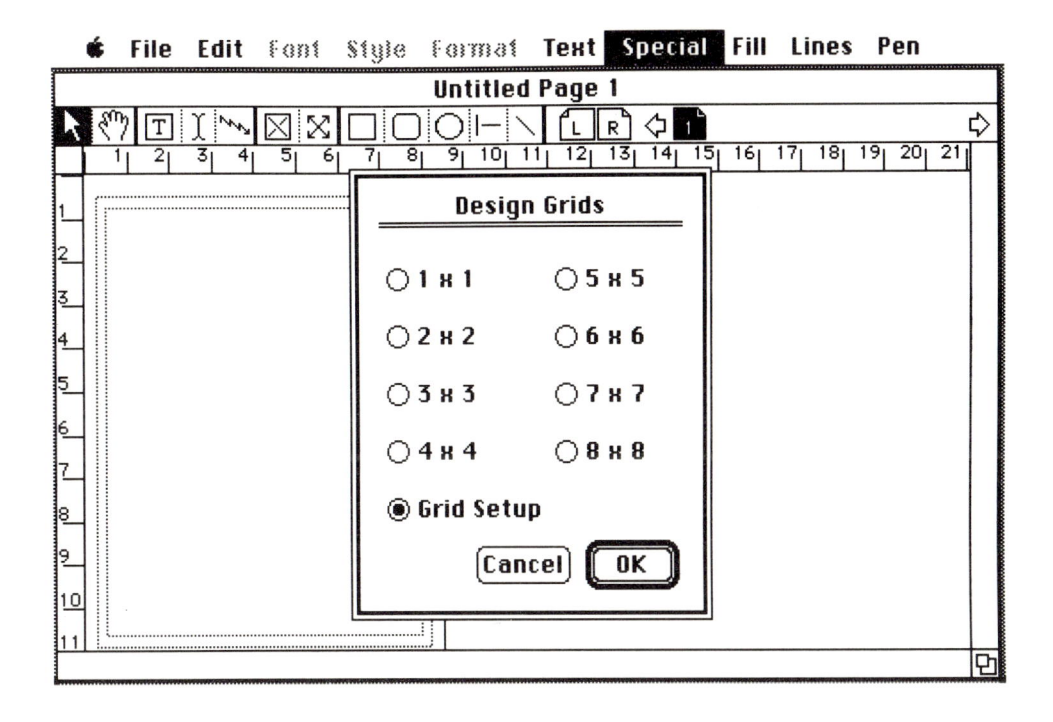

Figure 3.6 Built-in grids in Ready, Set, Go!

Figure 3.7 Design grids in Ready, Set, Go!

text tool – [T] – by dragging to create rectangles of the size required and the blocks can be small enough to contain a single word header or large enough to occupy the whole page. If the text blocks are to correspond to any sections of the grid then their creation is considerably simplified by using the 'Snap to' option from the Special menu.

Once the text blocks have been drawn on the page the text itself can be imported. Ready, Set, Go! will directly accept formatted text from three Macintosh word processors – MacWrite 4.5, Microsoft Word versions 1.05 and 3.0, and WriteNow – as well as text-only files. All compatible files are accessed via the 'Get Text ...' command from the File menu which, like PageMaker's Place function automatically recognises the different formats. No provision is made for directly importing from PC word processors and the files from these must be converted to ASCII before transfer. However, Ready, Set, Go! 4.5 shares with PageMaker 3.0 the ability to import tagged text and automatically format this according to pre-set styles. For users wishing to interface with PCs and non-compatible word processors this is worth a lot.

Unlike PageMaker, where default settings are used, text-only files can be placed on the Ready, Set, Go! page using the formatting information available at the insertion point. This means that the font, size, style and justification can be specified before the text is added to the document – an especially useful feature. Text can also be entered directly into Ready, Set, Go! and some of the word processing features are described in the section below on text editing.

*Chaining*

If the story to be placed is larger than a single block, the chaining of text blocks can readily be achieved using the linking tool – ⌇ – clicking on the mouse button in the order they are to be linked and then double clicking in the final text block. On transfer the imported text will then automatically flow into the linked blocks in the order selected until the whole story has been placed. This means that complex layouts can be produced easily but there is also the underlying assumption that the story length can be estimated accurately beforehand. For the inexperienced librarian who is still getting to grips with DTP this may not be easy. A further aspect of the chaining process is that 'Global links' can be specified in association with the insertion of new pages so that a long document with a single layout can be created with a minimum of fuss. Here again the surprising assumption has been made that the story or document length is known and that the precise number of pages can be created before the text is imported. This poor design feature makes the global links concept less suitable than PageMaker's Autoflow command or XPress' automatic text chaining, particularly for long documents.

*Exporting files*

Ready, Set, Go!4.5 permits the exporting of text from a single block or a series of linked blocks, but only as a text only file. Thus, if the original was imported as a formatted file from an 'approved' Macintosh word processor, there is no option but to keep two versions. Or import the text file into the word processor, reformat, and take it from there. The exporting is achieved using the 'Put Text ...' command from the File menu. The interesting option is also provided of saving a document as a tagged text file, based on the Ready, Set, Go! style sheets.

*Text editing*

In contrast to PageMaker, the program offers a number word processing features and in some respects can be considered an alternative implementation to MacAuthor and FullWrite which are word processors with DTP facilities. The suitability of this approach will depend on the type of job in hand and the relative advantages for writing books are discussed in detail in chapter 8. However, for some small jobs these features may be all that is required and may be sufficient to enable stories to be written directly into Ready, Set, Go!. Close control over type size is possible and a useful case conversion option is present, similar to that available in MacAuthor. However, the spelling checker and the find and replace function both have their disadvantages.

The **spell checker** acts sequentially throughout the document identifying misspelled words as it works its way from the current cursor position to the end of the linked block. This is not only a time consuming operation, it also requires an (almost) unnecessary degree of input on the part of the operator. On coming upon the first misspelled word the checker simply stops and waits for the operator to take action – by typing in the correct spelling or choosing 'Suggest...' from the pull down menu. When this has been done 'Check...' has to be chosen again until the next misspelled word is highlighted. This is a frustrating implementation and falls far behind the better spelling checkers that are available.

The '**Find**' function works admirably well and speedily throughout a text block – say a single page – or through a complete chain. The similar '**Replace**' function is curious for it does not highlight text to indicate the cursor position after the operation has been completed so that one is left scouring the page for the blinking cursor in a mass of text. This makes it very difficult to verify that the replacement has taken place and is particularly strange when highlighting is used in the 'Find' function. Neither of these functions have wrapround to return to the starting point of the search and so searches must always be carried out from the beginning of the text block, although the facility to find and replace the font, style and size of text could be useful in some instances.

Furthermore the 'Undo' command has been badly and inconsistently implemented in its linking to the replace function.

If a word is mistakenly replaced the standard way to return to the previous version of the text is through the Undo command from Edit menu. In Ready, Set, Go!, using Undo with 'Replace next', restores the original word in the text but it does not delete the substitute word from the Replace operation and so the two words co-exist in the sentence. Alternatively, when the standard 'Replace...' command is used the situation could be said to be worse, the Undo command being completely inactive.

*Style sheets*

In Ready, Set, Go! the 'Styles...' command available from the Text menu opens up a window with a list of existing style names. From here, and via the specifications box shown in figure 3.8, new styles can be created or existing ones modified. This specifications box represents an extremely effective implementation of styles in the package with the bulk of the parameters being clearly visible from the one window. A move to a secondary window is necessary for the setting of tabs, using the arcane symbols specially designed to confuse users, and for setting inter-character spacing.

In two other respects the implementation of style sheets in Ready, Set, Go! is disappointing. First, styles generated for use in a document are not available directly from a pull down menu as in PageMaker or MacAuthor but only through the Styles window. This slows down their use and makes them appear to be an afterthought in the design rather than an integral part of the program. Secondly, and more importantly, to use a style throughout an imported text-only file, sections of the document must be highlighted for the required style to take effect. This is also in contrast to other systems where the positioning of the cursor anywhere in a paragraph will implement a chosen style. Again, the procedure will slow down the user and in long documents with an abundance of different paragraphs and headings this constant operation will become very frustrating.

## Handling of graphics

*Formats*

Like imported text, graphics created in other packages can only be used in a pre-defined block. Once this has been drawn using the picture tool and then selected using the cropping tool, a pattern similar to television interference occupies the whole block and indicates that it is ready for accepting a graphic. Opening the 'Get Picture...' command from the File menu provides a list of available graphics in the compatible formats of MacPaint, PICT, PICT2 and EPSF.

Scanned files created in any of these formats as well as TIFF and RIFF can be imported using the same technique. The modification of scanned images is possible through the variation of brightness and contrast, and special effects such as posterisation and negatives can be created. As with PageMaker,

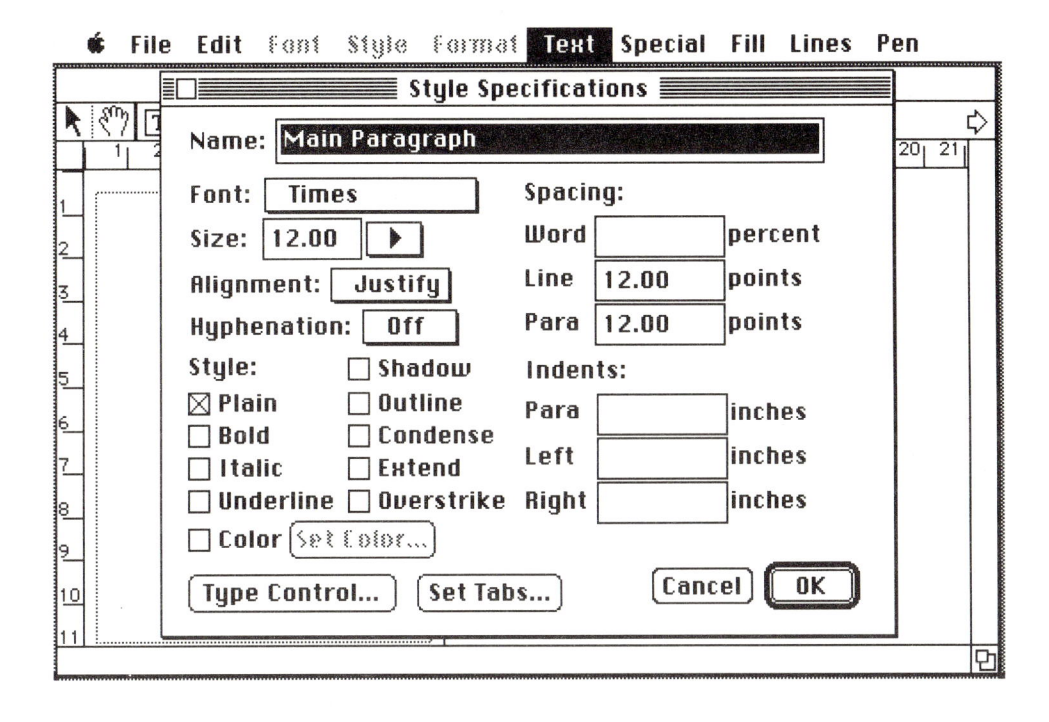

Figure 3.8 Style sheets in Ready, Set, Go!

variations are possible on the type of screen used for printing. However, it appears that Ready, Set, Go! is selective in its application of image control to TIFF files, for when the scanned image of figure 5.10 was imported it was not recognised by the 'Image control...' option. When a RIFF version was used from Letraset's own ImageStudio the 'Image control...' became operational. If a large amount of scanned work is planned, this feature would repay some investigation.

*Text wrap*

Runarounds are created in a fairly standard way. The graphic is imported into a picture block, dragged into place using the mouse and, assuming that 'runaround' is chosen in the picture specifications box, text automatically wraps round the graphic. The text repel distance can be adjusted to give the effect required but further adjustments similar to those available with PageMaker are not possible. If 'runaround' is not checked the text will flow only round the rectangular picture box itself.

In adjusting picture blocks and their contents a DTP user can take a while to position a graphic exactly. Unfortunately, in Ready, Set, Go! every alteration to a picture block, however small, causes a complete screen refresh. This is an operation which is distracting and which is painful to view, particularly on large screens when a complete page disappears and reforms before your very eyes. Furthermore, making these adjustments entails much to-ing and fro-ing between different tools.

*Integral graphics*  A range of basic geometric shapes can be drawn from within the program. The shapes available can be seen from the icons across the top of any of figures 3.4 to 3.7. The line thickness for any of the shapes, and the general line style – single, dashed, or double – can be specified from the 'Lines' menu but, ironically, one has to refer to the manual to determine the precise thicknesses of the selection. A further modification – available from the 'Pen' menu – can be made to any line by changing its pattern from black (the default) to pseudo grey shades or a set of uninteresting brickwork or ball patterns. The rectangle and circle shapes can be similarly filled with the same patterns but this time chosen from the 'Fill' menu.

**Overall view**

Ready, Set, Go! is difficult to sum up. It has many of the trappings of a good DTP package but it somehow falls short in the manner in which some of these have been implemented. It is difficult to know the reason for this, but perhaps it could be put down to the rush to have new versions of software on the market to maintain or improve market share.

There is a definite feeling when using the package that Letraset have attempted to come out from under the shadow of PageMaker with some deliberately different, if not novel, ideas on electronic page make-up. This must be good policy in the long term, for by providing different approaches, the user should be able to choose the interface (and the package) that is most suitable for his or her purposes. Unfortunately in Ready, Set, Go! some of these ideas have just not been thought through sufficiently and the conclusion must be that this is a potentially powerful program flawed by its implementation.

In the present version 4.5 there are just too many areas where the procedures surrounding operations are confusing for Ready, Set, Go! to be recommended for de-centralised library use (chapter 9). A program like XPress offers so much more with a friendlier interface that dedicated DTP sections within libraries are not likely to be attracted to the heavier approach of Ready, Set, Go!.

In spite of this, the program does score over PageMaker in its text editing features such as the spelling checker and search and replace. But again, these have not been well implemented – particularly the spell checker – and they are not as smooth as the equivalent functions in XPress. Thus, even with these advantages Ready, Set, Go! does not have enough going for it in its present version to make it a worthwhile purchase for most libraries.

# XPRESS

**Background**

From the time of its entry into the market place it always looked as if XPress would be a winner. While not everyone took immediately to it there were few of the equivocal remarks that are common in software reviews. Certainly the interface was different from that of PageMaker but once this had been appreciated and experienced most users adored the program and began to work with the extra power that lurked beneath the pull down menus.

The package was developed by the American company Quark who had already created a few programs for the Apple II range. XPress was their first Macintosh program and version 1.0 appeared in the early summer of 1987. A typical review of the time was that written by Hewson (1987) who later furnished an excellent book on version 1.0 of the program, the only offputting feature being the completely unnecessary comic-book cover. Since then bug fixes and a few enhancements appeared in revision 1.1 (year end 1987) and this was followed by the release of version 2.0 in autumn 1988. A cut down version of the program incorporating a large number of templates has recently appeared under the title QuarkStyle.

**User interface**

At first site the interface can appear both familiar and intimidating consisting of the usual page display but with several unusual tools in the palette down the left of the screen – figure 3.9. But this is a churlish complaint for when did the laws of computer software state that an icon had to be clear and easy to understand – as examples of recondite symbols look at the cropping tool of PageMaker and the chaining tool of Ready, Set, Go! It is just that XPress seems to have more than its fair share of these. Running through the tools they can be considered to fall into three sections. The topmost four-points-of-the-compass icon is the mover tool used for transferring boxes and lines on the page and this is followed by the text and graphics editing tool. The second group of tools is used for creating boxes – rectangles for holding text and three shapes for graphics – and then the by now standard icons for drawing basic geometric shapes. The final two chain icons are the tools used for linking and unlinking text between boxes.

Another point worth noting is that for a document comprising more than two pages, the pages are displayed below each other singly or in pairs depending on the document. In this way XPress resembles the display of word processors and permits the

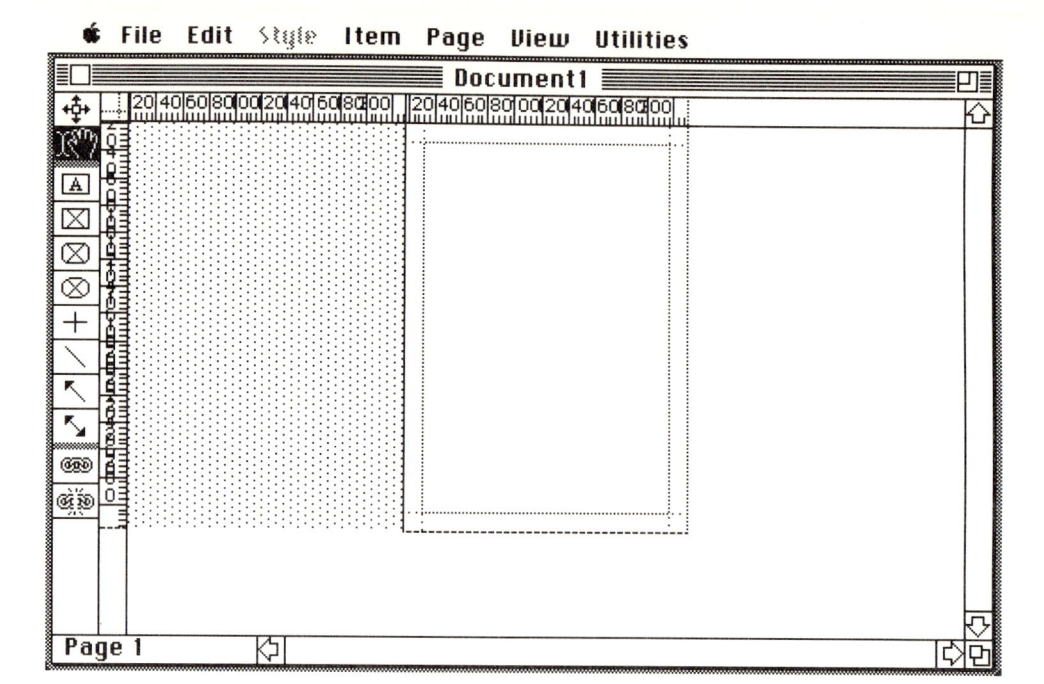

**Figure 3.9 User interface of XPress**

bottom of one spread to be viewed simultaneously with the top of the next. This is not possible in PageMaker and Ready, Set, Go! which treat single or double page spreads as discreet units.

The power of the facilities of this program and the thoughtful way in which these have been implemented only becomes obvious in use. For example, the cursor changes from the sinking-into-quicksand outstretched hand to a pointing finger when moved round the perimeter of a graphics box. This means that the graphic can be adjusted and then the box re-sized without having to move to the tool palette. Furthermore, although the mover tool has to be used in order to transfer boxes around the page, this can be temporarily selected by holding down the command key, the required item moved and then control returned to the previous tool. In PageMaker, processes involving the adjustment and movement of graphics can require frequent changing between the cropping tool and the pointer, but it is only after a period using the XPress method that this appears cumbersome. Pop-up menus have made their appearance in XPress but so far they are not use as extensively as in PageMaker.

The impression is gained from the first view of the screen that the pasteboard idea has been used in this program. On further investigation the area surrounding the page cannot in fact be used for holding stories and graphics while modifications are made to sections of a document. The fact that items cannot be moved from the page is at times a distinct disadvantage for, as explained earlier, one of the benefits of DTP to newcomers is that various trial layouts and graphic effects can be created before a final decision is made. The facility to move objects to a pasteboard enables them to be easily retained for future use. In XPress, if a graphic is to be moved to a different section of the text several pages away, the box containing it must first be deleted and then pasted into position on the new page. This functions well but it is an operation that works only on one graphic box at once and as a result the process can be laborious when moving several illustrations (or stories).

In common with Ready, Set, Go! XPress uses the box as its basic building block. However, the concept has fairly strict rules built into it, particularly in the case of embedded boxes, or parent-child boxes as the manual refers to them. The main restriction is on child box mobility for these cannot be moved outside the parent. This is no doubt one reason for the lack of an active pasteboard – any graphics boxes embedded within larger text boxes literally cannot be moved out of the parent box, let alone off the page. For those publications where the layout can be defined independently of content, or where the operator has a clear idea of both content and form from the beginning, this no doubt works well: the layout can be created and then text and graphics added to fill the empty boxes. For less experienced DTP users it is not as immediately easy to grasp as the working of PageMaker. In any event, this important piece of advice from the XPress manual should be borne in mind at all times: 'A child item can never be in front of another item that is in front of its parent'!!

The simultaneous working on multiple documents is possible as XPress permits up to seven documents to be open at once. Unfortunately, a window command is not available to facilitate easy swapping between these.

**Format**

On opening a new document a dialogue box is displayed for the user to specify a range of settings for page size, margins and general format. XPress has provision for five pre-set sizes of page: US Letter; A4; Tabloid; US Legal; and B5. Unfortunately, A5 is not pre-set but like most of the DTP programs there is the facility for entering any customised size that the user requires, up to a maximum of 48 inches square. When the chosen page size is smaller than the paper for printing, for example A5 on A4 paper, printing occurs in the top left hand corner of each sheet.

XPress offers a similar number of measurement choices to PageMaker: inches, decimal inches, picas, points, millimetres, and ciceros. In addition the possibility is provided for using picas along the horizontal rule and inches down the vertical – a traditional set-up in newspaper production according to the XPress manual. The measurements are altered in the Preferences dialogue box from the pull down Edit menu and act as default settings for all new documents until changed. Though the chosen settings apply to the rulers, values can be entered in the various dialogue boxes in any measurement unit and, as long as the accepted abbreviation for the unit is entered, XPress will accept it and act on the information given.

**Layout**

In setting up a new document the page size and the broad layout of the page – the number of columns and the margin sizes – have first to be specified. Once a representation of the first page appears on screen any features that are to be repeated throughout the document can be added to the master pages – in this case referred to as default pages. It is important that the user has a clear idea of the overall layout from the start because changes to the default page are not reflected in the existing document on screen but only in new pages added from then on. Page numbers, for example, must be placed on the default pages as the first operation otherwise they will only start part way through the document. This constriction can be useful in those cases where a change of layout is required for just a section of a document, but care must be taken in using the design of the default pages until one is familiar with their traits. Furthermore, as with many aspects of XPress there are work-rounds, and a method of reformatting a complete document to a revised default page is provided.

The other difference from the implementation of the master pages in PageMaker is that all items on a default XPress page can be altered, moved around and even deleted from individual pages. This applies equally to small graphics boxes and to the parent text box. If, to create interest on a particular page the number of columns in the parent box is to be changed, this is a simple operation calling up the Text Specifications dialogue box from the Item menu and altering a parameter for the single page – figure 3.10. When this is done there is no effect on the design of the default pages.

The 'standard' features of DTP programs – ruler guides, snap-to-guides, insert pages – are included in XPress but the deletion of pages can cause some problems for the uninitiated. If the default values of the program from the 'Preferences' dialogue box are used, deleting pages which result in a text overflow in a series of linked boxes will cause further pages to be inserted to handle the overflow. This can result in no changes being made to the document and can, until the cause had been deduced, be very disconcerting. As with page deletion, the XPress settings can be adjusted to obtain the required effect.

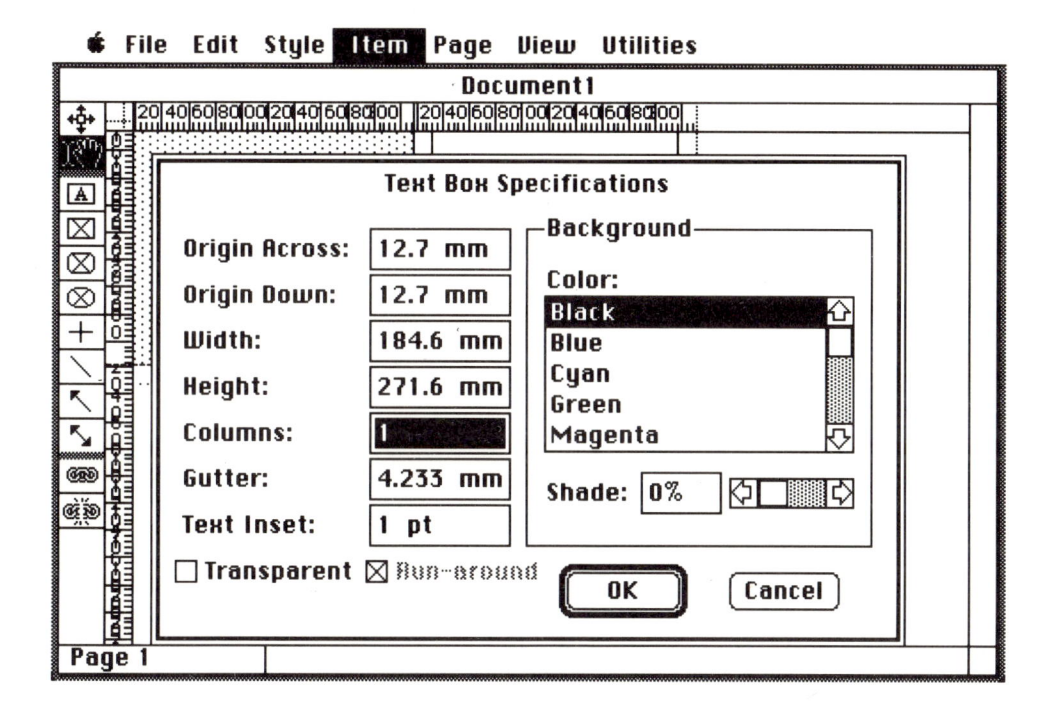

**Figure 3.10 The Text Specifications box in XPress**

## Handling of text

*Text entry*

As explained above, XPress is in some ways similar to Ready, Set, Go! in its use of boxes for holding text and graphics. Where it differs is in its well-designed interface which makes it particularly delightful to use in the case of text boxes. Thus, if no text boxes have been defined by the user, XPress assumes, by default, that the area bounded by the margins is one. The result of this is that for simple, single column layouts first time users can quickly create a document: by selecting the editing tool and clicking anywhere between the margins the box become active ready to receive text from either an external program or directly within XPress.

Also in common with Ready, Set, Go! is the easy means of adjusting the layout of imported text through modifications to the size of boxes. Any change in either height or width of a text box results in automatic text flow between all linked boxes and, where necessary, in the creation of additional pages to handle any overflow.

XPress will import documents created in MacWrite, Microsoft Word (including style sheets), Microsoft Works and WriteNow as well as standard ASCII files. Acceptable files in any of these formats are displayed in a transfer window once the 'Get Text' command has been selected from the File menu. A variant – 'Get Document' – allows part or all of another XPress file to be imported and its position specified in the active document.

Direct text entry from the keyboard is the other method available for adding text to an XPress document.

*Linking*

In documents where the layout remains unchanged throughout, automatic linking is incorporated into the default pages to facilitate the automatic creation of new pages during the importing of text. In its ever helpful manner XPress uses automatic linking as its default setting though like many aspects of the program this can be readily changed.

Where a separate linked series of boxes is required to provide contrast within a document, manual linking can be utilised. By using the chain tool and clicking on a sequence of boxes in turn, links will be created for the automatic flow of text. Existing links can be displayed by clicking the chain tool and the results from this can be visually arresting for complex layouts with arrows pointing in all directions around a document – figure 3.11.

*Exporting files*

The benefits of exporting to word processor formats has already been discussed in the section on PageMaker. In XPress a 'Save Text' command available from the File menu enables any selected text or an entire story to be saved in the usual range of formats: MacWrite, Microsoft Word, WriteNow, and as ASCII text.

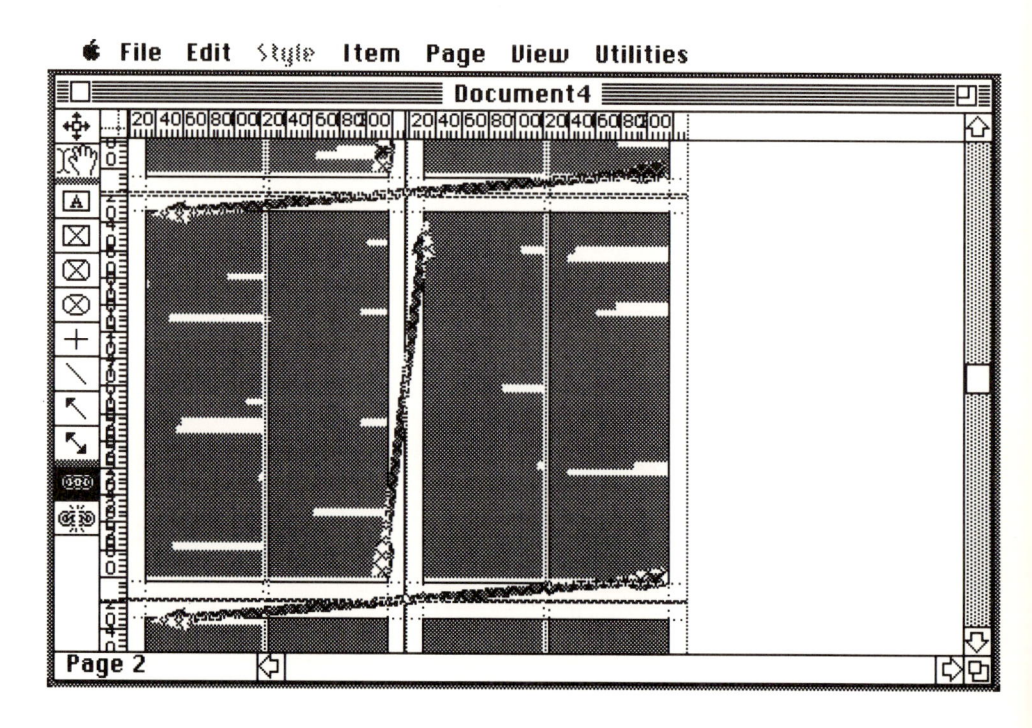

**Figure 3.11 Links displayed in XPress**

*Text editing*

XPress incorporates a spelling checker and a search and replace feature.

As with many things in this program, the **spelling checker** has been thoughtfully implemented to require as little input from the user as possible. Selecting 'Check story...' from the Utilities menu automatically spell checks the complete story in a set of active, linked text boxes. At the end of the search it returns a word count with the number of suspect words and then works systematically through the list of misspellings, highlighting the position of each within the document. Suspect words can be skipped if they are acceptable to the user or the dictionary can be used to make suggestions. Auxiliary dictionaries can be created to hold correct spellings for particular jobs or such things as English spellings. Unfortunately, if the user is working with a reduced view of the document at the start of the check, it is not possible to change to an actual size view when investigating the misspellings and the spell check has to be repeated. This is a poor feature but is partly counteracted by the speedy working of the checker.

Like Ready, Set, Go! the search and replace routine in XPress – referred to as Find/Change – has two operational levels. In the first of these the text strings are entered in the usual way and the search started by pressing the 'Find next' button. Only when the first occurrence of the string has been located is the option to change or change all given. The second level permits find and change of a much more detailed kind, and enables occurrences of text with particular attributes (font, style, size) to be located and altered. Wild card characters can be included in find dialogues but there is no wrapround and so searches must begin at the start of text boxes if a complete story is to be checked. Care must be exercised to ensure that the correct changes are being made to text as the ' Undo' command is inoperative in these circumstances.

*Style sheets*

The implementation and operation of these is very similar to the style sheets in PageMaker, being made up of three distinct dialogue boxes for the specification of typestyle, paragraph formatting, and tabs. The 'Character Specifications' dialogue box is the equivalent of the Text Specifications dialogue in PageMaker and is used for defining font, size, style and colour – figure 3.12. Left and right indents are defined through the 'Formats...' box which also provides the means of controlling the line spacing before and after paragraphs. As would be expected, different paragraph styles can have different spacings built into their style sheets. The usual variety of tabs – left, centre, right and decimal – can be set from the 'Tabs...' dialogue. Both paragraph formats and tabs are set visually against a ruler that is temporarily placed across the top of the relevant text box.

61

All three parameters are available separately from the 'Style' menu and all user defined styles are appended to this menu for selection in the usual way. Individual parameters can be overridden for particular paragraphs by selecting the appropriate one from the menu. The creation of new styles and the editing of existing ones is controlled from the 'Edit' menu when the characteristics of the chosen style are exhibited and the opportunity given to make amendments to each of the parameters in turn – figure 3.13.

## Handling of graphics

*Formats*

Picture boxes can be drawn in three basic shapes – rectangular, rectangular with rounded corners and circular – and once these are on the page they can be filled using the 'Get Picture' command. XPress is compatible with the usual graphics formats of MacPaint, PICT, EPSF and TIFF and also enables RIFF files to be brought in from ImageStudio.

Adjustments to imported graphics can be made in two ways. Where only a portion of a larger graphic is required this must first be positioned in the picture box. To achieve this XPress performs another of its cursor transformation tricks for on moving the cursor inside a picture box it changes shape to the grabber hand. By holding down the mouse button and dragging, the graphic can be pulled in any direction. In some cases – if for example the required section is a small diagram on an otherwise blank A4 page – it is not easy to locate the desired area and XPress provides a keyboard shortcut – Command-Shift-M – for centring the imported graphic in the box.

Once the graphic has been positioned, the precise size of the box can be finalised by moving the re-size handles on the picture box itself. Similarly, the mover tool can be used to adjust the box on the page (or within its parent box).

Like PageMaker, XPress enables some manipulation of scanned images but again, the effects of any changes can only be seen with grey scale or colour monitors and are really of use only to those with some experience of scanning. Controls are provided for adjusting colour, shade, and contrast – through the use of contrast curves – and a range of screening controls for printing is available.

*Text wrap*

Runaround an irregular graphic is straightforward. The graphic should be positioned in a rectangular picture box and the appropriate settings of 'runaround' and 'transparent' selected. 'Runaround' refers to the graphic shape and 'Transparent' tells the program to ignore the outline of the box. Once the text offset has been specified – the thickness of white space surrounding the graphic – XPress does the rest and flows the text. Text flow

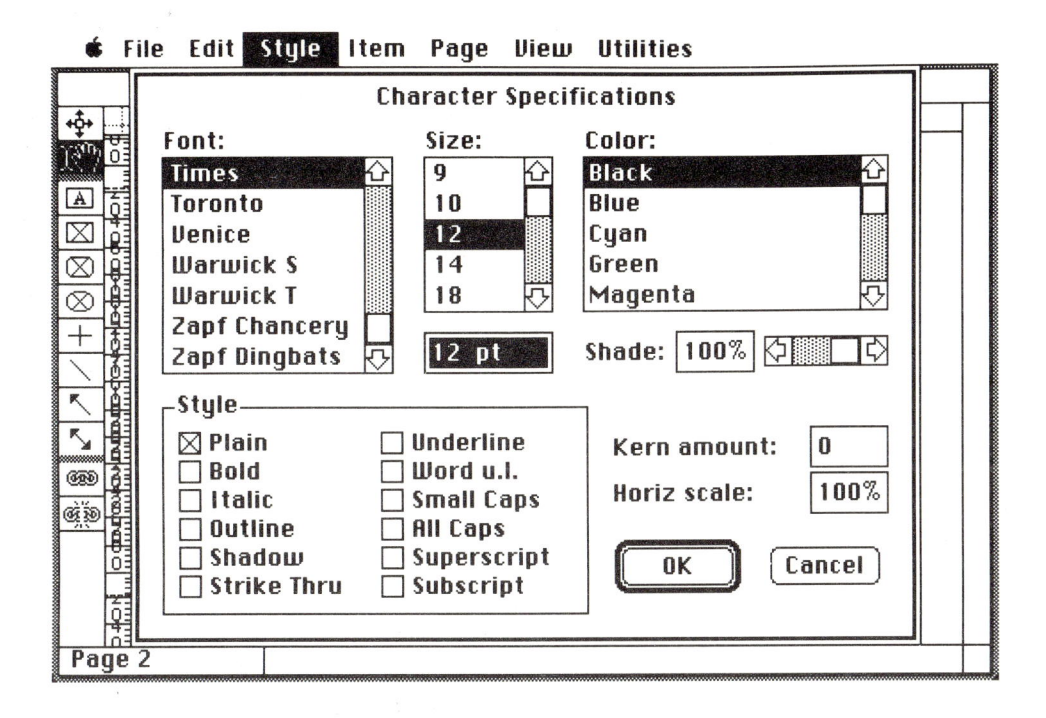

Figure 3.12 Character specifications in XPress

Figure 3.13 Style sheet creation in XPress

63

around variants of the graphic using PageMaker's 'skin' approach is not provided.

The text offset can also be used to repel text from rectangular boxes themselves – either picture or text boxes – but for some reason this feature has been omitted from text flow around boxes of other shapes. This is a pity for some nice effects can be obtained by importing graphics into circular shaped boxes and cropping. Unfortunately, the repel distance from non-rectangular graphic boxes cannot be changed resulting in text nestling too close to boxes for most aesthetic considerations. A tip culled from Hewson's XPress Companion (page 113–114) is useful here for by creating a larger white box and sitting the original inside, the desired effect can be obtained.

*Integral graphics*

Lines can be drawn in the expected way and in addition to the conventional selection of styles and thicknesses lines with arrow heads both with and without tail feathers are provided as standard. The characteristics of lines can be altered from the 'Style' menu or from a Line Specifications dialogue box available from the 'Item' menu.

Square and rectangular shapes are not directly available from the tool menu. However, as the majority of uses for these are as frames surrounding picture or text boxes, XPress deals with them in a different, and rather clever, way. A 'Frame...' command is available from the 'Item' pull down menu and the specifications of any enclosing border – style, size and colour – are fixed here. A frame editor is also available for the creation of elaborate shapes. When the characteristics have been finalised, XPress automatically draws the frame around the picture or text box and this then forms an integral part of the box and can be moved anywhere as a single unit. Background colour or shading of picture and text boxes are controlled via the respective dialogue boxes.

**Overall view**

There is little doubt that XPress is the most powerful DTP program running on the Macintosh. Just when the user has decided that it cannot cope with a particular requirement a study of the manual and a few tweaks make it burst into action. At the same time the user interface has been made as sympathetic as possible concomitant with the delivery of all this power. There is a feeling that the program has been *designed* rather than just thrown together to meet the needs of the emerging market for DTP products.

The one thing that XPress does not include (in the present version) is the ability to read tagged text which, as pointed out in the example in chapter 8, could be particularly useful in a library forced into using Apple and IBM-compatible machines side-by-side. Apart from this the only thing that lets XPress down is the manual which is appallingly indexed and contains a number of statements that seem designed to confuse the user.

In spite of this enthusiastic response, the question must be asked 'Is there a place for XPress in a library DTP set-up'. This is not as inappropriate as it sounds and the answer will be dependent on how DTP is organised in the library. XPress, in spite of its apparent ease of use but because of its complexity, is not the sort of program that would be suitable in a de-centralised DTP arrangement which was open to all staff. The training needs to ensure that all potential users were knowledgeable of the complexities would take up too many resources and if this training was not carried out, would result in a waste of time through too many questions. Where XPress should prove itself in library use is in a specialised DTP or publicity department which has large and varied publishing demands and where the staff time and dedication will not be a problem. In these circumstances the program will make many friends with its power and ability to do most things except get the librarian off your back. Hewson (October, 1988) was not overstating the case when he wrote that 'XPress 2.0 establishes Quark as the masters of professional page makeup on the Macintosh...'

**References**

Hewson, D. Measure for measure. *MacUser*, no. 13, July 1987, pp. 37–43.

Hewson, D. *The Quark XPress companion*. London, Heyden & Son, 1988. ISBN 0 86344001 0.

Hewson, D. XPress delivery! *MacUser*, no. 28, October 1988, pp. 47–49. Review on the release of version 2.0 of XPress.

Tyler, A. Hold the front page! *MacUser*, no. 3, November/December 1985, pp. 64–68.

Tyler, A. On your marks. *MacUser*, no. 10, January/February 1987, pp. 34–36.

White, J. V. *The grid book; a guide to page planning*. Paramus, NJ, Letraset, 1987. LC 87-82124.

# 4   Word Processing software for DTP

## MACAUTHOR

**Background**

When it first appeared, MacAuthor broke new ground for Macintosh word processors for it was the first to feature style sheets, incorporate a word count and enable flexible page layout between text and graphics. Several early reviews were enthusiastic (see, for example, Ritblatt) but the product did have a tendency to be slow and die on embarrassing and infuriating occasions.

When compared to some recent software its growing up period from fractious infant to responsible adolescent appears to have been fairly modest but its bug-ridden early beginnings are unfortunately still remembered by some. Towards the end of 1986 the 1.3ß version cured a number of problems associated with frames, but this was not officially released and most users had to wait until spring 1987 for version 1.4. This finally cured a number of other known bugs and was the first really stable version for users wanting to take full advantage of MacAuthor's many features. Much of 1987/88 was taken up with further refining the product into MacAuthor II.

MacAuthor and The Visual Arts discussed in chapter 5 share the distinction of being the only two British software products discussed in this section. MacAuthor has been developed by Icon Technology of Leicester, a company with a long history of Apple and particularly Macintosh associations. Attempts have been made to market MacAuthor in the United States – as Laser Author – but apart from a handful of enthusiastic users this venture has proved largely unsuccessful. In addition to

MacAuthor Icon Technology have recently developed an equation processor called Formulator.

The product has a dedicated (but not uncritical) following partly based on the flexibility of the software but also on the quality of support and after-sales service offered. Its gradual improvement over the last two years has shown that it is produced by a company who do listen to their users and who will incorporate enhancements and suggestions wherever possible.

**User interface**

Programs conceived as word processors present, superficially at least, a more straightforward interface to users than DTP-specific software. The general idea is that you should be able to start moving on the important job – writing – as soon as possible but when you need the more sophisticated tools, hey presto!, there they are lurking just below the surface. In practice they are sometimes buried so deep that even a JCB wouldn't find them in time to meet a deadline.

The MacAuthor interface is accordingly unremarkable with no toolbox or other icons to clutter up the screen. What is presented is a blank writing area with the usual pull down menus above and one important piece of information in the bottom left hand corner. This is a word count, a relatively minor but necessary feature which has given rise to much heated discussion and letters to journals, particularly in the Macintosh press, over the past twelve months or so. As with style sheets, MacAuthor was the first program to include this facility. Three of the pull down menus (Heading, Paragraph and Text) can be customised and used as templates or, in MacAuthor terminology, Stationery Pads (see below).

In common with all word processors MacAuthor provides a single-page scrolling display of the document and a page preview is available so that a two page spread can be viewed. Unfortunately, no aspect of the page preview screen is active and consequently layout decisions based on this – for example the positioning of pictures on adjacent pages – can only be made at the full document view.

**Format**

MacAuthor uses the standard Macintosh paper sizes which normally means the use of A4 paper on the LaserWriter and pin-feed paper on the Apple ImageWriter (unless a sheet feeder is connected to the ImageWriter). The printing area on either of these is defined from the margin settings which are adjusted from the 'Page setup...' command under the File menu (figure 4.1). Pre-set figures for common sizes such as A5 are not

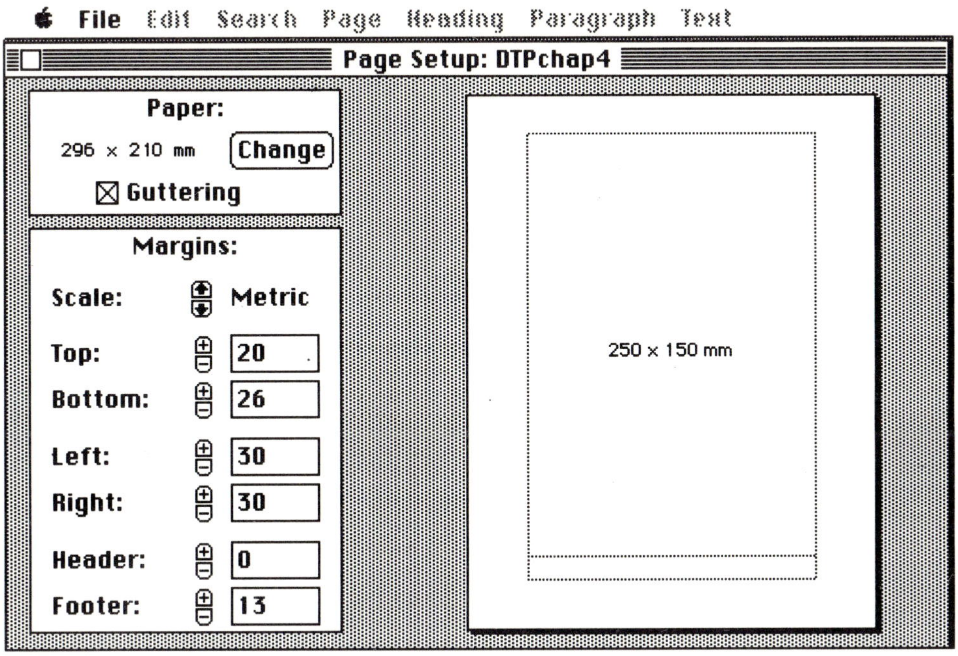

**Figure 4.1 Page setup in MacAuthor**

available and must be created from a knowledge of their dimensions. Working units of imperial, metric, picas and points can be chosen.

**Layout**

The standard way of laying out a page in MacAuthor is as a single column of text, but variants on this can be achieved in two ways. If the illusion of two columns is required then hanging indents can be created to separate the heading from the main section of the paragraph, as on this page. Where two or more columns are required MacAuthor uses the concept of frames. Thus, where linked text must flow between columns MacAuthor has an intelligent 'continuation text' option which automatically creates another column as required, whether on the same page or a new one. However, frames are more versatile than this for they permit virtually any arrangement on the page of graphics and text. A full description of their use for graphics is described below.

Another extremely useful feature is the incorporation of Stationery Pads which act as templates for previously agreed layouts that can be transferred from job to job. A Stationery Pad is usually a set of pre-designated style sheets which enable continuity of layout to be maintained throughout a single document saved as separate files or chapters. Without having to remember the format of all paragraphs and headings a Stationery

Pad of these is created to be called up as required as a new, blank document.

But a Stationery Pad can be more than this for an alternative is provided of saving an entire document as a template. This opens up a number of possibilities. If, for example, different issues of a document are to feature the same graphic on the same page an outline issue could be created and saved as a Stationery Pad. Alternatively, if a non-standard but fixed layout is required on one page – say the first page of each chapter – frames could be positioned on the page and then the complete (blank) document saved with the style sheets.

## Handling of text

*Text entry*

As MacAuthor is at root a word processor the clearly preferred form of text entry is direct from the keyboard i.e. do-it-yourself. Presumably for this reason MacAuthor is curiously xenophobic with regard to other formats, recognising only MacWrite and text-only apart from its own. In practice, this is not as bad as it sounds for most Macintosh word processors will save in MacWrite format and so some compatibility with other programs is maintained. Even small imported text-only files present little problem, being relatively easy to reformat with the help of style sheets. Only in large documents is the disadvantage obvious. However, MacAuthor is compatible with a number of outline processors – Acta, MORE and Voilà! – and an example of its use in this way can be found in chapter 8.

The other difference between MacAuthor and DTP programs is that external files cannot be appended to an existing document. Instead, they must be opened as a new file and then the appropriate sections transferred manually using the Macintosh cut and paste techniques.

*Exporting files*

In seemingly stand-offish fashion MacAuthor only permits the saving of documents in its native format and as text-only files. The reason for this is no doubt that a complex document comprising frames and different style settings cannot easily be reduced to the simpler MacWrite format and the files would lose some formatting information in the conversion process. As in the importing of files this is not of great significance but it should be realised that external use of a file produced by this word processor will entail more work than if some others were used. A comparison can be made in this respect with Microsoft Word which, as explained in chapter 3, has a format that is recognised by all three of the page make-up programs.

*Style sheets*

At the heart of all MacAuthor files lies the most fully conceived style sheets of any Macintosh word processor. This may be somewhat surprising considering that style sheets began with this product, but it simply emphasises the thoroughness of the original specification. The style sheets are impressive because all formatting information is visible on the screen at one time, and in an easily comprehensible and Macintosh-like (i.e. visual) way. The Style Editor is available from the Edit menu and on opening produces a screen similar to that shown in figure 4.2.

The style sheets of MacAuthor differ from those of other programs by being divided into two main types of 'heading' and 'paragraph'. At first sight there may appear to be little point in differentiating between the two, but in practice headings can be associated with particular paragraphs so that when one moves so does the other. This implementation also means that once a heading style has been used and its text typed in MacAuthor will expect it to be followed by a paragraph style and will default to the last one used. In a document with a large number of headings this can save considerable time and frustration. In addition to these two main types of style, a text style exists for the specification of customised lettering: superscript; boldface; italic etc.

The copy of MacAuthor distributed by Icon Technology has just one basic paragraph style and one basic heading style for it is expected that users will create their own for each job. This is achieved using the 'create' button on the top line of the style sheet. Most of the other information on the style sheet is relatively easy to interpret and consists of a ruler for the setting

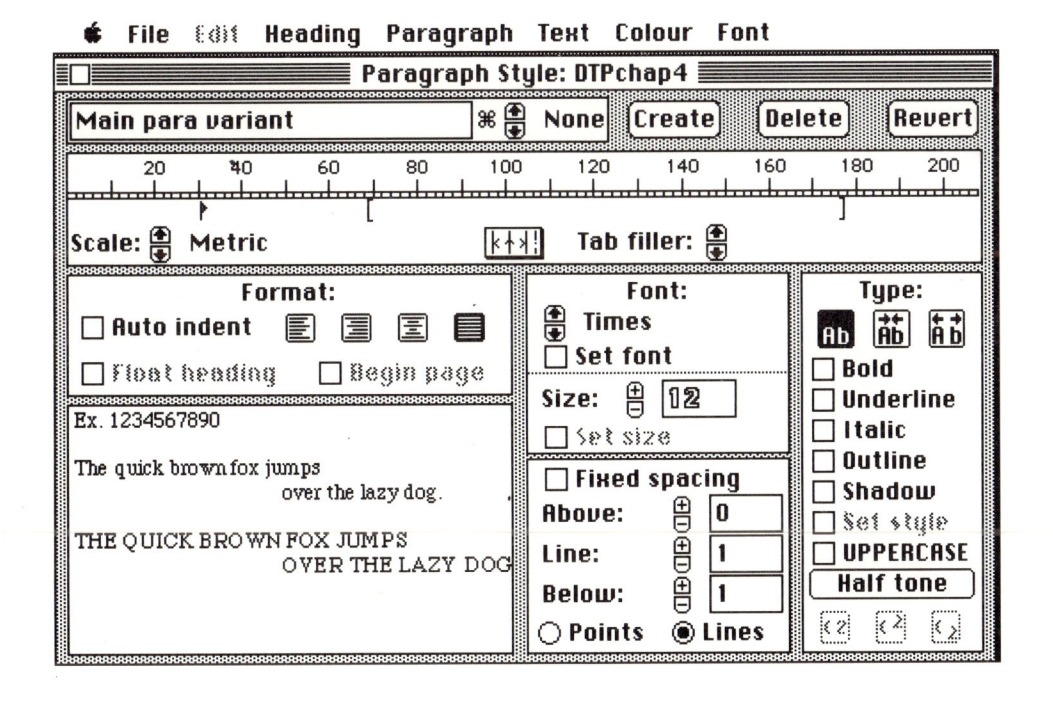

**Figure 4.2 Style sheet in MacAuthor**

of paragraph boundaries and tabs, a setting for the justification of text, the font style and size, and the line spacing above and below headings and paragraphs. So that the user can gain an idea of the appearance of the text a sample box is provided in the bottom left hand corner of the sheet. This operates dynamically and shows the results of any changes in the parameters of the sheet.

In MacAuthor II this idea of providing the user with a dynamic display to changes of style has been taken further and any alterations are immediately reflected in one paragraph or heading of the document itself. This can be viewed on screen by pulling the style window away to reveal the document beneath. Interaction of this kind is ideal when a number of alternative changes to a style sheet are under consideration but, unfortunately, the method of implementation in MacAuthor, or the lack of power in a standard Macintosh Plus, means that the changes on screen occur particularly slowly. Because of this the new feature is a mixed blessing and unfortunately there is no way of turning it off.

The main disadvantage of the MacAuthor style sheets is that no alternative or override has been provided. This means that whenever a different typeface or special effect is to be included within a paragraph a new style (generally a 'text' style) has to be created. Separate sheets must therefore be created for all little used styles and this drawback, coupled to the slowness of the interactive aspect, mars what is otherwise an excellent implementation.

*Text editing*

The **search and replace** routines are particularly strong, having been designed to incorporate wild cards and Meta-characters in addition to searches for partial words, case sensitive text and styles. The '=' is used as a wild card when, for example, the search is for two alternative spellings with one character different. Meta-characters are used for more complex searches and permit, for example, matches to be established based on groups of characters such as only numerals or vowels. Replace can operate sequentially or through a **change all** button.

Two useful features appear as '**Title**' and '**lowercase**' in the Edit menu. Lowercase converts all selected text to lowercase and is useful following a period of typing with the caps lock inadvertently pressed down; an '**Uppercase**' option is also provided. Title is used to convert the first letters of all selected words to upper case and, where appropriate, the remaining letters to lowercase. For example, desktop PUBLISHING would be converted to Desktop Publishing.

**Footnotes** can be inserted at any point in the text where they will be automatically numbered and the numbers superscripted and reduced in size. If text moves to another page the footnote moves with it and any adjustment in the numbering, due to other footnotes being present, is automatically taken care of.

**Indexing** of text is achieved in two stages. First of all the index terms have to be manually identified by using the 'Index' command from the Text menu; all indexed terms can be identified by having a dotted underline. The index is then created using the 'Build index' command from the Document Manager Hypercard stack.

The **Document Manager** enables a complete document to be built up from individual sections – probably chapters – saved as separate files. It causes global repagination and, as stated above enables indexing of the complete document to be carried out. Though it works interactively with MacAuthor II it is a Hypercard stack.

A **spelling checker** is not included as a part of MacAuthor, the original idea being that 'bolt-on' modules would be available to allow users to build up the kind of performance required. Since that time the situation has changed and most top-end word processors now include an integral spelling checker. Icon Technology has tested a number of checkers with different versions of MacAuthor and they currently recommend the use of Spelling Coach by Deneba. A variant, Spelling Coach Professional, includes a thesaurus. The operation of this package is described in detail in chapter 6.

## Handling of graphics

*Use of frames*

As explained in the section on layout, frames are used in MacAuthor for any change in page layout away from the normal for that particular document. However, they are especially useful for incorporating graphics into a document. Frames are created, rather unsurprisingly, using the command 'Make a frame...' available from the Page menu. Once the contents have been specified as text or graphics and the position linked to a particular paragraph or a fixed place on the page, the frame can be drawn to the size required – figure 4.3.

With a judicious use of text and graphics frames, quite flexible page layouts can be achieved. Furthermore, the user has the ability for moving graphics within their frames, adjusting the size of frames, and moving frames around the page. Where MacAuthor has not kept pace with developments is in limiting the way some of these effects can be achieved. For example, to alter the position of a frame on the page its top bar has to be first picked up by the cursor, an action that is irritating compared to the easy way in which other programs deal with a similar move. A further lack of development is the inability to flow text round

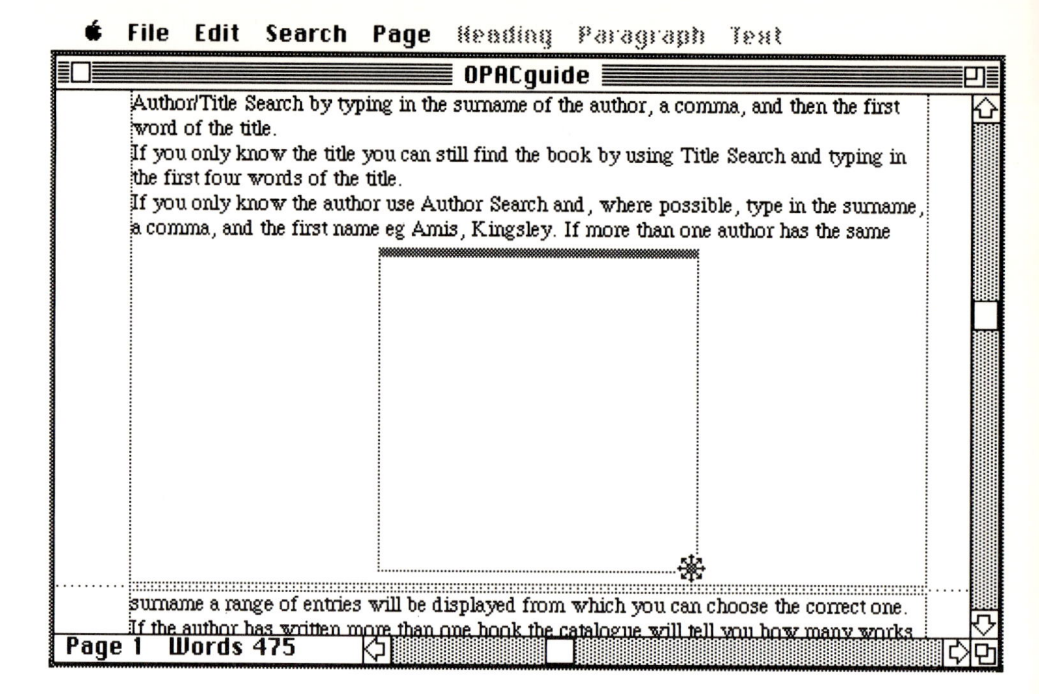

**Figure 4.3 Creation of a frame in MacAuthor**

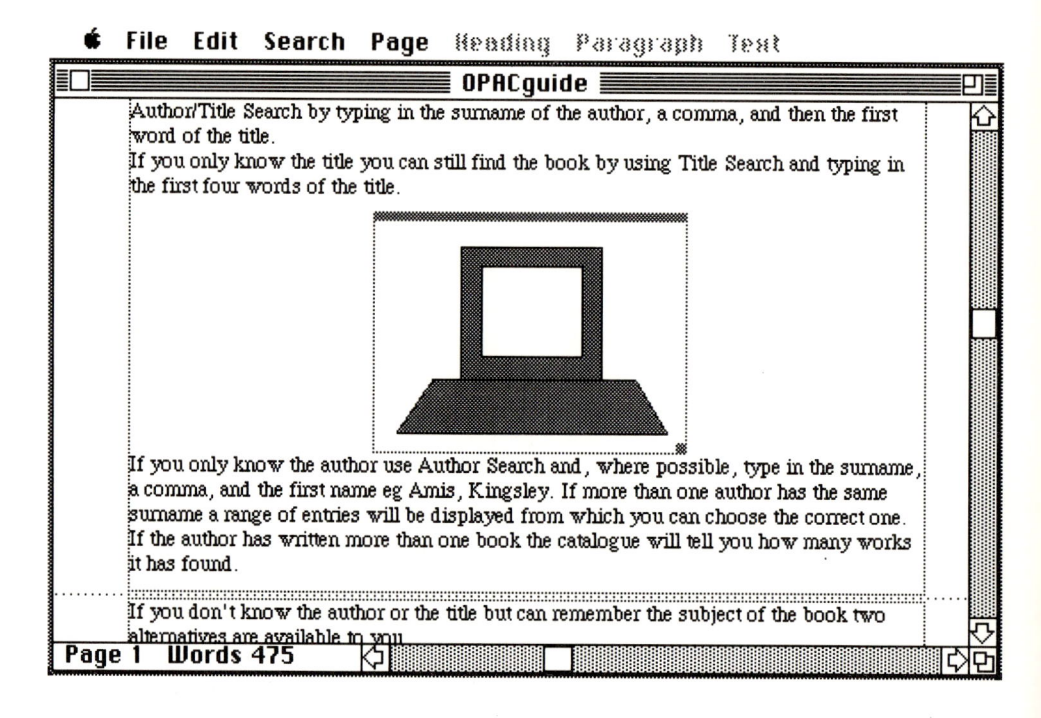

**Figure 4.4 Insertion of a graphic in MacAuthor**

graphics and if this feature is particularly important one of the other programs described should be considered.

*Formats*

Using the 'Insert graphics...' function it is possible to link the contents of a frame to a file from a draw program in the same way as the operation of PageMaker's 'Place' command – figure 4.4. MacAuthor directly supports only two of the range of graphics formats – PICT and EPSF – and all other images such as bit-mapped graphics from paint programs must be transferred via the Macintosh Clipboard. In addition two importing options have been included that are not available in other programs but are directly related to facilities provided by Icon Technology. The first of these is the ability to import Formulator files from the equation processor developed by the company. The second is the use of graphics written in PostScript, described in the 'integral graphics' paragraph below.

MacAuthor does not support the TIFF format and so the only way of importing scanned images is by saving them as EPSF files if the scanner software permits. This absence is unsatisfactory – for the additional reason that EPSF files are considerably larger than their TIFF equivalents – but if any serious scanning work is anticipated, users would be advised to use one of the specialised DTP programs.

*Integral graphics*

One of the recent facilities of feature-packed word processors is the ability to draw simple geometric shapes, although some programs (e.g. FullWrite Professional) have taken this idea further and incorporated a wider range of drawing tools. MacAuthor has adopted a rather different route. Instead of giving the user the facility for directly drawing lines and shapes these are provided from a set of PostScript routines which will create appropriate output when passed to a compatible printer. This means that the routines will not work with dot matrix printers such as the Apple ImageWriter. In spite of this the routines are genuinely useful, permitting the drawing of lines, for example, in and around frames, headers, and down the length of pages. To accept the routines into frames an import 'PostScript Text' option is provided. For users familiar with programming in PostScript this additionally means that custom effects can be created. Furthermore, if a utility is available for converting bit-mapped graphics into PostScript, these can be imported directly into frames and re-sized with no loss of resolution. The main disadvantage with all this is that graphics translated into PostScript text do not display on screen and the correctness of the output can only be confirmed by printing.

**Overall view**

MacAuthor is a sound word processor incorporating good, though not spectacular, DTP facilities. Its best features are the

Style Editor, extensive search and replace, and its ability to create templates through the use of Stationery Pads. Oh! and the word count. Its facility for importing graphics into frames coupled with the page preview display will provide many users with sufficient DTP power for their needs. In addition to these major features the program boasts a host of minor facilities that make working with it a real pleasure. For example, it uses an intelligent cut and paste for single words whereby one of the spaces between words is removed automatically; it has a keyboard shortcut for transposing mistyped letters; overtyping to produce accents is simplicity itself; and it uses a utility called smart quotes to ensure that real quotation marks such as ' and " are available.

It falls down in DTP terms by not providing first rate graphics handling capabilities, an active two-page spread, and in its inability to adjust copy to the space available either through tracking or the use of fractional font sizes.

Judging by the finished product the concept and design specifications for MacAuthor are first class. In practice, what has appeared has one drawback: a lack of speed. One of the reasons for this is said to be the automatic re-pagination which MacAuthor undertakes after sequences of text entry but the unsuspecting user can be left wondering what is happening to the program. This can also apply to the selection of text and to the cutting and pasting of text. It is true that this aspect becomes less noticeable and tiresome with familiarity but there are still irritating times when the flow of ideas can be interrupted by the thought processes of the program.

In terms of library DTP the usefulness of MacAuthor will depend on the composition of the staff undertaking the work and the jobs in hand. In a de-centralised set-up with a wide variety of professional and non-professional staff it would not be the most suitable program to adopt and, furthermore, it is not the sort of program to set in front of a trained typist who is likely to become frustrated with its slowness. If make-up comprises a large number of complex pages with text wrap MacAuthor also would not give the desired result. Where it can shine is in the hands of individual librarians who have the time to get to grips with its many features and who also will be sympathetic to its foibles. And a particularly impressive library application, in conjunction with Acta, is described in chapter 8.

# FULLWRITE PROFESSIONAL

**Background**

One of the first inklings of this product appeared in an advertisement in the US version of MacUser magazine in January 1987 where it was seen as 'a third generation document processor ... expected to obsolete all existing text based products'. Interested parties were encouraged to rush along to the Ann Arbor Softworks stand at the MacWorld Exposition in San Francisco to see the beast in full flow. In spite of mouth-watering adverts appearing in subsequent months, including one stating that 'we'll be at your store in 60 days' (MacUser – US edition, April 1987), the only thing that appears to have been finished was the specification. Along the way, this product alone seems to have given rise to the term 'vapourware', meaning a piece of software that has a written specification, has been demonstrated at shows, has been advertised by both software developers and distributors, but which remains unavailable to the public. Most end-users had begun to believe they would never see it.

One of the features that gave rise to a great deal of interest at the time of the program's initial announcement was the inclusion of an integrated drawing layer with text wrap around any graphics created – a concept that was quite revolutionary for a word processing program at the time. Other features such as posted notes ensured that this was just about the most eagerly awaited word processor of all time.

In February 1988 FullWrite was bought from Ann Arbor by Ashton-Tate, somewhat of an irony given that this company had themselves taken twelve months between showing ß-test versions of their first entry into the Macintosh market – dBase Mac – and releasing it to the public. In this case however, Ashton-Tate lost no time in completing the product and shipping it to the market place. Version 1.0 was officially released in the UK at the beginning of August 1988. A number of, by and large, favourable reviews have appeared since then (Bywater; Gabaldon; Weber) but one of the most interesting articles has been a comparison of FullWrite, Word, and WordPerfect by Heid. An Ashton-Tate book backing up the information given in the manual has also appeared from Thompson and Paterson.

**User interface**

Most of what was said about the initial screen display of MacAuthor also applies to FullWrite – basically it is unremarkable yet functional in appearance. As would be expected, some of the menu commands are different and, moreover, there is an interesting collection of small icons along the bottom of the screen. These represent the four different views that are available for any FullWrite document. The first one shows the full text with a vertical bar running down the left hand side of each column indicating where any of the varied notes available in FullWrite have been attached. It is known as the icon bar display. The second icon represents an outline view, where this has been created, and the third indicates changes that have occurred since the last use of the document. The final view provides a display of the document as it will be output to the printer. These four icons can be seen at the bottom of figure 4.5 where the icon bar display is selected and two icons can be seen in the top left hand corner, one indicating a sidebar – in this case containing a picture – and the lower one indicating a posted note. An explanation of both of these terms will be found in the sections that follow. A second icon bar runs down the centre of the page and splits the diagram in two; it is used to indicate notes and sidebars that are included in the right-hand column of text.

The standard menu bar extends across the top of all documents. In addition, FullWrite has many features lurking under the surface, many of which relate to their use at particular times in a job. In such instances an additional menu item appears to the right of the standard terms and provides commands specific to that aspect of the program. For example, whenever a diagram is to be drawn a 'Picture' menu appears on the menu bar as shown in figure 4.9.

Though not directly related to the user interface it is worth pointing out the memory requirements of FullWrite. Although the program can run on a 1 megabyte Macintosh not all the facilities are available at all times and one of the consequences is that chapter lengths have to be kept to a minimum (6–10 pages). FullWrite really needs at least 2 megabytes of RAM to operate in all its glory. Even then it is choosy who it shares memory with when run with other programs under MultiFinder.

**Format**

As with MacAuthor only the usual printing sizes associated with the LaserWriter printer driver are available with FullWrite. As it is seen as a writers' tool it is a pity that none of the standard book sizes (or A5) have been implemented as defaults, particularly as the majority of these are smaller than A4 and could easily have been accommodated. In printing, FullWrite provides two non-standard options of 'Print collated' and 'Print both sides'. Working units are inches, centimetres, picas, points, and pixels. The chosen unit is selected from a 'Document setup' box but any unit can be entered in the various dialogue boxes as long as the correct abbreviation is specified.

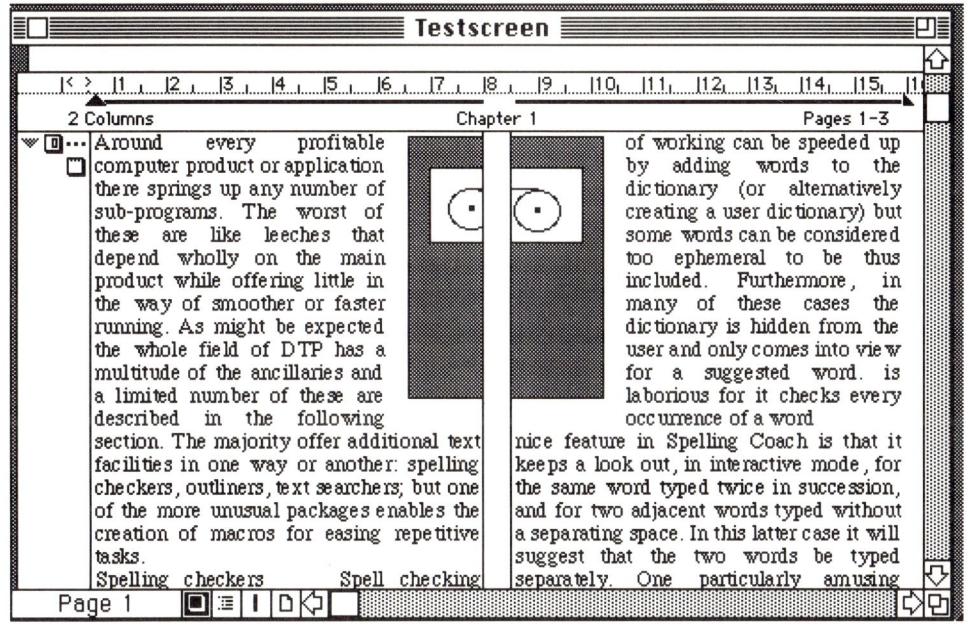

**Figure 4.5 Icon bar display in FullWrite**

Interestingly, margins are set from a dialogue box accessed via the 'Page setup' command used for selecting paper size. This gives no indication of the height or width of the column into which the user will be typing, dimensions that can be important in a variety of jobs and that are requested in some specifications sent to authors for the production of camera-ready copy.

**Layout**

Any further layout adjustments, once the margins have been specified, are controlled primarily through the Layout command of the 'Format' menu – figure 4.6. It is from here that the number of columns and the sizes of any header and footer are specified. The creation of columns is especially easy and any changes can be made either from the main ruler of the document – refer to figure 4.5 – or from the Layout dialogue box.

Where non-standard layouts are required on pages, these are achieved through the use of sidebars – rectangular boxes of user definable size which can be positioned anywhere on a page and can accept text or graphics. In many respects they are similar to the frames in MacAuthor. When a new sidebar is required a dialogue box opens similar to the Layout box of figure 4.6 and this enables the size of the sidebar to be specified and its position to be fixed relative to the page or to any text containing it. FullWrite indicates that a sidebar is present by placing the appropriate icon in the icon bar – figure 4.5.

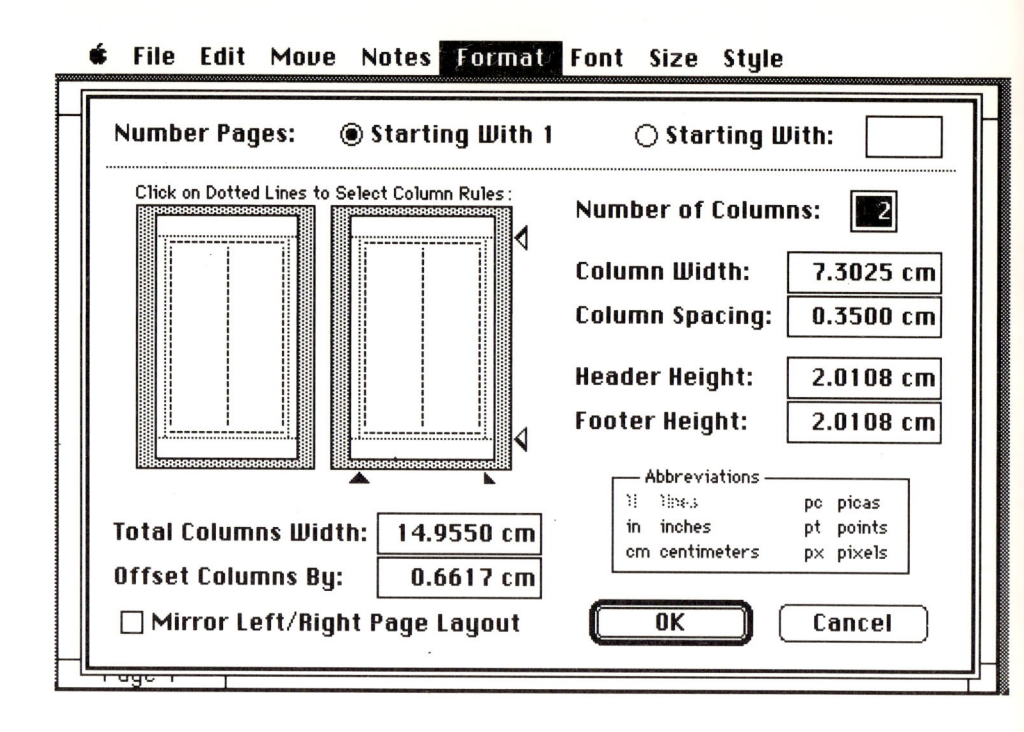

**Figure 4.6** Layout dialogue box in FullWrite

To reposition sidebars entails opening the 'Place' command from the sidebar menu and making the necessary adjustments. Though one becomes used to this indirect method, modifications to page layouts containing sidebars continues to be somewhat cumbersome, even with experience. The main disadvantage is that the sidebars are not active from the document itself and so any changes have to be made at one move from reality. Ashton-Tate say that sidebars will be active from within a document in version 2 of the program.

FullWrite uses the chapter as the basic divider within a document but one has the feeling from studying the manual that this is more to do with the design of the program and its memory requirements rather than as a convenience for the author. The reference guide section of the manual states (page 7–12) 'when working with long documents, it's also a good idea to start a new chapter periodically to allow FullWrite's virtual memory system to segment the document and increase efficiency'. The fact that the demands of writing can result in chapters of quite different length appears to be irrelevant and this is one example of technology-led rather than user-directed developments. It also ignores the fact that for security reasons some users may prefer to save a long document as individual chapters, though in those cases some of the advantages of FullWrite's active linkages will be lost.

If FullWrite's chapters *are* utilised a number of other options exist for controlling the layout of the complete document.

Endnotes and bibliographies can be placed either at the end of chapters or the end of the document, and a preface and appendix can be incorporated where necessary. FullWrite will see to it that the document is compiled with the specified requirements.

Throughout FullWrite a wide variety of features is available that gives the impression of the program being able to cope with any writing task. However, in spite of its great flexibility the program is curiously limited in a number of areas. One of these is the automatic positioning of the preface before the table of contents, and the facility for only a single appendix. In many books – for example the Gower series on library automation systems – it is customary for the preface to appear *after* the table of contents, and it is strange that FullWrite does not offer this as an option.

A variant of master pages is available with FullWrite with its ability to save basic templates as stationery.

## Handling of text

*Text entry*

In addition to the obvious method of entering text directly from the keyboard, FullWrite can open files created in other word processors and convert them to FullWrite documents. Microsoft Word and MacWrite files can be opened and, not surprisingly, files from Ashton-Tate's PC word processor, MultiMate, are also compatible with the program. As usual, text files can be opened.

*Exporting files*

The possibilities for exporting in different file formats is limited, mainly for the reason that other formats would not be able to handle the detailed make-up of a FullWrite document. In spite of this an option for saving in MacWrite 4.5 format is provided, in addition to text only and text only with line breaks (ASCII).

*Style sheets*

Style sheets in FullWrite operate unlike those in any other program discussed in this book. One example of this is the differentiation between 'Base styles' and 'Custom styles'. Separate Base styles are defined as defaults for the main text of the document and for each of the types of note available. For example, footnotes and bibliographies can be specified in a completely different format to that of the main work. Base styles comprise the usual elements of font, size, style (bold, plain, etc.) and justification and also allow for different paragraph spacing between the different parts of a document. The main disadvantage with this approach is that it limits the writer to a single Base style for the main text so that any variations – including those for paragraph headers – have to be added as 'Custom styles'.

Custom styles are defined in a similar way to Base styles but they omit one vital piece of information which limits their usefulness considerably. No allowance has been made for variable paragraph spacing so that if a header is required with two lines above and one line below at least one carriage return has to be entered manually. In a long document with a variety of styles such a limitation would give rise to a large amount of work during any major re-formatting. A further restriction is that any indents imposed at the beginning of the Base styles paragraph are automatically carried through to all the Custom styles in the document and there is no means of setting the first line indents of Custom styles individually. It may appear extreme to say that the limitations of the Custom styles make FullWrite of little use for complex work but it is a fact that these limitations throw a great deal of responsibility onto the writer that should be an in-built part of the program. It is ironic that a program with so many features should be deficient in such a vital area.

For the writer familiar with the style sheets of other programs the practical use of the FullWrite styles also leaves something to be desired. All Custom styles can be included in the 'Style' menu and selected in the usual way but again most things rotate around the Base styles. When moving from a paragraph written in the Base style to one of the Custom styles the Custom style is applied without problem. However, the writer cannot move *between* Custom styles simply be choosing a new style from the menu. If this is attempted the second style is applied on top of the first and some very strange – or at least unexpected – results can occur. To prevent this nasty shock one has to revert to the Base style, after first highlighting the paragraph concerned, and then apply the appropriate Custom style from there. This becomes second nature after a time but familiarity does not make the procedure any the less frustrating.

*Text editing*

In addition to 'standard' text editing facilities such as search and replace, and an excellent spell checker and online thesaurus, FullWrite is loaded with features to help the overburdened writer. It is impossible to provide full details on all of these and so the discussion below concentrates on two of the more unusual and potentially helpful features.

One of the problems facing any writer of illustrated works is how to keep track of the diagrams and, sometimes more importantly, how to keep a grip on the numbering scheme used. There is always the underlying worry that numbers will be repeated or overlooked and last minute checks of the manuscript are inevitably needed to overcome any lingering doubts. FullWrite has largely solved this problem through the use – unlikely though it may seem to librarians – of classification and citations.

**Classify...** is the command used to define a group of objects to which reference will be made throughout a document, for example, figures, tables, graphs, illustrations. Once a group has been defined its classification can be applied to all individual members of that group – for instance, all figures – and FullWrite will keep a record of the items and number them accordingly. If a new figure is inserted between existing ones FullWrite will adjust the numbering scheme to take account of this.

Once individual items have been classified any number of references can be made to them by using the 'Insert citation' command. When making a new citation a dialogue box similar to figure 4.7 allows the manner and terminology of the reference to be tailored. The clever bit is that a new dialogue box opens for each citation to the same item so that the reference can reflect the different contexts in the text. Thus, the first reference to a diagram will generally be simply to its number – figure 10 – but when referring back an indication of page number can be especially helpful to the reader. The only minor drawback to this feature is that a numbering scheme similar to that used in this work – figure 4.7 – cannot be accurately represented for FullWrite inexplicably enters a space before its sequential number in all classified sequences, thus making the example figure 4. 7.

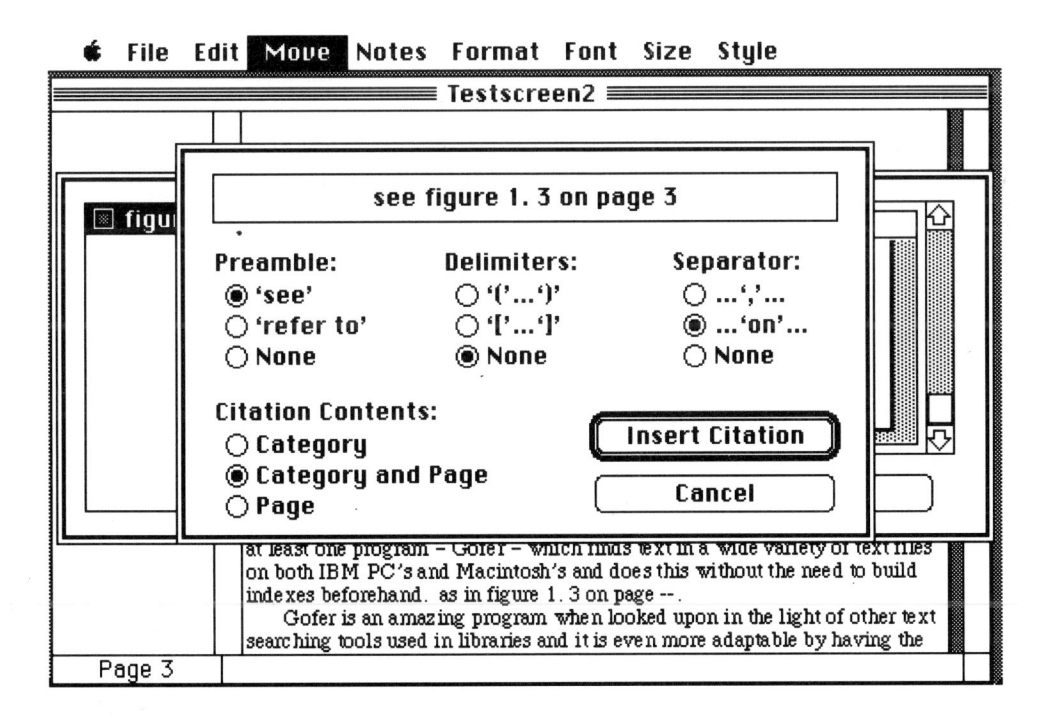

**Figure 4.7 Insert citation in FullWrite**

The other novel feature of the program is the variety of notes that have been made available: endnotes; footnotes; bibliographic notes; posted notes; indexes; and contents notes. FullWrite notifies the presence of these from the icon bar display and additionally all notes of one particular type can be browsed and located directly. Of the many notes available, the posted notes are the most fascinating and the bibliographic notes are the ones that many librarians will be interested in putting into practice. These latter are discussed in detail in chapter 8.

**Posted notes** can be added anywhere in a document and can be used for writing notes to oneself relating to different drafts of a section of the text; reminders; references to other chapters; and so on. All writers will have their own use for them and they appear to have been included partly to enable working groups to signal suggestions for change to each other within one copy of the document – assuming the document is networked. The author has used posted notes for keeping a record of citations to software reviews which were needed for reference but which would not be included in a final bibliography. An example of a posted note is shown in figure 4.8.

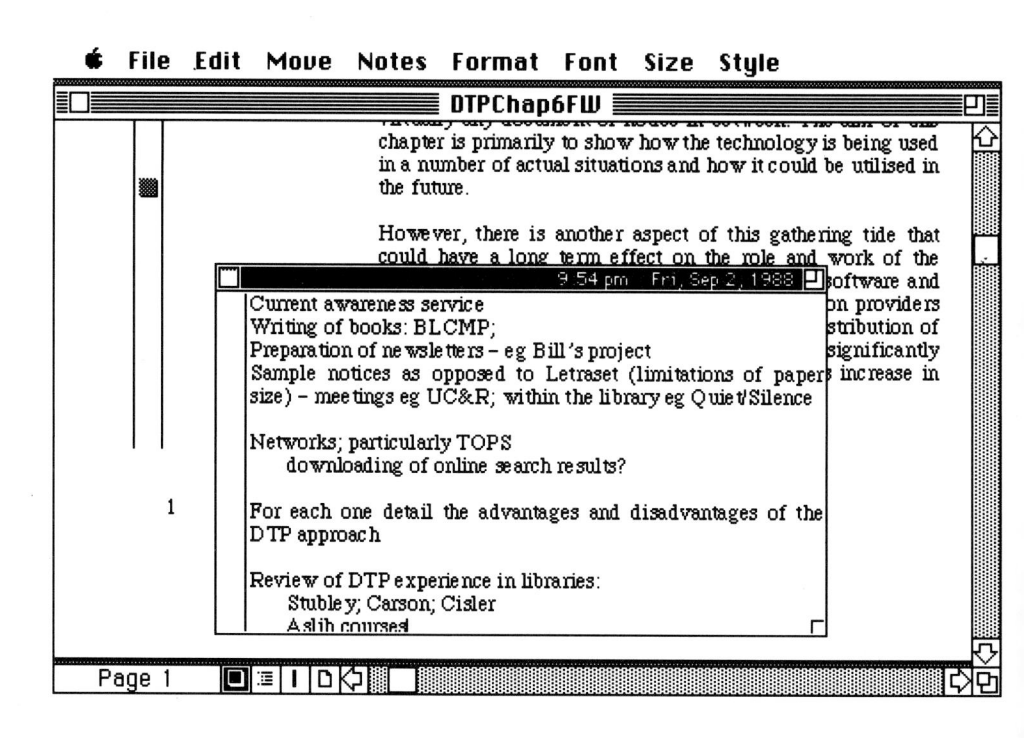

**Figure 4.8 Posted note in FullWrite**

## Handling of graphics

*Formats*

The operation of FullWrite's integral drawing program is outlined below. No doubt as a result of this feature Ashton-Tate has not felt the need to make FullWrite compatible with the full range of graphics formats. Accordingly, only PICT and bit-mapped graphics can be introduced into FullWrite documents and even these only indirectly via the Macintosh Clipboard. This severely limits the DTP capabilities of the program especially with the increase in EPSF clip art and the use of scanned images in TIFF format.

*Integral graphics*

In the DTP programs described in chapter 3 the drawing tools are available for use anywhere within a document, almost without exception. FullWrite's graphics come in three forms: column rules; borders and shadings for sidebars; and the separate drawing facility, and the first two of these have distinct and limited uses. For most cases any flexibility that appears to have been lost will be more than made up by the capabilities of the integral drawing program.

**Column rules** are normally set and edited from the layout dialogue box (figure 4.6) and a small variety of styles is provided including a number of double line combinations. While this system is extremely easy to use it does have its limitations through being tied to columns. For example, it is not possible to use this method to create a horizontal rule across the top of only the first page in a chapter (as used throughout this book) because column rules always appear on all pages. The only way of achieving this would be to draw a line in the drawing program and position it as required but this seems to somewhat defeat the object. A further drawback is that the vertical rules will not extend into headers and footers.

**Borders** around sidebars are equally easy to specify and come with a range of options for square and rounded corners and with different degrees of shadow. These are available from a 'Format' box specific to each sidebar and from where the background grey scale can also be specified.

By far the most interesting of FullWrite's graphic capabilities is its **integral drawing program**. This has many of the tools available in the early versions of programs such as MacDraw and SuperPaint in addition to providing facilities for manipulating the images produced. The tools and the commands available from the 'Picture' menu can be seen in figure 4.9. A Bezier tool is provided which makes the drawing of curves a real pleasure and, as would be expected, text can be incorporated into pictures.

The drawing program is summoned from the 'Notes' menu using the New Picture command and this results in the opening

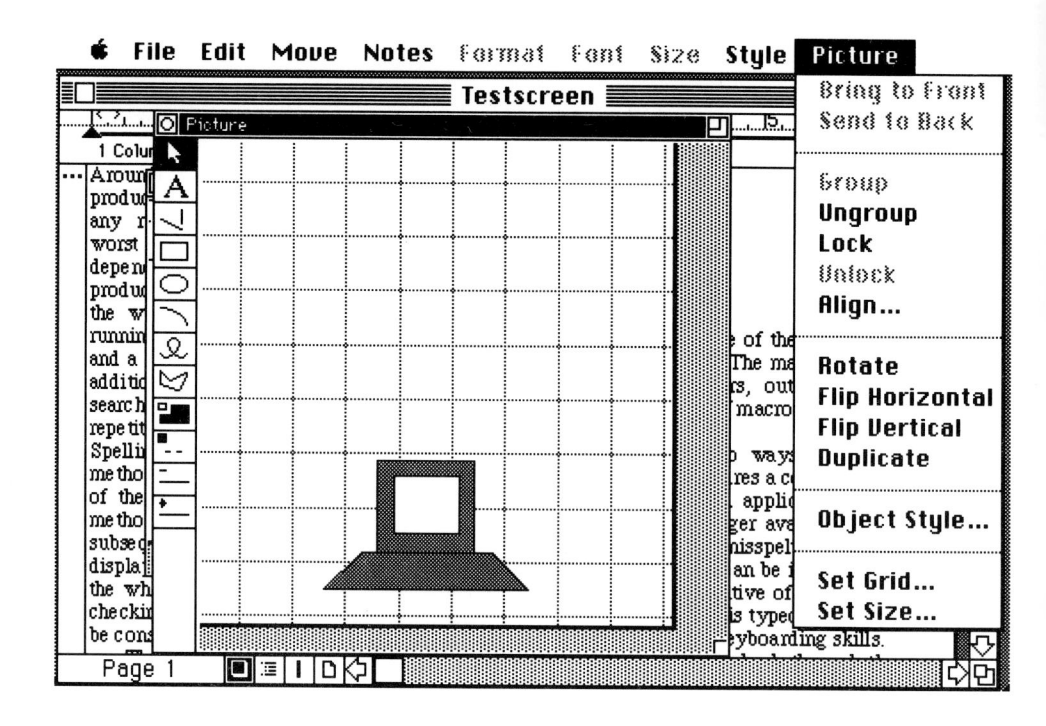

**Figure 4.9 Drawing facility and Picture menu in FullWrite**

of a window of disconcerting smallness. How can graphics creativity flower when it has been reduced to this scale? After a while common sense dawns and it appears quite reasonable that the dimensions of the drawing fit in with the size of the page. Furthermore, the drawing area can be adjusted – and the window opened – to the size required.

Once it has been completed, the drawing is added to the document in one of two ways. The simplest is to add the picture at the text insertion point and FullWrite will then float the picture with the surrounding text. The other method, and the only one in which text wrap can be obtained, is to first place the picture into a sidebar. The difficulties of placing sidebars on the page have already been pointed out and similar problems can arise when positioning pictures within the sidebars. The picture is added at the insertion point but this means laboriously making manual adjustments until the correct location is obtained, followed by positioning of the sidebar itself. To assist in this operation an outline of the picture is provided in the sidebar 'Layout' box but overall the positioning of graphics in FullWrite is not a smooth business.

*Text wrap*

This is only possible if the picture created in FullWrite has been embedded in a sidebar and then text wrap can take place surrounding the sidebar or around the graphic itself. Text wrap is controlled using the Format command of the 'Sidebar' menu where a repel distance – referred to in this program as 'whitespace' – can be specified.

**Overall view**

FullWrite was obviously conceived as the word processor to top all word processors and so it is not surprising that it falls down in some areas. What is available in version 1.0 is good but, even with all the features, rarely outstanding and it has some limitations for serious DTP work. In many ways this may appear to be an unfair assessment for FullWrite is being criticised for its limited implementation of facilities that are not available in most other packages. However, it is being sold on these features and some of them are essential for effective DTP. At the same time, those that do work well, such as the posted notes, are extremely impressive and smooth in their operation.

The use of this program for DTP work – as opposed to word processing – therefore depends on the type of DTP work undertaken. In broad terms the main disadvantages are the limitation on imported graphics formats and the poor style sheets. And while the drawing facility is a boon in some instances, its real value must be questioned in the face of high end packages like FreeHand (chapter 5) which offer far greater possibilities.

Many reviews have criticised Ashton-Tate for making this, in effect, a 2 megabyte program and admittedly it is frustrating to receive the 'there is not enough memory to complete that operation' message. But criticism of this sort is pointless when, over the next few years, personal computers will be supplied with up to 8 or 16 megabytes of RAM and software will expand to use this. FullWrite is unfortunate in being the first of the new breed.

In terms of library work the use of FullWrite will depend, like XPress, on the organisation of the DTP function for it is an extremely complex program that would appear intimidating to newcomers and require substantial training. For these reasons it will probably not become the DTP program of choice for libraries and neither will it act as the library work-horse word processor. Consequently, the most suitable use for FullWrite will be as the chosen DTP software for the individual librarian who will have the time to get to grips with the many features and use it to best advantage. In a few versions time it might well be the world beater it would like to be.

**References**

*MacAuthor*   Ritblatt, S. The Write stuff. *MacUser*, no. 5, March/April 1986, pp. 18–21.

*FullWrite*   Bywater, M. The Write stuff. *MacUser*, no. 25, July 1988, pp. 43–49. In spite of its unimaginative title (refer above) this really is about FullWrite.

Gabaldon, D. Features vs. speed. *Byte*, vol. 13, no.12, November 1988, pp. 241–246.

Heid, J. The Great write-off. *Macworld*, November 1988, pp. 123–135. A detailed look at how three top-end word processors – FullWrite, Word, and WordPerfect – fared under seven comparative tests.

Thompson, K. and Paterson, T. *FullWrite Professional: a users guide*. Torrance, California, Ashton-Tate, 1989. ISBN 1 55519 070 7.

Weber, J. FullWrite Professional. *Personal Computer World*, February 1988, pp. 148–152.

# 5     Graphics software

**Types of graphics software**

*Draw versus paint*     In the early days of the Macintosh graphics were defined by the MacPaint program and however artistic some of the creations appeared the software was limited in its usefulness for serious academic and business applications. Also, while MacPaint was supposed to unleash the latent artist in all of us, it is likely that what it really created was a jumble of unusable squiggles produced in frustration rather than artistic abandon. This is not to underestimate the impact that MacPaint had on the computer world or belittle the paintings of value that were produced. It is just that freehand sketching is not for everybody and is of considerably less use than was made out at the time.

MacPaint and similar packages produce what are known as bit-mapped graphics. Every line or shape of a paint document is made up of a pattern of dots or pixels determined by the resolution of the computer screen, and herein lies the main disadvantage. The screen resolution of the Macintosh is 72 dots per inch and consequently most paint programs cannot take advantage of the 300 dots per inch resolution of the LaserWriter. Scaling of paint images will not produce quality results and distortions frequently occur. While editing of the picture is possible individual elements cannot be adjusted independently of the whole. MacPaint, however, created a standard file format which has since been supported by most, if not all, subsequent paint packages from all suppliers.

MacPaint was soon joined by MacDraw and for the first time here was a program that could be used to draw circles, squares and other geometric shapes. It was the (almost) ideal tool for those needing to create flowcharts, plans and engineering drawings but suffered, at this early stage, from an inability to produce truly accurate work. It also had the remarkable ability to fill any of the forms created with unbelievably boring patterns of bricks and other simplistic shapes. A program that vacillates so widely between the two extremes of usefulness and idiocy should never be underestimated.

MacDraw produces what is known as object-oriented graphics. In contrast to MacPaint this software recognises objects such as lines, squares, circles, and polygons as complete individual units which can be modified without affecting the entire drawing. One of the main advantages of this type of graphic is that the resolution of the printed version does not depend on the resolution of the screen and it can utilise the full 300 dots per inch of most laser printers. Another graphics format was created from this program, which saves files in PICT (for picture) format and like MacPaint this has also been adopted by other software producers as a standard. Even when newer drawing packages produce output in their native format they usually provide the option of saving in PICT for transfer to other programs.

MacPaint and MacDraw were developed by Apple Computer and MacPaint was 'bundled' free with all new Macintoshes sold. (In 1987 Apple off-loaded its involvement with software and passed these two products to a new company, Claris, for further development and marketing). As the Macintosh began to be taken seriously, and Apple unbundled MacPaint, so a wide range of competing and gradually improved products came onto the market from third party software houses. The names of some of these were obviously chosen to indicate advances over the limitations of the Apple products: FullPaint, SuperPaint, while others took a less obvious path with names such as Cricket Draw, Canvas, and GraphicWorks.

Most of the packages could produce output that in one form or another – usually in MacPaint or PICT format – could be used by DTP programs and in the early days of the technology this was all that was required. However, it gradually became apparent that more sophisticated facilities were required for some applications and out of this need came the top end drawing packages such as Illustrator and FreeHand.

These more sophisticated programs use PostScript to take full advantage not only of laser printers but also of imagesetters. The main disadvantage of paint images is that they do not scale without suffering from distortion. Draw images fare a little better as they are stored as mathematical expressions but even here significant size adjustments can cause loss of clarity. The way around this is to translate all drawing actions into PostScript code and this is what Illustrator and FreeHand do. While saving files in their native format they also permit exporting in Encapsulated PostScript Format (EPSF), again to enable transfer between programs and particularly into DTP software such as PageMaker.

*Graphs*

The other obvious need in corporate and academic institutions is for graphs to highlight the relationship (or lack of it) between figures and, although a cliché and open to derision, in these circumstances a picture really could be 'worth a thousand words'. On the Macintosh only two specific graphing packages are available – Microsoft Chart and Cricket Graph (MacUser October 1988) – but this is no doubt largely due to the fact that an increasing number of spreadsheets (Microsoft's Excel; Ashton-Tate's Full Impact; Informix's Wingz) are incorporating graphing facilities.

*Clip art*

An alternative to creating your own images – a particularly attractive one for those with absolutely no drawing or painting talent, is to use pre-drawn graphics created by commercial artists. This has come to be known as 'clip art' and is usually available as sets of floppy discs. The usefulness and quality of clip art has more or less followed the development of painting and drawing packages, with much of the early material being frankly embarrassing or having a very limited appeal. A brief review of packages available in 1987 was carried out by Burton and since then a few collections have even become available on CD-ROM (Fenton). If you can face over 500 megabytes of clip art then these are obviously for you. With the advent of the top end drawing packages so the quality has improved and a particularly impressive set is a British production entitled 'The Visual Arts'.

*Scanned images*

This is the area that has seen the greatest growth in the last twelve months with the increased availability of both cheaper and improved quality scanners. It is also the area that will separate the DTP professionals from the others, partly through the cost of the top quality hardware, but also through the expertise required to get the most out of the investment. For, in addition to the hardware a range of software has been developed for manipulating photographic images – ImageStudio; Digital Darkroom – which, while being relatively easy to use, does require techniques that differ from most of the other packages described in this book. Realistically, it is unlikely that many libraries will be able to justify, or in fact have a real need for, top quality scanners in the immediate future. In spite of this it is felt important that this area is covered so that information is available when libraries take the plunge. This is very much the area that serious DTP is moving very seriously into.

*Another warning!*

The production and application of each of these types of graphics is described in the sections that follow but one important point should be made, particularly for librarians coming to this software for the first time. The fact that all these possibilities are available does not mean that they have to be used, and care should be taken with graphics in just the same way that it was recommended for text: if in doubt, keep it simple.

There is no problem in getting to grips with basic paint and draw programs, and the preparation of graphs is a straightforward matter for those familiar with spreadsheets. However, Illustrator and FreeHand are not intuitive. They have been conceived as tools for graphic artists and will require a considerable amount of training to be used to their fullest advantage. This is not to say that they are out of bounds for librarians but they should not be considered the graphics programs of first choice.

Similarly, scanners offer a marvellous way of incorporating 'difficult' graphics such as logos and photographs into publications and, at a basic level they are easy pieces of equipment to operate. But again, to reap the full benefits they require more than a passing knowledge of halftones, continuous tones and the capabilities of different printers.

*More on scaling*

Much has been made in the previous three pages on the ability of graphics packages to scale images without their suffering from distortion. The importance of this is never fully recognised until an illustration has been created to fit into a fixed space on the page when there are three practical alternatives: clipping; scaling; and re-drawing. At this awkward time a sense of frustration may also lead to the fourth course of action of excluding the drawing altogether. This point is worth stressing for even with a fair amount of experience it is still difficult to judge the finished size of a drawing when the first shapes are created on screen.

Clipping will obviously be used when the need is to incorporate a section of a larger drawing. To utilise the whole of a graphic, scaling is the only real solution and the effect of a scaling down to 48% of the original size for three versions of the same illustration is shown in figure 5.1. At a cursory glance there is little to choose between the three but a closer inspection reveals that only the PostScript version has retained all the fine detail in a precise replica of the original. Both the MacPaint and the PICT re-sizings have coarsened the text and introduced differential shading into the graphic and the scroll bars along the bottom and side. For some work these differences may be thought too subtle for serious consideration but the point of DTP is that for many jobs it can provide a low cost alternative to conventional printing at little or no loss of quality. Scaling MacPaint and PICT images does not allow this quality to be maintained. However, the differences are primarily noticeable when outputting to a laser printer (figure 5.1) and if an imagesetter had been available many of these small differences would not have appeared.

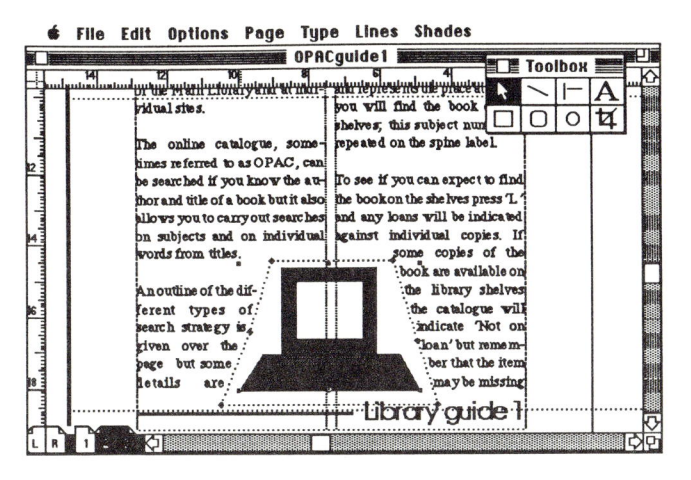

MacPaint graphic scaled to 48% of original

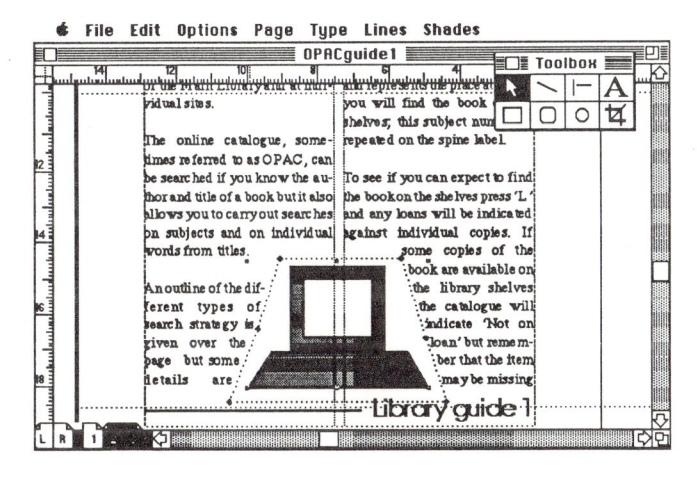

PICT graphic scaled to 48% of original

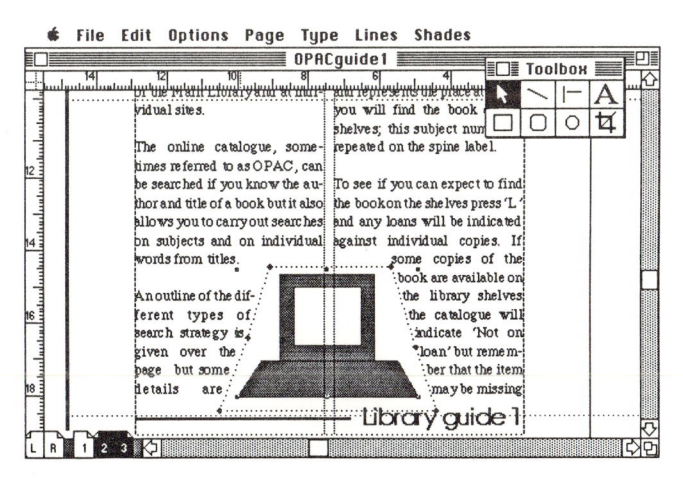

PostScript graphic scaled to 48% of original

**Figure 5.1 Effect of scaling on MacPaint, PICT and PostScript graphics**

**Graphics file formats**

A whole range of file formats has grown up for saving graphics images and transferring them between programs. These have arisen largely out of the limitations of the early formats for handling the more complex information contained in PostScript-related graphics and graphics produced from scanners.

**MacPaint** The original bit-mapped format limited to 72 dpi. When used by scanners only dithered greys are possible.

**PICT** A picture format developed by Apple to permit the exchange of object-oriented graphics between programs. As with MacPaint only dithered greys are permitted in scanned images. It is supported by most draw programs.

**PICT2** This is an extended version of PICT which was developed to handle a full 256 grey scales.

**TIFF** The Tag Image File Format was developed by Aldus in cooperation with Microsoft and some scanner vendors in an attempt to standardise on a format for scanned images. Its disadvantage is that it is an open ended graphics standard with a number of variations, not all of which are recognised by all the software described in this book. In particular compressed TIFF files cannot be imported into Digital Darkroom.

**RIFF** The Raster Image File Format was also developed to handle scanned images. Files in this format are produced by ImageStudio.

**EPSF** Encapsulated PostScript Format was developed to allow a PostScript description and a PICT image to exist in the same file. In so doing two advantages are evident: PostScript can be used to fully define complex graphics and permit them to be scaled; and the PICT version enables a crude approximation to be viewed on screen. It is supported by Adobe Illustrator and Aldus FreeHand.

**PostScript** For those familiar with PostScript it is possible to write a program to create virtually any special effect; some utilities are available which will convert bit-mapped graphics into PostScript text to utilise the advantages of this format. When this text is imported into a DTP program nothing is displayed on screen – hence the usefulness of EPSF.

It is useful to compare the disc space required to save different formats of the same graphic and for this purpose the full A4 version of the scanned photograph of figure 5.10 was saved in a variety of file formats directly from the scanner software. The results are presented in table 5.1 and show a number of interesting features, most notably the extremely large size of the

EPSF file. When saving in SuperPaint format the scanner software split the illustration into seventeen separate files but at least retained the detail from the original. MacPaint, on the other hand, while looking an extremely economic format from the figures lost a great deal of information and rendered the image useless.

| | |
|---|---|
| MacPaint | 32K |
| SuperPaint | 460K |
| TIFF | 963K |
| Compressed TIFF | 440K |
| EPSF | 1990K |

**Table 5.1 File sizes of scanned image in different formats**


## Paint and draw programs

The use of these two types of program will obviously depend on the artistic ability of individuals and the job in hand. However, for the majority of library applications draw programs are likely to be of greater usefulness than painting software. They can easily be used for creating the geometric shapes needed in library floor plans and suchlike.

There is not a great deal to choose between many of the first generation draw programs for they all provide similar basic tools. Where some packages score is in their smooth implementation of the facilities and for the purposes of an example SuperPaint has been chosen. It is a program that offers particularly good value by enabling both draw and paint graphics to be created. The description of its features is followed by a discussion of FreeHand, one of the second generation graphics packages.

*SuperPaint*    Version 1 of this program appeared towards the end of 1986. It is a product of Silicon Beach Software, a company that over the past three years has developed an impressive range of Macintosh software, not to mention a small number of highly addictive games. SuperPaint offers what have become the standard drawing tools such as all types of straight line (horizontal, vertical and diagonal), squares, rectangles, rectangles with rounded corners, ovals, circles, polygons and arcs. These are simply chosen by clicking on the appropriate tool icon on the left of the screen, as shown in figure 5.2.

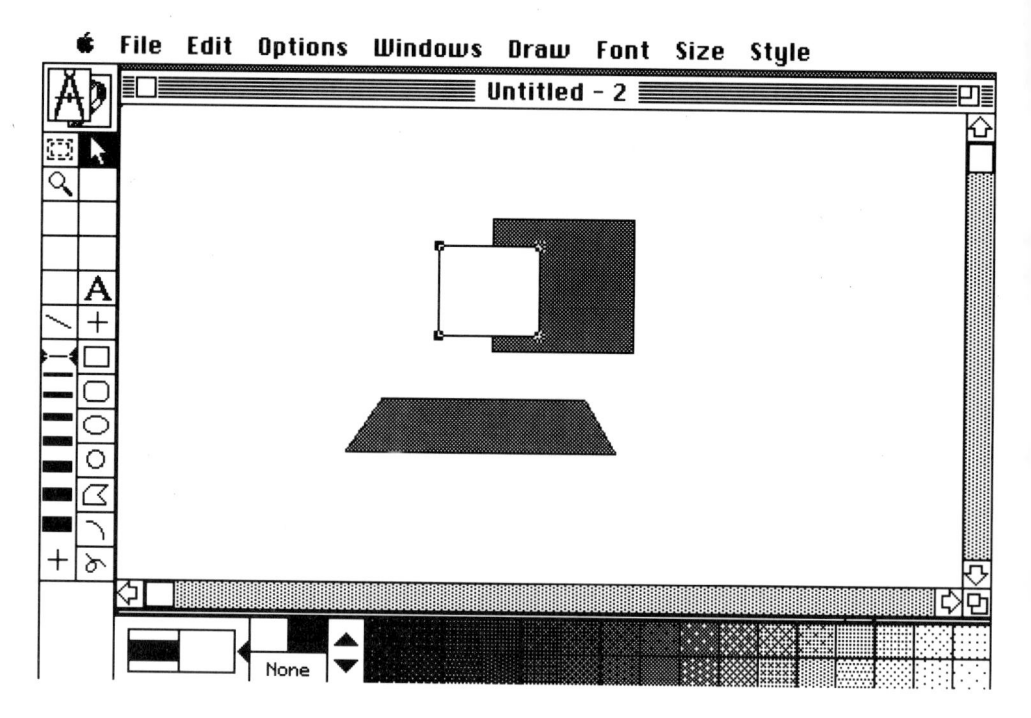

**Figure 5.2 Creation of a simple drawing in SuperPaint**

The callipers in the top left hand corner indicate that the draw layer is active. To switch to the paint layer the paintbrush icon partially obscured by the calipers is clicked with the pointer. This dual functionality does have advantages over and above the fact that two programs have been purchased for the price of one. For example, it is possible to create special effects in the paint layer with the commands such as rotate, stretch, distort and slant and then copy these to a drawing. Unfortunately, sections so transferred remain bit-mapped objects that will not always blend with re-sized drawings.

The great advantage of a draw package is that compound items can be created by drawing the component parts separately, dragging these into their final position, and grouping them. 'Group' is a command available from the Draw menu which glues the component parts together so that they can be moved about the screen as the complex object. If modifications are required at a later date the object can be 'Ungrouped', the changes made and the separate parts glued back together as required. Thus, the simple representation of a terminal in figure 5.2 is created from three shapes: two squares and a polygon dragged together, filled with patterns to differentiate the screen, and then grouped.

A range of fill patterns for objects is available varying from simple black and white through the usual boring lattice-work and brick patterns of little use to the librarian (and probably anybody else) to a more appropriate – and professionally sober – range of greys.

Among the other features, the most useful for librarians involved in a large amount of repetitive work are the 'Duplicate' command and the ability to rotate objects horizontally and vertically. These enable, for example, rectangles representing rows of shelving and seating to be created from a limited set of templates rather than drawn afresh each time. An interesting text editor is also available (interesting when one is used to its idiosyncrasies compared to the expectations formed from contact with word processors) which, through the use of boxes, enables text to be accurately positioned inside graphic objects.

Version 2 of the program was released at the end of February 1989 and incorporates so many enhancements that it could almost be considered a new program. Perhaps to emphasise the difference the patterns palette has been moved from the bottom of the screen to the top, but more importantly, both this and the tools palette have been changed to windows to permit them to be moved anywhere on screen. A third, coordinates, window is also available to track the position of the mouse for work requiring particularly fine control.

On the surface, the draw layer is substantially unchanged. The tool window now includes a 'Multigon' tool to create equilateral polygons with a definable number of sides, and a freehand Bezier curve tool, but a number of features have been added to make its operation easier or to provide greater precision. For example, it is now possible to transfer directly to the selection tool (the arrow pointer) immediately following use of another tool, and the replicate command enables complex patterns to be created from simple geometric elements.

However, it is in the paint layer that most of the advances have appeared with, in particular, inclusion of a wide range of 'plug-in' paint tools. These allow special effects to be easily achieved – balloons; raindrops; charcoal; toothpaste; three-dimensional boxes – the assumption being that other software developers will create more as time goes on. These may not have a great deal of practical application for the sober public face of libraries but they are fun to use. An example of three of the plug-in paint tools can be seen in figure 5.3.

In addition, powerful ways of duplicating selected sections of a painting are provided and several of the tools have parameters which can be customised. For example, the airbrush tool can be set by varying the spray area, the nozzle shape, the flow, the spray pattern, and the dot size, all through a single dialogue box. With this flexibility inevitably comes a steeper learning curve but, overall, SuperPaint is an extremely impressive package.

**Figure 5.3 Plug-in paint tools in SuperPaint 2.0**

*FreeHand*

This was the first package to be released under the Aldus banner since the success of PageMaker although much of the development work was actually carried out by Altsys Corporation. It was released in the first half of 1988, just before version 3.0 of PageMaker, and was seen as direct competition to Adobe's high end graphics package, Illustrator.

FreeHand borrows a number of features from PageMaker's user interface. Each document opens with a setup screen from which page size and other parameters are chosen (A5 is again a listed size option), and the pasteboard metaphor is also utilised. Most attempts at user friendliness end here, for FreeHand, in fact, is quite difficult to get to grips with, especially for those used to the simpler paint and draw techniques pioneered by MacPaint and MacDraw.

The opening screen of a FreeHand document is included as figure 5.4 and a comparison with the SuperPaint display of figure 5.2 shows that the similar basic drawing tools are supported for the production of lines, rectangles and ellipses. In addition five 'freeform drawing tools' – looking like do-it-yourself plumbing connections – and four 'transformation tools' – indicated by icons with strategically placed arrows – are provided.

It is the freeform tools in particular that can cause some confusion and difficulty for the newcomer. Where the basic

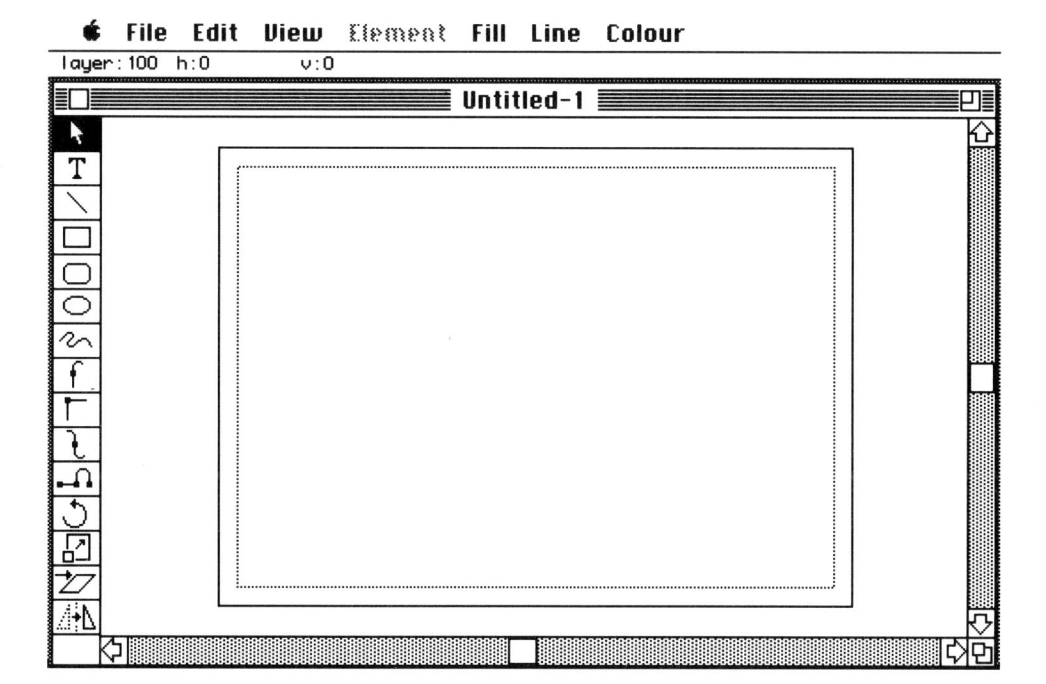

**Figure 5.4 User interface of FreeHand**

tools can be used to create the required shapes, or at least close to these, by dragging the cursor on the screen, four of the freeform tools do this more by implication. For example, to draw a curve using the appropriate tool the anticipated position of the curve is indicated by placing marks along its route which are then automatically connected by the program.

The manual that comes with the package refers to this as a 'connect the dots' method and that is what it is. The main difference from that child-like way of drawing is that in this case the user has to possess a good eye for line and form to anticipate the position of the next sequence of dots. The line of the resulting curve can readily by modified by changing the position of individual dots or their anchor points at tangents to the curve but even this does not always provide the curve in the user's mind. An alternative is to draw using the freehand tool and let the program smooth the curves and supply the dots, but again this does not easily provide the shape required. Having said this, after some practice the tools can be used in a basic way even if the feeling persists that they are not fully mastered.

The other freeform tools work in a similar join-the-dots manner, from the corner tool, to the combination tool for shapes comprising curves and straight lines, to the connector tool for creating smooth joins between curves and straight segments. One of the other problems here is that, even from a study of the manual, it is not always clear which tool should be used to best draw a particular shape and it could be argued that too much flexibility has been provided to the user. One or two tools enabling all the shapes to be created by utilising command or option key combinations might have provided a smoother interface.

One of the most novel aspects of the package, and one that proves a boon in even simple drawing, is that of layer control. This feature enables an illustration to be built up in sections, or layers, in a manner similar to the overlays used on a set of overhead transparencies. The main advantage is that the layers can be edited independently thus reducing the possibility of inadvertently changing sections of a complex drawing and having to begin all over again. The approach does not rule out editing a drawing as a whole if required. One of the other advantages of layers is that a non-printing layer is provided which can be used to hold say, imported drawings or scanned images for tracing and converting into FreeHand documents.

On its release, Adobe's successor to Illustrator, Illustrator '88, contained a number of features that surpassed those of FreeHand (McMahon; Fenton). However, in the ongoing software war of features Aldus regained the lost ground with the release of version 2.0 of FreeHand in early 1989. But even in version 1.0 the Aldus package was superior in its ability to handle text in a variety of ways. In particular, text can be made to flow on any path, including round a circle. Admittedly, this is another of those powerful features that could quite easily be abused unless handled with care, but there is no doubt that it can liven up otherwise dreary posters. Even simple graphics can be improved and given a more professional air with the addition of some curly text.

Other noteworthy features of FreeHand include an information bar which gives the current position of the cursor so that precise adjustments can be carried out, the incorporation of user-defined fills (limited to white, black and greys if no colour system is available) and the ability to scale.

As FreeHand uses PostScript, its files are compatible with any programs that will import EPSF. The only (minor) disadvantage is that a FreeHand file stored as EPSF is considerably larger – up to ten times – than the native file size. One thing that is not possible in FreeHand is the modification of MacPaint or PICT images. These can be imported into FreeHand's non-printing background layer and traced to effectively convert them into EPSF but then, of course, the original format is lost and they cannot be subsequently opened by the originating program.

Examples of the potential of FreeHand in libraries can be seen in figures 5.5 and 5.6. The diagram of a circulation counter could have been created in other programs but FreeHand's features rendered some aspects, such as the floor shading and the counter cut-outs, easier to achieve. Layer control was also useful in gradually building up the drawing from scratch. What FreeHand will not provide – as has been repeatedly stressed – is the talent for drawing human figures, and it could be argued that this sketch would not be a good advertisement for the library: would you let your daughter take a book out from this person? Figure 5.6 could perhaps be used as a notice to attract people to the library and is an example of the power of FreeHand's skew command, used here to rotate the image of the falling book without distorting it, and of the ability to write text along any path. Neither of the drawings are meant to be of professional quality but rather are intended to demonstrate the types of material that might be produced.

**Figure 5.5 Drawing of library counter produced in FreeHand**

Figure 5.6 Library notice produced in FreeHand

**Graphs**

Graphs are the stock in trade of most librarians for presenting data such as output statistics, and if they are not their stock in trade then they really should be. As already pointed out most modern spreadsheet packages incorporate graphing facilities but Cricket Graph is a package that can be used as a self contained unit.

*Cricket Graph*

This was the first product in what has become a successful range of graphics and presentation packages for the Macintosh developed by Cricket Software. Like most graphing facilities it is extremely easy to use and consists of a spreadsheet-type grid into which data can be entered manually or imported from another program. Twelve graph types are available but for most library purposes the column/bar charts, the line graphs and the pie charts will probably be sufficient. The graphs are plotted automatically when the type has been selected but a range of tools can be used to modify the appearance and highlight different aspects using arrows and a system of flexible text entry. As in the example of figure 5.7 'depth' can be added to the graph to provide a 3D view. The only disadvantage is that

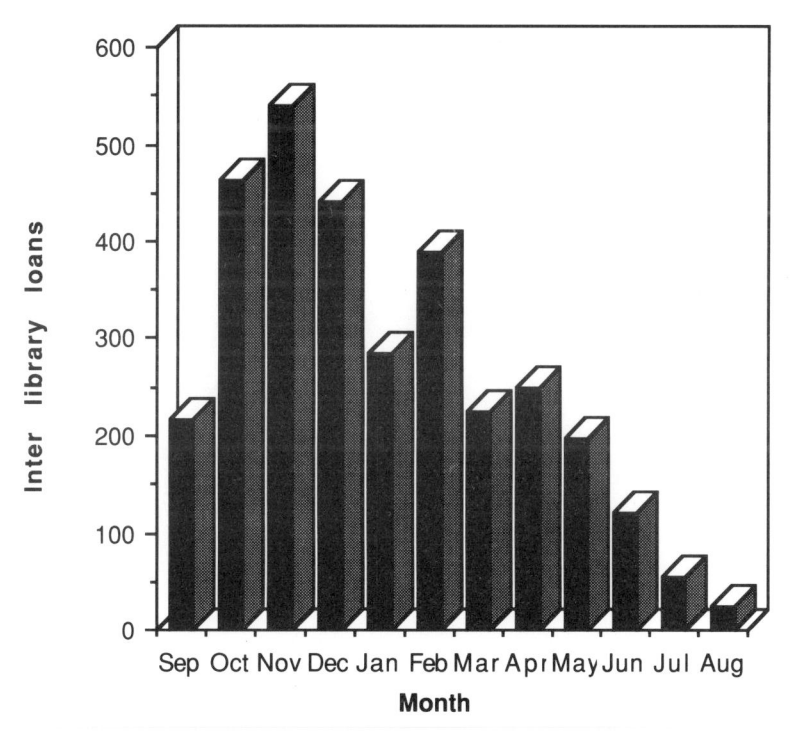

**Inter library loans for academic year 1988/89:
West Midlands Polytechnic Library**

**Figure 5.7 Bar chart drawn in Cricket Graph**

there is no dynamic link between the data and the graph so that if one cell of the spreadsheet is changed the graph will not be automatically adjusted but must be re-drawn. Graphs can easily be re-sized on screen and saved in PICT format so that they can be imported by most DTP programs.

## Clip art

There are two main problems with this type of graphic: finding clip art that is relevant to the particular application; and finding illustrations of a high enough quality. A third consideration is whether the illustrations will fit into the space allocated on the page – yet again the scaling factor comes into play. No one has yet, to the knowledge of the author, produced a clip art package dedicated solely to the needs of librarians. It is equally likely that one will not appear in the near future because the pursuit of personal fortunes does not lie in this direction. That is not to say that existing clip art cannot be utilised and adapted for library applications, and in some cases it can provide a novel, or at least different, slant on affairs.

*The Visual Arts*

This collection is produced by a British company, Electronic Pen Ltd., as an alternative to the high volume and sometimes low quality of much American-oriented clip art. Apart from their British and European bias their other advantage is that the images are produced using Adobe Illustrator and saved as EPSF files so that they can be imported into a wide range of DTP programs and be scaled without loss of clarity. The first collection – The Visual Arts, Set One – appeared in spring 1988 and a second group followed in the autumn. A wide variety of images is provided ranging from computer hardware, office equipment, sketches of people at work and play, to the more flamboyant drawings of Lamborghinis and helicopters. A range of borders, drop caps, dingbats, and background shades are included as DTP aids. All are excellent, with the possible exception of the hamburger (not shown) – although it is unfair for a vegetarian to take a moral stance on the drawings – and samples of those that could be utilised by librarians, including one or two illustrations of less specific usefulness are included as figure 5.8. The illustrations of Macintosh hardware in chapter 2 are also taken from The Visual Arts.

## Scanned images

There has always been the desire, if not the need, to convert traditional printed documents into machine-readable form so that they can be manipulated on screen. This applies equally to illustrations and text but it is only recently that the hardware to achieve this end has been reliable and (almost) cheap enough to be purchased by owners of personal computers. With this reduction in price has come greater sophistication in the ability

**Figure 5.8 Clip art from 'The Visual Arts' Sets One and Two**

to handle increasing levels of grey scales and a wide variety of typed material through enhanced optical character recognition (OCR). To permit further manipulation of scanned images on the Macintosh two software packages in particular appeared in 1988: Digital Darkroom from Silicon Beach Software (the producers of SuperPaint) and ImageStudio from Letraset. In one respect these could be a sign of programs to come, but one alternative line of development might lie with the hardware producers themselves who could develop increasingly sophisticated software for the manipulation of the images scanned with their own equipment.

*A bit about greys*

An important ingredient in the operation of scanners is an understanding of the techniques used by computers to simulate the continuous tones of photographs. Obviously line art such as drawings can be scanned but these do not in general present the same problems.

The basic element on the computer screen is the dot or pixel which can generally have one of two values assigned to it to represent black or white. However, in more sophisticated systems it is possible to assign more than a single value to each pixel so that a limited range of shades are possible between the two extremes. The Macintosh Plus and the SE are single bit systems and are consequently limited to black and white displays, with greys being simulated by a controlled mix of black and white dots known as dithered greys. For the Macintosh II and the SE/30 a range of add-on boards are available for the representation of grey scales. Boards permitting the display of 4 bits per pixel allow 16 ($2^4$) grey levels to be recognised while those representing 8 bits per pixel (256 grey levels) are becoming increasingly popular. 24 bit boards are also available giving 16,777,216 greys.

In transferring a photograph into digitised form the computer has to break down the continuous greys into the limited number (even 16 million is limited!) that can be recognised by the system. The drawback is that, although the scanner and the Macintosh screen may be able to recognise and display a wide range of greys, laser printers and imagesetters are single bit devices and so must approximate the output. Because of the small pixel size on these printers – particularly on imagesetters – moderate to acceptable results can be obtained if one is prepared to wait for the output to be delivered. For high quality publications it appears likely that the traditional method of stripping in photographs will be used for some time to come. As Matazzoni comments: 'Replacing conventional halftones with grey scale scans turned out to involve a few problems: nothing important, it just took longer, cost more, and looked worse'.

Further readings providing a good background to scanning and grey scales can be found in Heid, Hewson, Lu (pages 195–207), and Tyler. An overview of image processing systems in a wide variety of application areas with the intention of investigating their relevance to library work, is provided by Petrie.

*Digital Darkroom/ImageStudio*

The difference between these programs and the graphics software already described in this chapter is that, by and large, their purpose is to modify existing images rather than create them from scratch. ImageStudio can be used to create graphics, utilising a range of effects not available elsewhere, but its strengths really lie in image modification. Thus, before anything can be achieved scanned images must be imported, an operation that obviously requires compatibility between the programs and the file formats available from the scanners. TIFF is the generally accepted standard in this area but there is no single TIFF format and neither of the software packages can automatically assess the saved format or estimate the number of grey scales used at the time of scanning. This has to be stipulated by the user at the time of importing.

Once the image is on screen one of the main disadvantages of a traditional Macintosh setup is immediately apparent: the inability of the standard screen to display true grey scales. What appears is a rough and ready version of the scan with only the broad areas of contrasting blacks and whites being distinguishable through dithered greys. The fine detail that is present on both the original and the printed version of the image just cannot be seen. To make full use of image modification software on the Macintosh a grey scale screen and video card connected to a Macintosh II or an SE/30 is essential and this is equipment that does not come cheap (including the cost of the Macintosh). A view of a scanned image of students studying in a library as displayed on the standard Macintosh Plus screen is shown as figure 5.9. It is shown imported into Digital Darkroom.

Following on from this it is clear that if the original image cannot be displayed with full clarity then the effects of software that subtly alters this image will equally be difficult to see. As one example, brightness and contrast controls are available with both programs but on a standard Macintosh setup gross changes have to be made to achieve a noticeable difference. The only real way of viewing the changes is by frequent outputting to a laser printer but this option does little to keep down the toner bills and gives no indication of the subtleties that may be apparent when printing on an imagesetter. At present, and for the foreseeable future, scanning is not a cheap business.

It is not possible to describe all the features of these programs but between the two, major changes to scanned images can be undertaken. Sections of an image can be selected by a variety of means and then cleaned up, removed, rotated, distorted, scaled and even transferred to other scanned graphics. All of these

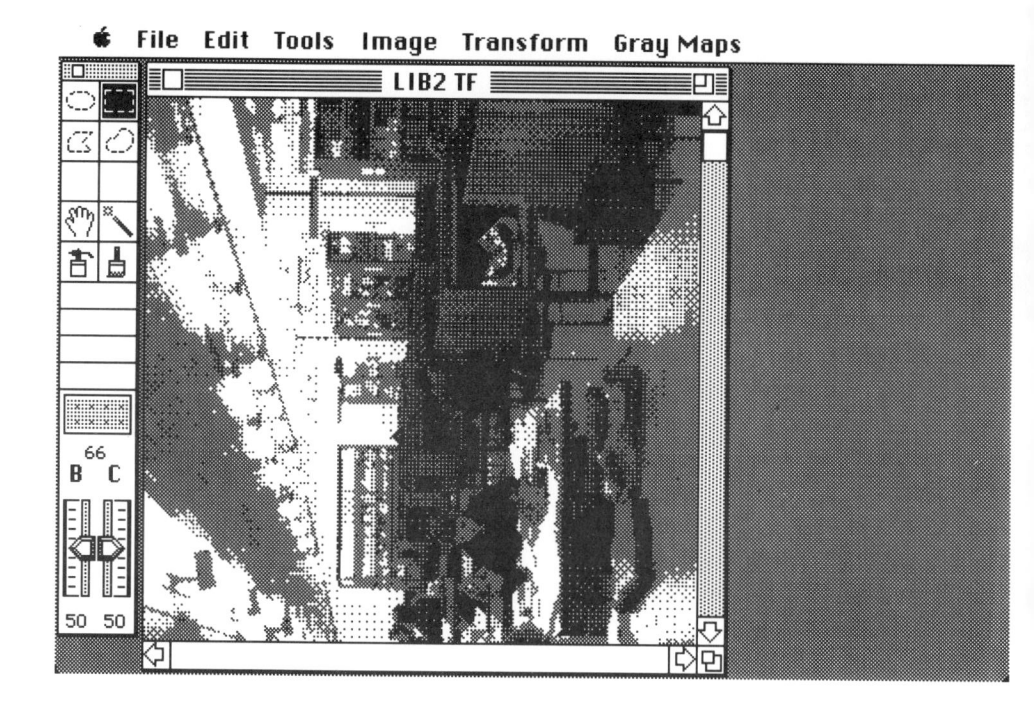

**Figure 5.9 Scanned image in Digital Darkroom**

features can be combined to produce composites from several pictures in order to make a point that is difficult to achieve with a single image, although skill is required to achieve anything like professional results. In addition several of the operations can be slow on the Macintosh Plus due to the high degree of processing required. A further consideration is that Digital Darkroom in particular keeps the entire image in memory (for faster processing) and as scanned images produce large files a large RAM is generally required to use the program to best advantage. Very little can be achieved with 1 megabyte and it is generally understood that at least 4 megabytes are required before any serious work on scanned images can begin. With anything less the scanner's own software will probably not operate, making it impossible to digitise the original illustration in the first place.

As an indication of the effects that can be obtained, two scanned images are presented as figures 5.10 and 5.11 and then combined into a composite of figure 5.12. Both photographs were scanned on a 16 grey scale scanner and saved as TIFF files, figure 5.11 being full size and figure 5.10 being reduced 50% via the scanner software. As shown they have been imported from their original TIFF files and printed directly in PageMaker without using any image manipulation software. Interestingly, when both images were imported into Digital Darkroom and ImageStudio as TIFF files and then printed with no modifications a definite blurring occurred. This difference in

**Figure 5.10 TIFF image saved from scanner software**

109

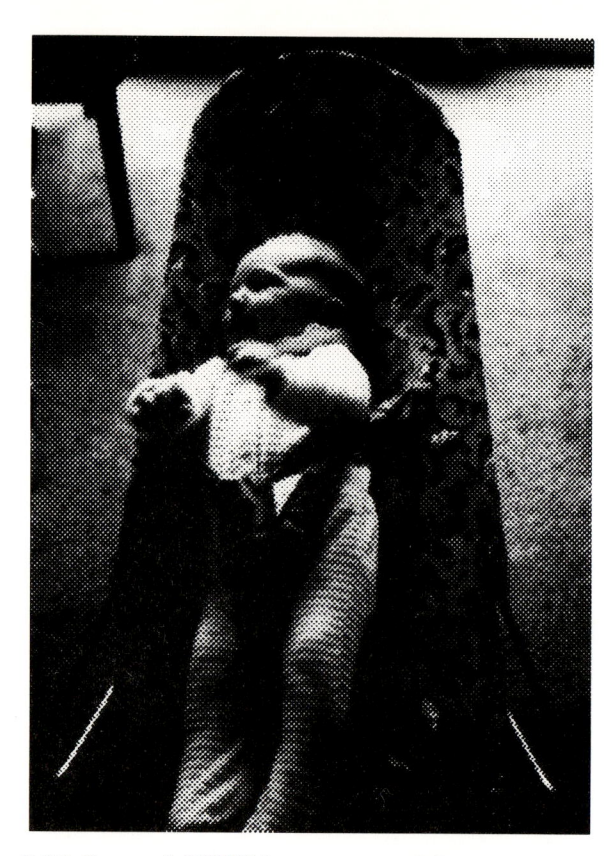

**Figure 5.11 Second TIFF image saved from scanner software**

**Figure 5.12 Composite image created in Digital Darkroom**

clarity can be seen by a comparison of figures 5.10 and 5.12 where there has been a definite loss in the amount of grey scale information. On the other hand the versatility of Digital Darkroom is well illustrated by its ability to isolate the baby and baby bouncer from the rest of figure 5.11, reduce this image significantly and then add it to the library next to an unsuspecting reader. In spite of this, Digital Darkroom has at least one surprising omission for it will not resize the page when an image is rotated through 90 degrees and, accordingly part of the original image can be lost. This explains the difference in size between the two figures.

It may appear that, both here and in chapter 2, the disadvantages of scanning have been stressed too strongly in comparison to the obvious benefits that can result. It is not the intention to dissuade anyone from investigating scanning for themselves but rather to present a realistic picture for those unfamiliar with the technology. This is an enormously complex area that is going to take a few years yet to really come into its own and before then many DTP users are going to spend an awful lot of money and time attempting to get to grips with it. It is probably the only area of DTP where enthusiasm will not carry one through and where careful training is essential. What is required is a thorough understanding of the technology and until this is achieved many users of DTP may prefer to stick with conventional photographs.

## References

*Clip art*   Burton, R. A cut above. *MacUser*, no. 18, December 1987, pp. 47–49.

Fenton, E. Miles and miles of art. *Macworld*, vol. 5, no. 8, August 1988, pp. 131–133. A review of two CD-ROM packages: Artroom and Art Department.

*FreeHand*   Fenton, E. The big match: Illustrator 88 vs. FreeHand. *Macworld*, vol. 6, no. 2, February 1989, pp. 180–187.

McMahon, K. Battle of the graphics giants. *Desktop publishing today*, vol. 3, no. 8, September 1988, pp. 14–17.

*Scanning*   Heid, J. Getting started with scanners. *Macworld*, vol. 5, no. 11, November 1988, pp. 235–250.

Hewson, D. Industrial resolution. *MacUser*, no. 265, August 1988, pp. 31–3.

Lu, C. *The Apple Macintosh book*, 3rd edition. Microsoft Press, Redmond, Washington, 1988. ISBN 1 55615 110 1.

Matazzoni, J. A halftone handbook. *Macworld*, vol. 5, no. 10, October 1988, pp. 116–123.

Petrie, J.H. *An overview of image processing and image management systems and their application.* London, British Library, 1988. ISBN 0 7123 3160 3. British Library Research Paper 40.

Tyler, A. Grey expectations. *MacUser*, no. 31, January 1989, pp. 79–82.

# 6    Ancillary programs

**Do we have to purchase more software still?**

Around every profitable computer product or application there springs up any number of sub-programs. The worst of these are like leeches that depend wholly on the main product while offering little in the way of smoother or faster running. As might be expected the whole field of DTP has a multitude of ancillaries and a limited number of these are described in the following section. The majority offer additional text facilities in one way or another: spelling checkers, outliners, text searchers; but one of the more unusual packages enables mouse movements to be substituted by keyboard commands and so ease repetitive tasks.

**Spelling checkers**

Most Macintosh word processors now incorporate a spelling checker and consequently the outlook for third party checkers would not appear to be especially bright. Spell checkers, however, are a little like DTP programs – similar in principle but different in their mode of implementation and the operation of the checker supplied with the word processor may not suit all users.

Spelling checkers can operate in one of three ways. The first two batch methods are substantially similar. In the first the whole document, or a selected portion of it, is checked and a complete list of the misspelled words is prepared for subsequent action. Amongst Macintosh applications this method was implemented in the spell checker MacLightning (no longer available) and subsequently used as the base for Spelling Coach from Deneba. The fact that all the misspelt words are displayed at the end of the spell check means that those that are valid can be ignored in one go and the whole process is correspondingly speeded up. XPress also uses this approach.

113

The second batch method of operation is a sequential check through the document with a display of every misspelt word as it is discovered. On the face of it this would seem little different from the first alternative but its drawback is that words not recognised by the dictionary but still valid for the document can significantly slow down the procedure by being repeatedly highlighted. This way of working can be speeded up by adding acceptable words to the dictionary (or alternatively creating a user dictionary) but some words, for example authors' surnames, can be considered too ephemeral to be thus included. In many of these cases the dictionary is hidden from the user and only comes into view for a suggested word and this again can be frustrating when scanning of the dictionary might be all that is required. This method of operation is used, in varying ways, by Ready, Set, Go! and FullWrite.

The third alternative uses interactive checking, whereby the spelling checker keeps an eye on your typing *as you type*. Whenever a misspelt word is typed the checker can either beep to show you what an incompetent person you are, or suggest an alternative spelling. The idea of an imperious piece of software warning you of misspellings was met with disdain when it first appeared but the more one becomes used to this type of help the more it is missed when it is not around. The approach was pioneered by MacLightning and has since been used by its successor, Spelling Coach.

*Spelling Coach*

No doubt to ensure as wide a market as possible for this product, its developers, Deneba, have undertaken an aggressive advertising campaign in the American Macintosh press – see, for example, Macworld, December 1988, p. 27. What started off as two packages – Spelling Coach as a dictionary and spelling checker and Spelling Coach Professional incorporating a thesaurus – now appears to have been transformed into one product with a larger checking dictionary, a reference dictionary (including definitions etc.) and a larger thesaurus. At the time of writing version 3.1 of Coach Professional had been released with a 193,000 word spelling dictionary, an 85,000 word reference dictionary, and a 100,000 root word thesaurus. By comparison, FullWrite uses a spelling dictionary of 100,000 words and a 15,000 root word thesaurus. The main drawback of Coach Professional is that it requires up to 3 megabytes of hard disc space if all the components are used.

Coach Professional – figures 6.1 and 6.2 – can be used in both interactive and batch modes and offers a certain degree of user customisation. For example, in interactive mode it can be set up to show suggested spellings for typos, phonetic possibilities or the dictionary itself when a misspelt word is encountered. It also allows for interactive grammar checking and will notify the user whenever the same word is typed twice in succession, and a new

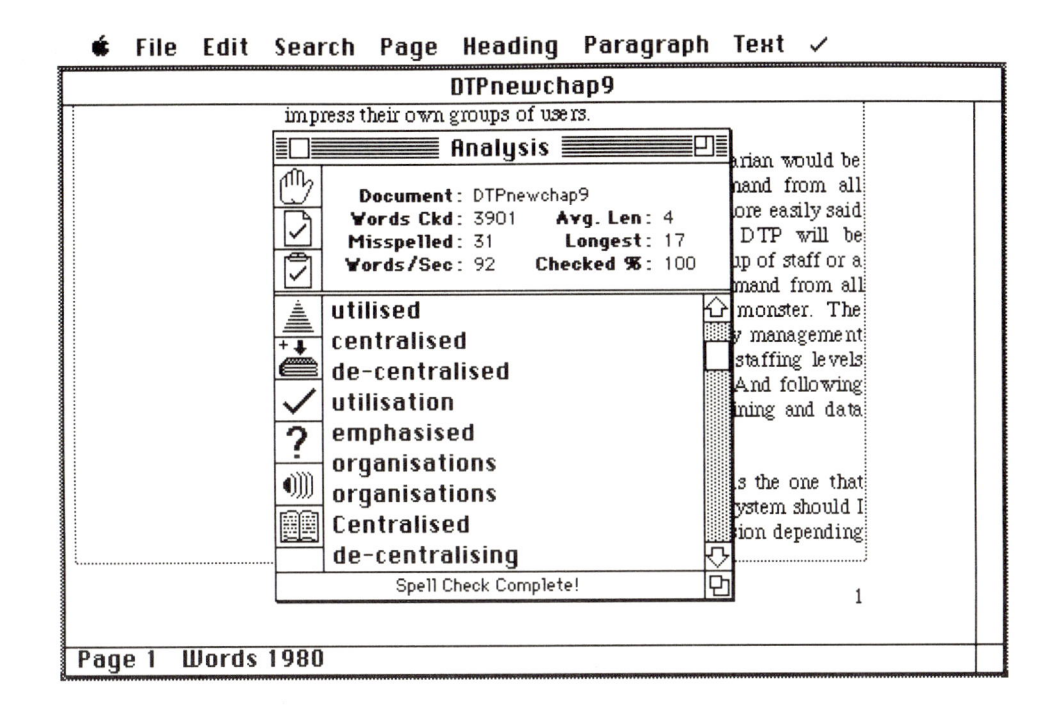

Figure 6.1 Analysis window in Spelling Coach

Figure 6.2 Spelling replacement in Spelling Coach and MacAuthor

115

sentence begins without a capital. Where it does not recognise a word it will at times, as an alternative to suggesting a spelling, decide that a space has been omitted and suggest that the single word should actually be two. One particularly amusing example is that the word librarianship is not in the original dictionary and the suggested spelling is 'librarians hip'. This may be true in a number of cases, man, but it is not an aspect that is made a lot of in the professional press. Or perhaps a medical reference was intended.

As can be seen from figure 6.2, options are provided for adding the word to the dictionary, ignoring it (when it is placed into a temporary buffer so that another occurrence in the same document is not signalled as a misspelling) or skipping it, when further occurrences are signalled. One of the disadvantages of the interactive mode is that it does not give the option of deleting the misspelt word and so if none of the suggestions are suitable the word has to be removed manually.

In its batch mode Coach scans all selected text and gives notification of the progress of spelling and a list of misspelled words through an analysis window – figure 6.1. In its *automatic* batch mode (there is also a manual option) it then summons the search and replace function of the word processor (in this case MacAuthor) enters the first misspelled word in the find box and opens a pop-up menu with a list of spelling suggestions. Quite impressive this as it all happens in one operation. If the suggestion is acceptable the native word processor replaces the word and then Coach resumes with a suggestion for the second misspelling, and so on until all have been dealt with. At any time the automatic operation can be interrupted and then resumed as required. Furthermore, the second occurrence of the same misspelt word is not notified but is replaced automatically.

But Coach Professional is more than just a simple spell checker for it has as additional features the reference dictionary and the thesaurus. By incorporating these it shows the way to the future because this is the beginning of a complete reference system at the point you need it – immediately to hand rather than an arm's length or room's length away in the form of hard copy. At present the electronic versions are not as comprehensive as the paper ones but given time and users' acceptance of paying for hard disc space to hold these, improvements should occur. Of course, Microsoft has already come out with its reference system on CD-ROM – Bookshelf (DeMaria) – but at the time of writing this is only available for the PC. But as with the other features of Coach, the reference dictionary and the thesaurus are sorely missed when working on a Macintosh without them.

Overall, Spelling Coach/Spelling Coach Professional is an excellent spell checker and a good embryonic reference system. It is another of those programs that has been thought out rather than been thrown together. In addition to the features mentioned above it can be automatically loaded – with all programs or only selected ones – so that it really does feel part of the basic application. Its only real drawback is that it is American (!) and in its original form it does not recognise English spellings – refer figure 6.1. While these can be added to the dictionary this is a frustratingly time consuming operation.

**Outliners**

The intention of these packages is to permit ideas for any writing project to be set down in a relatively organised way at the start of work and so form an outline for the whole operation. Of course there is nothing to stop the outline being modified as work progresses. A good outliner will permit changes to be made at any time, easily, and in any direction. That is, it should be possible to move a section originally intended for one chapter readily to a different position in another chapter. Many word processors now include integral outliners e.g. FullWrite Professional, but one or two programs are still available operating as either desk accessories or as stand-alone packages. In the experience of this writer the desk accessory approach makes a great deal of sense, particularly when working in a range of different packages, for great, or even useful, ideas do not only occur while writing. They can easily appear during other work and the presence of a desk accessory outliner will help to make sure that they are committed to disk. For the Macintosh an excellent desk accessory outliner is Acta.

*Acta*

The creation of an outline will depend on the method of working of the individual, on the flow of ideas, and on the work at hand. In some cases a topic and all its sub-topics will be listed first whereas in others the outline could consist of simply major terms or headings to be completed at a later date. Acta permits both of these approaches to be used, for once ideas have been set down they can be moved around at will to fine tune the results. The program has been written to follow the Macintosh interface closely and so topics can be easily moved into new places in the hierarchy with the help of the mouse or by using commands from the Acta menu.

An outline created in Acta as an early synopsis for the present book, together with the Acta pull down menu, is included as figure 6.3. From here it can be seen that Acta creates outlines using a kind of family tree of mothers, sisters, daughters and aunts. While this helps to define the way in which Acta works, in some respects an awareness of the terminology is unnecessary to understanding the operation of the program. However, this does have one useful spin off. As aunts, sisters and daughters all have command-key equivalents – using keys that are next to each other and, furthermore, are hierarchically correct – a new

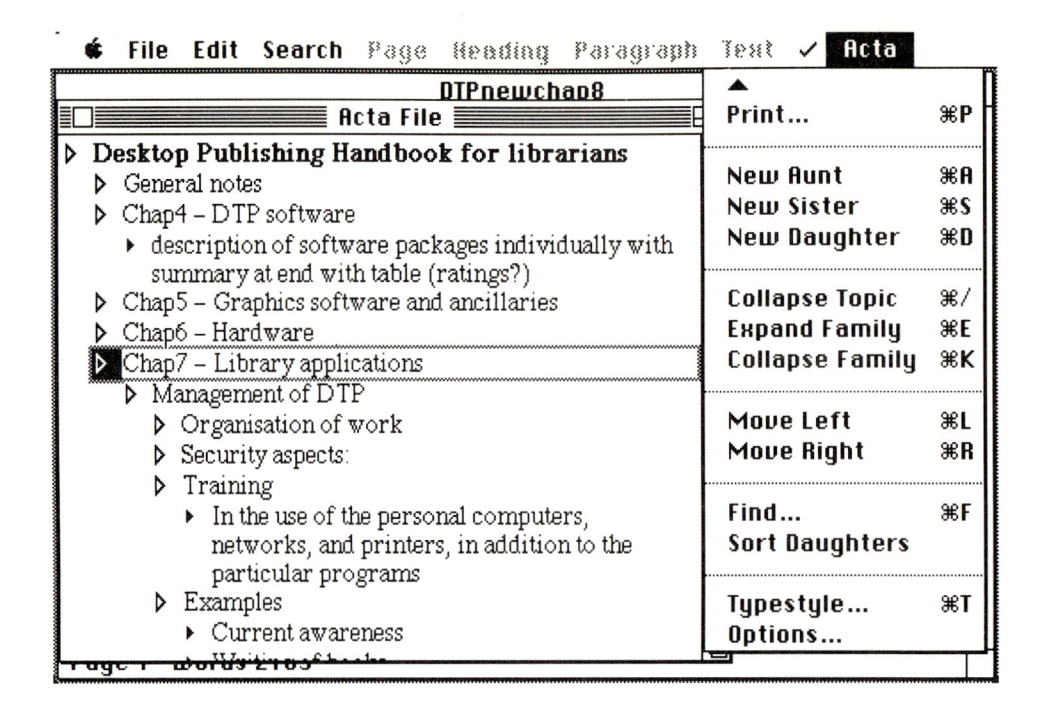

**Figure 6.3 Outline created in Acta**

topic can easily be chosen from the keyboard. This is a shortcut which enables fast working when the ideas really start to flow.

At any time during the creation of an outline, the display can be adjusted to provide the most apposite view. Any topic with daughters can be compressed or expanded to provide any view from major topics only (e.g. chapter headings) to the full outline fully expanded. Two types of arrow are used to denote topics: a hollow one to indicate that sub-topics exist; and a solid one to indicate no sub-topics.

Acta is currently in version 2.0 and is a pleasure to use by virtue of its thoughtfully implemented interface. But in addition to its obvious outlining features, Acta can also act as a mini word processor by incorporating facilities such as 'find', 'sort' and smart quotes (see page 76 on MacAuthor) and enabling the typestyles to be varied to correspond to most writing needs. For example, the same typestyle can be chosen for all topics at a particular level so that these are easily differentiated on screen and Acta will automatically implement the typestyle when new topics are added at this level. The outlines can be printed directly from the program using a variety of paragraph markings from bullets to decimal numbering.

The sort facility is one of the most useful features and again enables Acta to be used for jobs other than straight outlining. By permitting the sorting of topics at one level throughout the outline, a kind of selective sorting can be achieved whereby related topics at a lower level remain attached to their parents. This is not possible with the standard sorting capabilities of most word processors which apply sorts to all lines following a carriage return. When Acta is coupled with a word processor that can recognise the various levels in an outline, this facility can be put to good use and an example of the production of a current awareness bulletin using these techniques is described in chapter 8.

Acta documents can stand on their own on many occasions, but there are times when an outline needs to be incorporated into a word processor for subsequent modification. To facilitate this, a number of filters (format drivers is the terminology used in the Acta manual) are supplied so that Acta can open and save in a variety of formats including MacWrite, MORE, WriteNow and Microsoft RTF.

## Text finders

All word processors that are to be taken seriously incorporate a search function that enables the rapid location of text strings. To make full use of search implies that the writer has a good memory, is extremely organised and logical regarding the naming and storing of files, and that all information relating to similar material has been committed to the same word processor. There can be times in any writing task when the memory recalls that a relevant paragraph or phrase from another document could be utilised in the present work, but the location of the file and its saved filename prove elusive. On these occasions search can be of little practical use because it means opening and searching through all relevant files and ends up being an extremely time consuming business.

A package is needed which allows a search to be carried out across, if necessary, all the text files on a hard disc, in much the same way as one search strategy can be used on all the databases of a single host in online searching, or a keyword search operates through all bibliographic records in an online catalogue. The disadvantage of any search methodology on a library stand-alone computer is that indexes rather than the bibliographic records themselves are searched and these have to be built separately. This process takes time and the indexes account for a considerable amount of disc space. If such an approach was used on a microcomputer with a 20 megabyte hard disc, or on floppy discs, it would probably be considered impractical because of the valuable disc space required. Fortunately, there is at least one program – Gofer – which finds text in a wide variety of text files on both IBM PCs and Macintoshes and does this without the need to build indexes beforehand.

*Gofer*

Gofer is an amazing program when looked upon in the light of other text searching tools used in libraries and it is even more adaptable by having the ability to structure boolean searches. At last, true online (or CD-ROM) searching applied to all your microcomputer files. Its has two disadvantages, neither of which effect its functionality. Firstly, the name. One would like to think it had been christened after nice little furry creatures scuttling through holes and searching for nuts but its origins unfortunately appear to be in an American corruption of 'Go for it'. Secondly, while it will happily search through drawers of files on hard discs it finds it impossible to locate lost socks and screwdrivers and so will not make your day-to-day life totally trouble-free. To be fair, the manual makes this perfectly clear.

Gofer works as a desk accessory. Thus, whenever you wish to locate a section of another saved file it can be used without quitting the main program, making the incorporation of the old material as smooth as possible. When summoning Gofer a screen like that of figure 6.4 appears.

In this case the search string of 'FullWrite Professional' has been entered in the 'What' box. Search strings may contain any combination of up to eighty characters, numbers and symbols, and where more than one keyword is involved, these should be entered as normal English phrases with spaces separating the words. The only other parameter that Gofer needs is the location of the files to search, and the folders on the hard disc can be worked through and relevant ones selected after clicking the 'Where' button. The 'How' option in the top right hand corner tells Gofer how to display the search results, the default being a display of part of the text file in the window with the keyword highlighted. If there is more than one hit within a file these are all displayed in the same way, one after the other, and the program then passes to the next file until the search is over. At the end of the search the files with hits are listed and their full contents can be viewed at leisure – figure 6.5.

Gofer then allows one further stage to be undertaken: the selection and copying of any relevant text from the file for its subsequent transfer into the current document. Many of the formatting codes used by individual programs come into view but these can be ignored and paragraphs of text are normally presented intact. Gofer comes with a number of 'defaults' which make it immediately compatible with a wide range of word processors and DTP programs but these can easily be changed to make it adapt to read other formats such as MacAuthor II. It can be particularly useful when used in conjunction with PageMaker which is limited to one open document at a time. In addition to acting as an indirect replacement for a search function, Gofer can be used to transfer text between PageMaker documents while always having the current document open on screen.

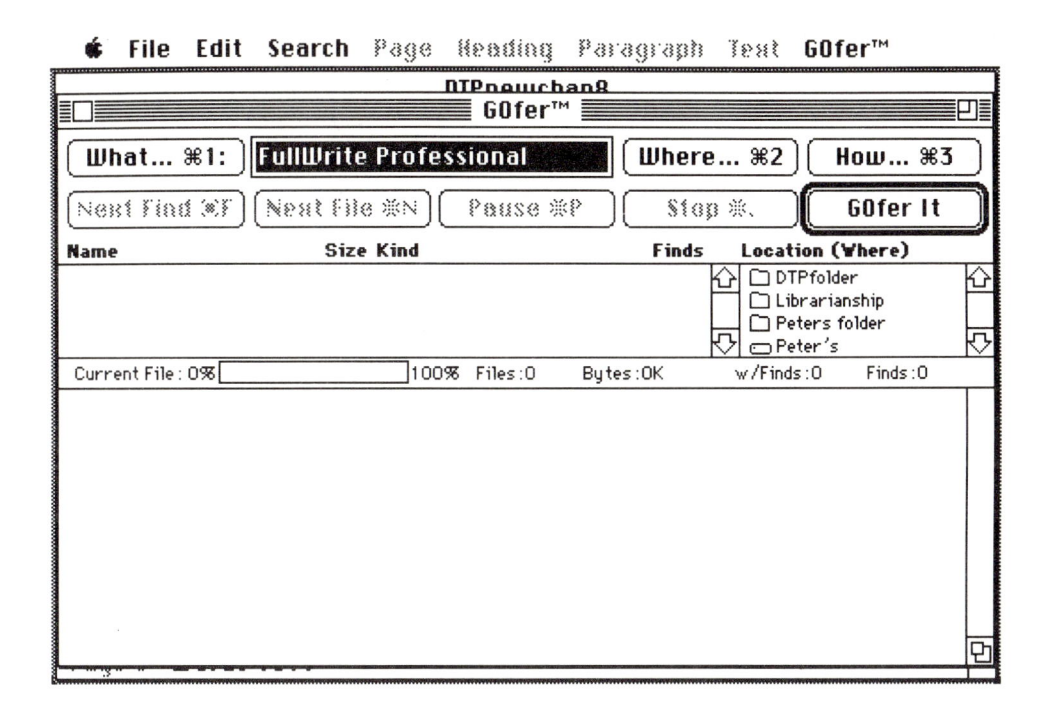

**Figure 6.4 Start of text search using Gofer**

**Figure 6.5 Results of text search using Gofer**

121

**Keyboard enhancers**

It seems fair to say that the mouse has been one of the key components in transforming the user interface of computers from being an offputting to an encouraging attribute. In spite of this, the very fact that one hand has to be removed from the keyboard to manipulate the pointer means that work is slowed down and, as a result, there has been an anti-mouse backlash in some quarters. Hewson (page 143) is only one writer who has railed against the beast: 'there are two things that don't work so well with the mouse ... : moving through lengths of text and accessing dialog boxes'. The way round this is to use keyboard shortcuts for selecting commands but some programs are limited in their implementation of these. In addition there are many operations – transferring between programs; selecting desk accessories – for which keyboard equivalents are not generally available. A number of packages have come onto the market which enable virtually any operation to be controlled from the keyboard and one of the most useful is QuicKeys.

*QuicKeys*

It can be seen from the main QuicKeys panel – figure 6.6 – that a wide range of mouse or related operations can be translated to keyboard functions. Top of the list is a feature that allows a text string of up to 71 characters to be saved and then played back at a single keystroke. For example, the term 'desktop publishing' could be allocated to a text QuicKey so that whenever, say Option–D was pressed, the complete two words would appear on screen. File and Menu/DA work similarly by enabling any program or document to be launched from the keyboard and permitting pull down menu commands not normally available from the keyboard to have Command keys assigned to them. Figure 6.6 shows a number of 'mousies' that are supplied with the program and which enable basic movements around documents to be achieved from the keyboard. Some of these operations may appear superficial but, like most of the ancillaries described in this chapter, the QuicKeys shortcuts are sorely missed when they are not available. A longer discussion of the various options in QuicKeys can be found in the article by Hahn.

But QuicKeys is more than a way of translating mouse movements to the keyboard, for sequences can be built up so that a complex series of operations can be carried out with the minimum of fuss. In this way repetitive jobs can be planned in principle, translated to keystrokes, and then played back at will and without the deadening of the mind that can happen on these occasions. These sequences for specific repetitive tasks are known generally as macros and some programs (Excel; WordPerfect) have this facility built in.

An example of a section of a sequence created to build up the list of figures and tables in this book is shown in figure 6.7. A

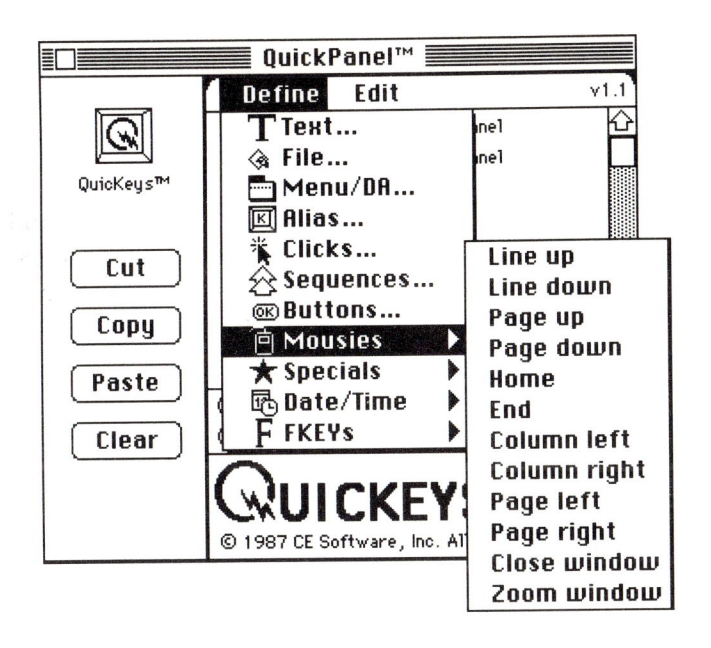

**Figure 6.6 QuicKeys window showing 'mousies' options**

**Figure 6.7 Macro sequence created in QuicKeys**

123

sequence is created by stringing any number of individual QuicKeys together and some of those that have already been assigned and are available for use are indicated on the right hand side of the window. These are a mix of those created for use across all programs and those specific to MacAuthor.

The actual sequence is built up in the left hand window by highlighting the required QuicKeys in turn. In this instance the first element is the copying of the title of each figure to the Clipboard and the Copy command is assigned a key using the QuicKeys 'Menu/DA' option. The next step is a transfer to the file which holds the list of figures and tables – Contents – and then the pasting of the title into the document. At this stage MacAuthor brings up a dialogue box asking if the Clipboard formatting should be retained and the response to this – No – has also been assigned to a QuicKey. The pause of 2 seconds simply gives MacAuthor time to display the dialogue box. The rest of the sequence tabs across to the right margin, pauses while the page number is added manually, adds a carriage return and then transfers back to the relevant chapter ready for the next title to be located and highlighted. This sequence totals ten elements which can be summoned by one keystroke. In addition to automating a very repetitive procedure this has the advantage that the titles are precise copies of the originals and so no mistakes are made in what would otherwise be a large re-typing job. Unfortunately, no way has been found of fully automating the operation by including the page number in the QuicKeys sequence.

This is all very well and QuicKeys works like a dream in these situations. The main drawback is that complex sequences are just that – complex, and when creating these users must be extremely clear-headed about what they want to achieve. If they are not, unexpected results will occur. Also, it must be stressed that the savings achieved with macros are never as great as one would expect because of the time taken to create error free sequences in the first place. The end products of macros must always be checked to make sure that the anticipated results will in fact be achieved.

*Tempo*

Another third party program that was designed to specifically create macros from any sequence of mouse and keyboard operations is Tempo. This excellent program was used to automatically create the charts included in Stubley's BLCMP book from data maintained as a spreadsheet. When over fifty bar charts are to be prepared from spreadsheet data some means of automating the procedure is required both to save time and prevent the operator going round the twist. Tempo permits a sequence of operations to be recorded and then played back to completion or halted for user input part way through. In this respect it is more suited to users who have complex and repeated operations to perform than is QuicKeys which only permits pauses of specified duration to be incorporated into sequences. Tempo II is now available, essentially an upgraded version of the program described so favourably by Whitby.

**References**

*Spelling checkers*  DeMaria, R. Microsoft's Bookshelf. Byte, vol. 13, no. 1, January 1988, pp. 176–178.

*Keyboard enhancers*  Hahn, R. Insights on QuicKeys. *Macworld*, vol. 5, no. 7, July 1988, pp. 229–238.

Hewson, D. *The Quark XPress companion*. London, Heyden & Son, 1988. ISBN 0 86344001 0.

Stubley, P. *BLCMP: a guide for librarians and systems managers*. Aldershot, Gower, 1988. ISBN 0 566 05512 0.

Whitby, M. The Ghost in the machine. *MacUser*, no. 6, May/June 1986, pp. 48–50.

# Section 3

# DTP in the library

# The gathering tide

Any librarian with an IT background or a knowledge of microcomputer software will readily adapt to DTP and easily come up with any number of practical applications in their own organisation. There is already evidence through the literature and the number of specialised courses and seminars that many enterprising librarians are already using DTP or are interested in learning the techniques. Cisler probably wrote the first article on DTP that appeared in a librarianship journal, and in this country there have appeared papers by Carson, Stubley and Tuck. Books are similarly beginning to appear with recent titles from Carson, and Johnson and Johnson.

Since October 1987 Aslib has been running one day seminars twice a year on 'Desktop publishing for effective presentation' and in September 1988 the Library Association Information Technology Group organised a one day course entitled 'Desktop publishing: is it for you?'. The British Library have become interested and involved at various levels and have produced a Library and Information Briefing on DTP (Howells). In addition, a number of papers on the subject have been presented at a variety of seminars and conferences on the use of microcomputers in libraries.

It is thought that the first desktop published book on a library topic was Stubley's work on BLCMP and it is known that others are in the pipeline, not to mention the present book! By desktop published is meant a book that has been wholly (or largely) prepared on a microcomputer using DTP techniques with camera-ready copy submitted to the publisher for subsequent printing.

DTP techniques can thus be used by librarians for producing anything from notices to complete books and virtually any document in between. The aim of chapters 7 and 8 is primarily to show how the technology is being, or could be, used in practice. Chapter 8 concludes with a resumé of library DTP applications and a subjective view of the most appropriate software for each.

But probably the most important aspect of this gathering tide is the way in which the technology is organised and managed in libraries. This pressing matter should be the concern of all librarians and should be considered seriously before the hardware appears on the doorstep. The various aspects of the management of DTP are covered in the final chapter.

## References

Carson, J. Desktop publishing: a technology waiting in the wings. *Library Association Record*, vol. 90, no. 2, February

1988, pp. 95–97. This was a resume of a report subsequently published as the following monograph.

Carson, J. *Desktop publishing and libraries*. London, Taylor Graham, 1988. ISBN 0 947568 34 4.

Cisler, S. Desktop publishing in libraries. *Online*, vol. 11, no. 5, September 1987, pp. 64–72.

Howells, L. *Desktop publishing*. British Library Research and Development Department, 1988. Library & Information Briefing 4.

Johnson, H.H. and Johnson, R.D. *The Macintosh press: desktop publishing for librarians*. London, Meckler, 1989. ISBN 0 88736 287 7.

Stubley, P. *BLCMP: a guide for librarians and systems managers*. Aldershot, Gower, 1988. ISBN 0 566 05512 0.

Stubley, P. Desktop publishing on the Macintosh: six questions answered for librarians. *Program*, vol. 22, no. 3, July 1988, pp. 247–261.

Tuck, W. Desktop publishing: what is it and what it can do for you. *Aslib Proceedings*, vol. 41, no. 1, January, 1989, pp. 29–37.

# 7 The Library Guide: a practical DTP example

**The library guide as the subject of DTP**

The library guide is the one publication that most libraries have in common. In spite of this it appears in a most uncommon range of sizes, formats, type styles and qualities, ranging from the truly dismal (could the Penny Dreadful have been named after the library guide?) to excellent professional productions. Most librarians feel that they should have a guide but it must be a rare number indeed who do not become depressed at the prospect of producing one or updating their publication from the previous year. A good guide requires a meticulous attention to detail, coordination of input from a wide range of library staff and other sources, and liaison with printers either internally or outside the institution, all carried out to an extremely tight time schedule. In addition, in the absence of professional help, many librarians have to draw on design skills they never knew they had and probably don't possess.

Many of these problems will still be around with desktop publishing – in possibly a rather different form – but there are, in addition, a number of advantages that make the preparation of the guide a much less demanding proposition. Aspects such as the incorporation of new information into an existing guide are fairly obvious, being the stock in trade of most computerised operations, but the major benefits are the increased control that can be exerted by the originator of the material – including influence over the time scale – and the improvement in final quality.

This chapter is taken up with a detailed description of the use of the software to produce two pages from a hypothetical library guide. The idea of producing a guide for 'West Midlands Polytechnic Library' seemed quite amusing at the time the chapter was written and it was only later that one institution decided it wished to be known by this name. In spite of this, the fictitious name has been retained. The DTP software used in the example is PageMaker.

This consideration of the library guide continues the basic approach used in analysing the software in chapters 3 and 4. Thus, it discusses the format (i.e. general page size), the layout (e.g. one column or many), the method of text entry, and the production of diagrammatic material.

**Format**

It has already been stated that DTP gives greater control over much of the publishing process. What it cannot do – at least for the foreseeable future – is to make intellectual decisions over such questions as 'what is the most appropriate format for the library guide in my own institution?' and 'what layout should be adopted to actually encourage use of the guide by the library clientele?'. Where the staff time is available DTP can assist in these decisions by enabling the preparation of a range of sample formats for comparison but the final decision must obviously rest with the librarian or designer.

A further consideration is the format in which the master copy produced by the librarian is to be presented to the printer or the local reprographic unit. Even if the final size of the guide is to be less than A4 there can be instances when it will be preferable to produce A4 output from the DTP system so that the final reduction takes place elsewhere. Obviously a decision should be taken on this matter before work is started by discussing all implications with the people concerned. This should ensure that valuable time is not wasted creating a guide that is impractical to handle later on in the overall process.

*Page size*

Once decisions have been taken on these two factors the shrink-wrap can be ripped from the PageMaker box for work to begin. Sensibly, no work can be started on a new PageMaker document until the page size, the paper orientation (landscape or portrait), and the margin widths have been specified – figure 7.1. In this case the decision has been taken to produce the master copy of the guide as single A5 sheets and PageMaker allows us to work with this size on-screen and, if desired, view facing pages. The master copy does not have to be printed on A5 paper and in most instances A4 will be chosen and trimmed at the printers. To aid in this process PageMaker provides an option for the printing of crop marks when the finished masters are output from the laser printer.

As an alternative the A4 page size could have been selected with a 'landscape' orientation and then treated as two separate pages

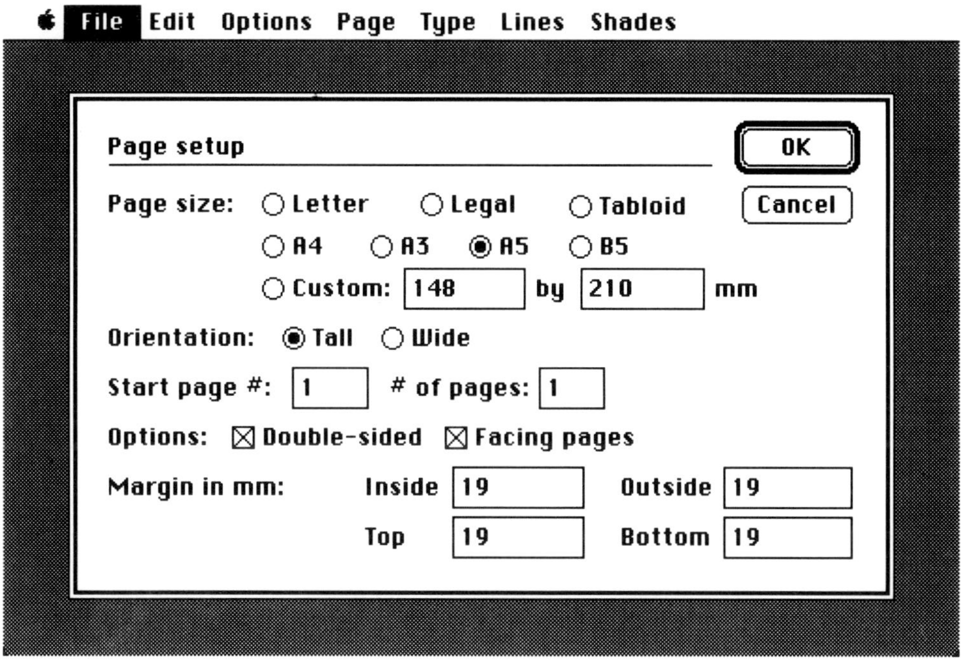

**Figure 7.1 Variations of page size available with PageMaker**

using some of the features described below in the section on layout. It will be seen from figure 7.1 that non-standard sizes can also be used by selecting the 'custom' radio button. Selecting the 'double sided' box has the effect of alternating the inside and outside margins between left and right pages so that the gutter or binding margin is even.

*Overall format*

Once the size has been selected attention can turn to the layout of individual pages. However, a further factor that needs consideration is the overall format of the guide, that is, will it comprise loose-leaf sheets slotted into a single cover, or will a single bound or stapled publication be most appropriate? High printing costs coupled with the difficulty of communicating to the printer the small changes required from multi-site working have led to many librarians choosing the loose-leaf alternative. With DTP the production of publications directed at specific groups becomes that much easier and in a few years we may see a bound library guide produced for each site or even for specific groups of users.

The choice of format will not alter the detailed design of the guide but it might influence the way PageMaker is used. For example in a loose-leaf guide the display of facing pages (see figure 7.1) will have no meaning as all pages will be seen by the users as single sheets and can accordingly be designed individually. In spite of this it can prove useful to design back and front as a two page spread, even though the librarian is the only one who will see the unity of the two parts. A further factor is that the space available for text and diagrams in loose-leaf guides will be limited to two sides whereas a bound guide offers much greater freedom or, to take a different view, allows ample space for waffling. In this example the loose-leaf single sheet approach has been adopted.

**Layout**

The 'traditional' layout for the library guide is single column text separated by diagrams where clarification of some detail is required e.g. in the explanation of catalogue entries or the inclusion of a floor plan. Only occasionally, with the incorporation of tables such as lists of staff or subject areas will more than one column be used. These restrictions are not imposed by the content or purpose of the guide but rather spring from the limitations of the traditional equipment and in particular the difficulty of producing multi-column text on a typewriter.

Page make-up programs like PageMaker permit the use of a virtually unlimited number of columns per page although for most sensible designs library guides will be limited to between two to four columns depending on page size. In designing the A5 guide of this example two columns would appear to most appropriately fit the needs of the publication.

*Master pages*

With a loose-leaf guide some uniformity of design is advisable to bring together the individual pages into a whole in the minds of the library users. This can be achieved in a number of ways – similar headings, use of the organisation's logo – but one obvious method is to utilise the same columnar layout from sheet to sheet. To achieve this easily PageMaker uses a facility of 'Master pages' to incorporate all the features that are to be repeated throughout the publication. This facility can be used in two ways. It can be stored as a separate file and then used as a template whenever a new copy of the publication is produced – the approach for a loose-leaf library guide. Alternatively it can simply form part of the overall document so that when new pages are added they possess all the basic characteristics of the masters. Independent left and right master pages can be created and the master can also be overridden if a non-standard design is required in some parts of the publication.

Within any PageMaker document access is gained to the master pages by highlighting the 'L' and 'R' pages in the bottom left hand corner of the screen. As shown in figure 7.2 the number of columns and the distance separating them is controlled from the 'Options' pull down menu. PageMaker automatically creates columns of equal width but if unequal spacing is required this can be achieved by simply dragging the column outlines across

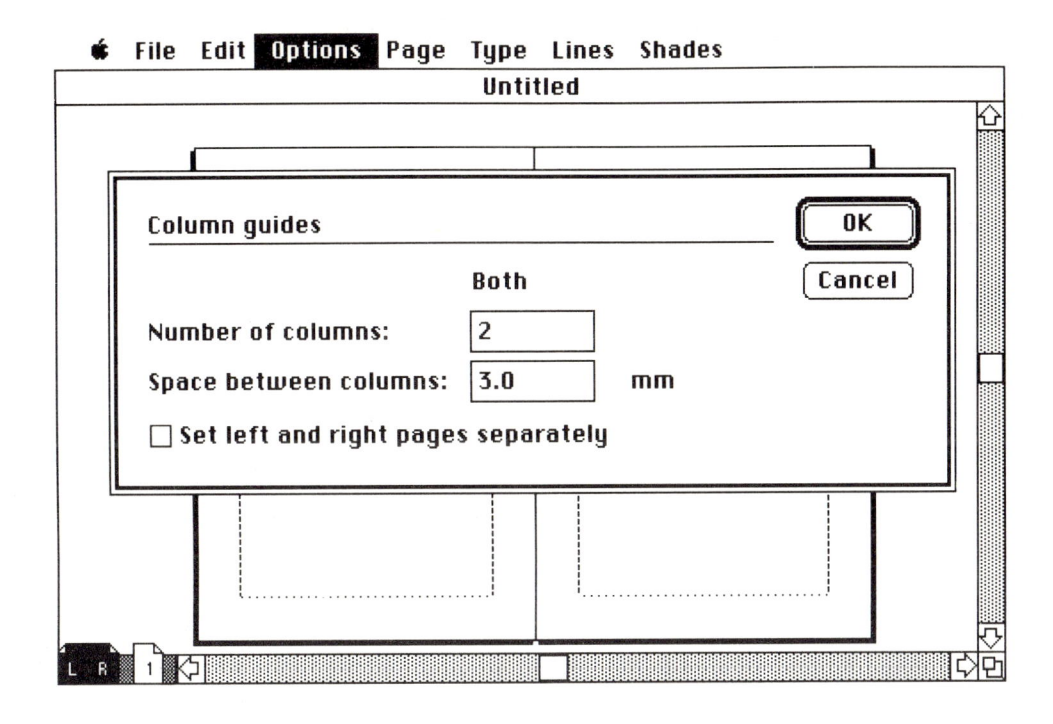

Figure 7.2 The creation of columns in PageMaker

*Toolbox*

the page with the mouse. For the purposes of the library guide left and right pages (or in this case, front and back) have the same number of columns and column spacing.

So far use has been made exclusively of the pointer to select pull down menus and begin the layout of the guide but from this point on other facilities will be required. These will be found in the Toolbox. The most widely used of these is the text tool – designated by 'A' – which is used in the selection and editing of all text. Additionally, lines can be drawn in a variety of styles and thicknesses, and boxes can be created to highlight text and diagrams or be filled with a range of patterns to add interest to the page. The final hieroglyphic (an ancient fertility symbol?) is the cropping tool used to adjust the size of imported graphics. The Toolbox is shown in figure 7.4 and it can be hidden from view when not in use or moved around the screen as required.

*Type styles*

Other features that can be included on the master pages of the guide are a heading e.g. the name of the library and, possibly, an identifier of the page number or name at the bottom of the page. Details on the text entry for the main content of the guide are given in the section below but headings are best input directly in PageMaker. Once the text tool has been chosen by clicking on the Toolbox, the selection of the style and size of typeface is controlled from an item on the 'Type' pull down menu. In this case the Avant Garde typeface has been chosen out of personal preference and an attempt to get away from the more traditional

135

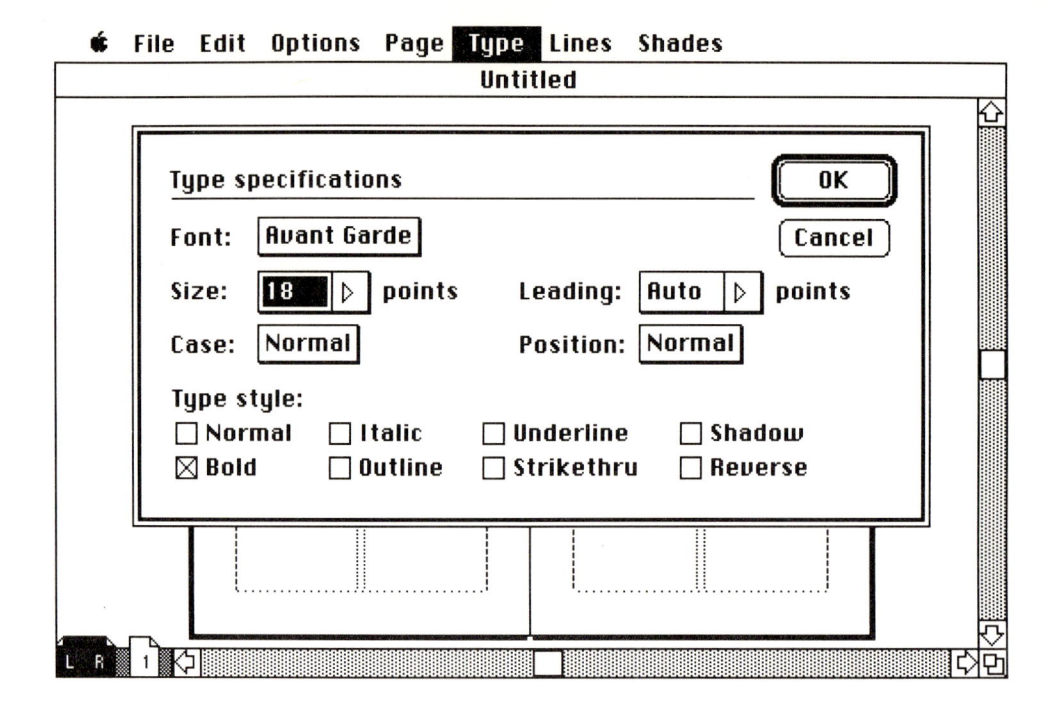

**Figure 7.3 The selection of type styles in PageMaker**

faces of Times or Helvetica. To make an impression a relatively large size of typeface (18 point) has been chosen and the heading has been further set in bold (figure 7.3).

PageMaker uses the concept of the pasteboard and, accordingly, the whitespace on screen surrounding the displayed pages can be used to store text and graphics when not in use on the actual document. Thus, the heading, the name of the library, can be typed anywhere on screen and subsequently dragged into position. It easily spans the top of the guide and does not have to fit into the columns already created to take the main body of text. As this heading will be needed across only one side of each page of the library guide, it is incorporated into only the left master page.

*Page view*

When used with the standard Macintosh screen it is not possible to display two full-sized A4, or even A5, pages side by side. To compensate for this PageMaker provides a range of working views of the document varying from 50% to 200%. 100% or 'Actual size' is used for the majority of work to ensure the accurate placing of text and graphics, while the reduced views are especially useful during the overall design of single and two page spreads; subsequent fine tuning can be achieved at the larger views and for precise positioning the 200% view is especially useful. To speed up the screen display in the reduced views text below a certain size – varying with the view – is displayed as 'greeking' or simulated text – grey representations

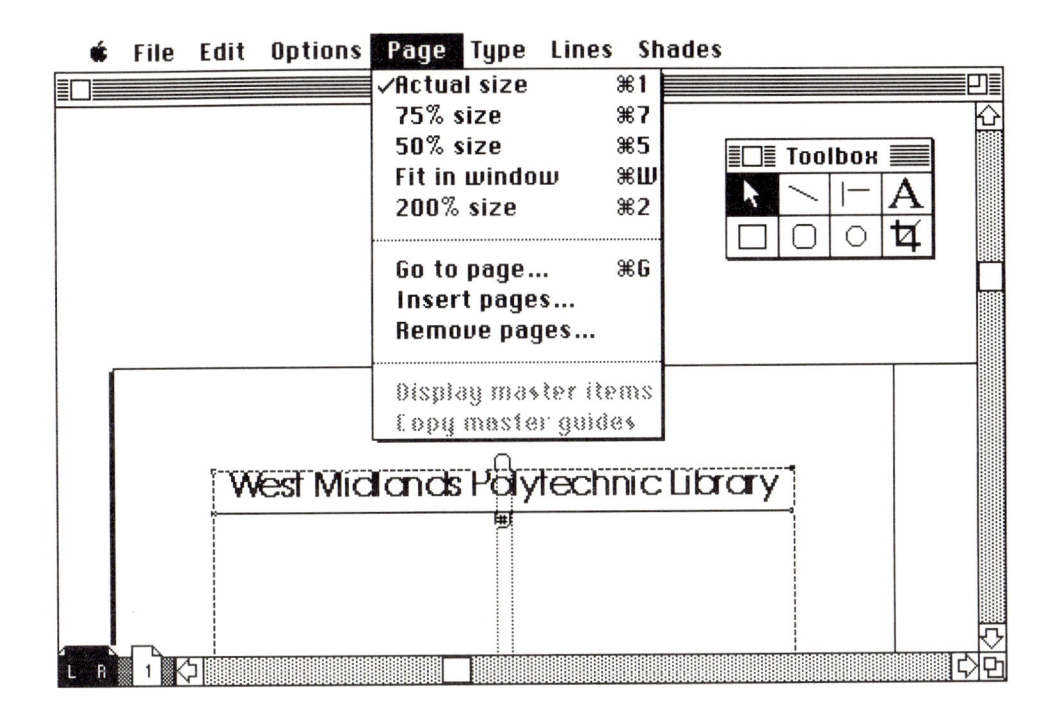

**Figure 7.4 Page view and the toolbox in PageMaker**

of both the thickness and length of lines of text (figure 7.8). The contents of the 'Page' pull down menu, with a portion of the left master page of the library guide viewed at actual size, are displayed in figure 7.4. This diagram also shows the name of the library being placed at the top of the left master page as a heading, just below the dotted top margin guide.

*Lines*

Below the library name it will be usual to have a sub-heading giving the title of the particular sheet, for example, 'The online catalogue'; 'Library staff', 'Library rules and regulations'. In order to emphasize the difference between the two headings a horizontal line will be drawn across the page and because this is required on every leaf of the guide it is again attached to the left master page. The selection of line thickness is made, unsurprisingly, from the 'Lines' pull down menu and then drawing on the screen with a cross-hair pointer from the Toolbox. In an attempt to move away from a closely-typed mass of text and bring more space onto the page, the line motif is repeated across the bottom of the sheet and coupled with the sheet number.

*Ruler guides*

The final addition to the master pages are ruler guides to ease the alignment of text and diagrams either on a single page or from one page to another. In this case two ruler guides are used, to position the sub-heading below the line across the top of the page and at the start of the main text block. The guides appear

137

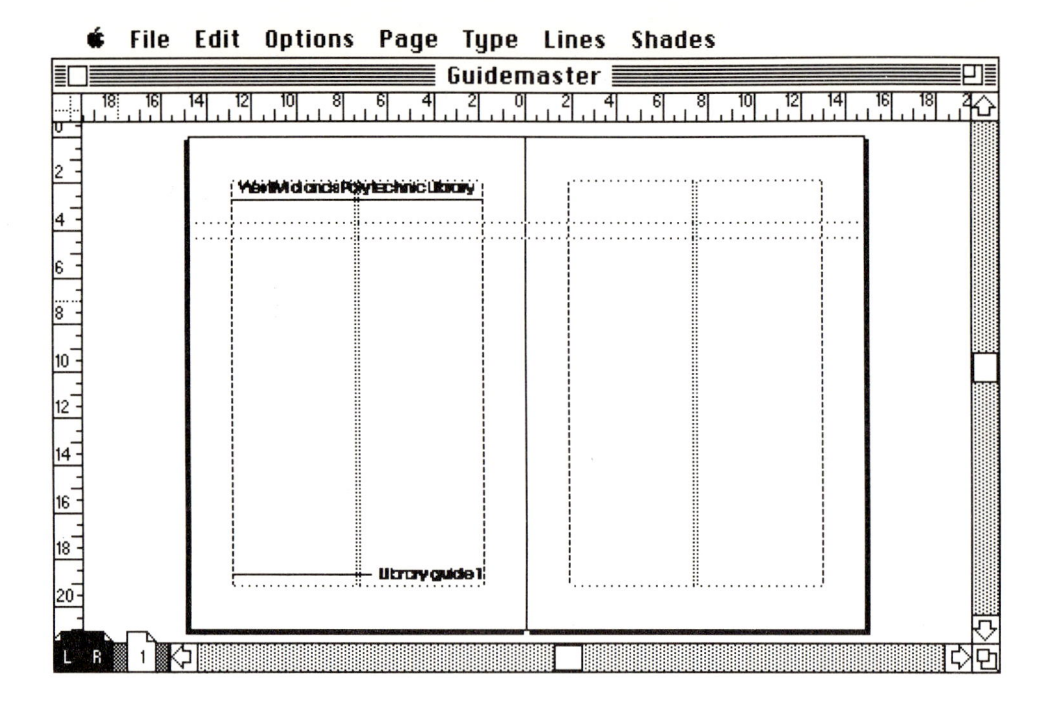

**Figure 7.5 Completed master pages in PageMaker**

after first selecting 'Rulers' from the 'Options' menu and they can then simply be pulled into position using the pointer tool.

The master pages, complete with headings, lines and guides are then ready to receive the main text, and are presented in figure 7.5 using the 'Fit in window' page view. As explained above, this would normally be saved as a template for use as the basis of each loose-leaf sheet of the guide. To facilitate use of the template PageMaker incorporates an 'Open copy' command so that the original is left intact and unaffected by any unintentional changes.

**Text entry**

In any consideration of the desktop published library guide it is preferable to see the document as a whole so that decisions can be taken rationally as the publication proceeds. This may be at odds with the somewhat *ad hoc* approach that can be more freely adopted in manual preparation where the most important aspect is generally the content and written style of the text. Even with DTP the two methods of attack are not mutually exclusive and it is possible to have one part of the team working on the content while another is finalising the layout and format.

PageMaker, in common with other DTP packages, incorporates a number of word processing features but these are best used for making relatively minor changes to the text. Accordingly, the approach adopted by many practitioners of DTP is to write directly into a word processor and then transfer the text as a separate operation into the DTP program and concentrate on layout as a separate issue. PageMaker recognises a number of word processors and can thus import text fully formatted but failing this the text can be saved as a text file and formatting carried out within the make-up program.

The text for the current two pages of the library guide – an introduction to the use of the online catalogue – was prepared in MacAuthor II, a word processor whose formatting is not recognised automatically by PageMaker. However, as the features of this word processor were known in detail by the writer it enabled the text to be input extremely quickly and with little consideration being given to the formatting and layout, although, as discussed in chapter 4, MacAuthor II can for some jobs be considered a page make-up program in its own right. The separate preparation of the content is likely to be used in many libraries, where the text may even be written on paper (!) and input by a secretary or typist. The text is subsequently saved as a text file, an option provided by most word processors. If a PageMaker-compatible word processor had been used the text could have been saved in 'native' format.

*Place command*   The beauty of most DTP software is that text and graphics created in other programs can be imported directly and then be manipulated without leaving the main application. Thus, returning to PageMaker and using the Place command it is possible to pick up the OPAC text file created in MacAuthor II (Figure 7.6). In this instance it makes little sense to 'Retain format' and the text is transferred into the document using the PageMaker default values for type style, size and text alignment. Fortunately, in this example the chosen type face – Times 12 Point – is the same as the default and no further formatting is required. If a different typeface had been required this could have been applied with the style sheets or through the 'Type specifications' box. So that the front and back pages of the guide can be viewed side-by-side two new pages have been added – with all the attributes of the master pages – by choosing 'Insert pages' from the Page menu (Figure 7.4). The previous page 1 then becomes a blank and unused page.

Before the text is placed on the page the Autoflow Option is selected to flow the text from column to column until the document is complete. This rather obvious feature deserves particular mention for it has only been introduced in the latest version of PageMaker and previously text had to be manually transferred throughout the document one column at a time. Many people still seem to think of PageMaker as a package for making up single sheets but this is no longer the case. Accurate

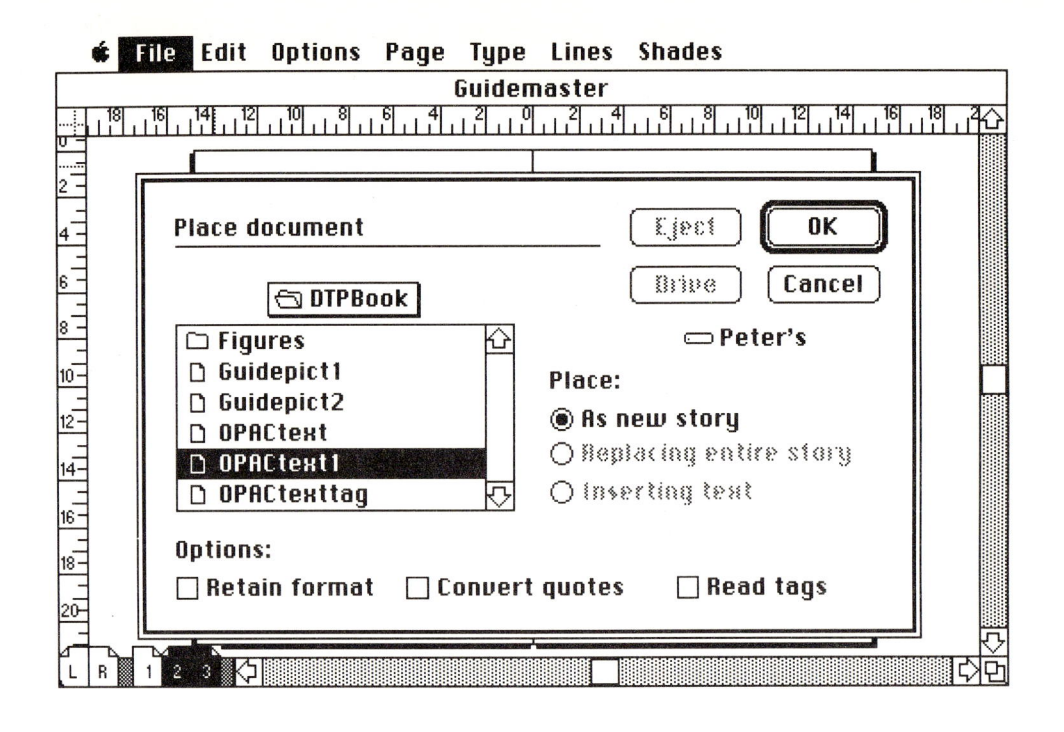

**Figure 7.6 Place command in PageMaker**

positioning of the start of the text on the front page of the library guide is aided by a 'Snap to guides' Option which, as explained in the PageMaker manual, acts as a magnet for the incoming text. This feature will be particularly appreciated by those with shaky hands who find it difficult to accurately control the position of the mouse. The flowing text keeps within the column guides but overruns into the heading at the top of the first page, and adjustments are made by moving the top and bottom boundaries of the text boxes to clear the heading. At this stage the added text occupies only a portion of the total available space, as frequently happens when preparing the text of the library guide manually. However, with DTP it is much easier to adjust the text to the available space and one of the other advantages of the software is that steps can be taken to fill out the page with graphics and so give a more interesting and, hopefully, professional result. Ways of doing this are described in the section below.

Before consideration is given to graphics, the sub-heading needs to be added to indicate the content of our two pages (The Online catalogue) and this is achieved in much the same way as described for creating the heading. In fact the same type style and size ( Avant Garde, 18 Point, Bold) has been used.

In the previous description it will be apparent that DTP enables the use of a much wider range of type styles and sizes than is normally available on electric typewriters with their standard Courier font.

**Graphics**

The handling of graphics in PageMaker can mean one of two things: the importing of illustrations from external packages or as scanned images in much the same way as already described for text files; and the creation of geometric shapes within the program to enhance the overall look of a document. This section will concentrate on the former.

Several packages exist for producing drawings and other graphic effects which may be suitable for incorporating into library publications and some of these have already been described in chapter 5. None of the packages will turn librarians who happen to be computer freaks into artists, just as the ownership of Dewey would not transform an artist into an expert classifier. What it is possible to achieve, though, and with only a limited amount of talent, is the transformation of some design and graphics ideas into reality. For this example a simple online terminal shape was created in the program SuperPaint, saved in the PICT format and picked up by PageMaker using the 'Place' command. As with text PageMaker automatically recognises a variety of graphics formats of which PICT is but one.

The initial positioning of imported graphics from the Place command is rarely accurate and the diagram invariably has to be dragged into place using the pointer tool. The fact that the text has been flowed into columns does not affect the positioning of the graphic which can easily be centred on the page between columns. Two other adjustments can also be made: cropping, and wrapping the text round the graphic. Cropping, using the cropping tool from the Toolbox, is what it sounds like, and consists of reducing the size of the graphic so that it will fit more easily into the space available. It is especially useful if only a portion of a larger diagram is to be incorporated into a publication so that re-drawing or modification in the external program is not required.

*Text wrap*

Text wrap, or runaround, is a feature that has come to be sought after by most users of DTP software and the usefulness of most programs sometimes seems to be judged on whether or not it is available. It is the ability of the program to follow the contours of a diagram of any shape and PageMaker's manifestation is found from the Options menu under the term 'Text wrap'. Full text flow around a graphic need not necessarily be chosen, so if you wish to be totally unfashionable, always a good thing, you can simply decide to finish the text above the graphic and start again below. Or even flow the text over the graphic used as a backdrop. The choice of any alternative is available at all times

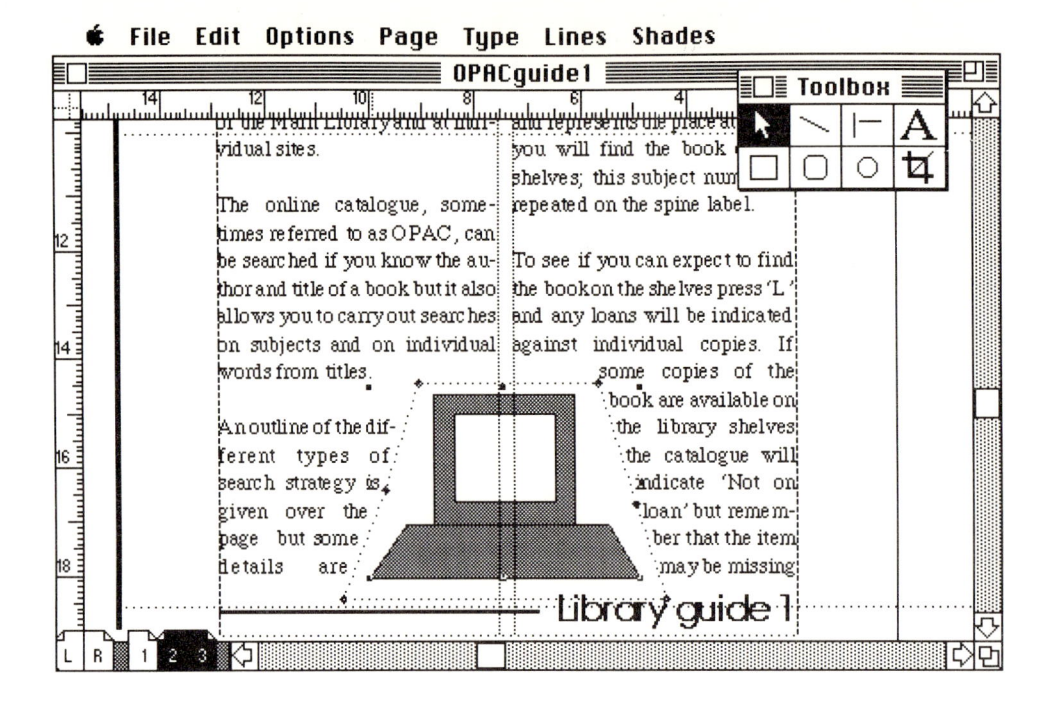

**Figure 7.7 Text wrap around graphic in PageMaker**

and so the result of different effects can be viewed before the final judgement is passed.

If full text wrap is chosen PageMaker creates a skin around the graphic and scatters this with diamonds at strategic places – a rather pleasing effect! By dragging the diamonds on screen the shape of the skin varies and the text can be made to flow around any shape irrespective of the shape of the graphic itself – figure 7.7. To a person with little professional page layout experience, this appears an extremely elegant solution to the text flow problem, while at the same time providing the user with an element of creative control not previously available.

**Final adjustments**

In this example the length of text – the description of the online catalogue for the library guide – has been kept to a minimum and does not fill the space available. The two pages of the guide with the graphic and the imported text are shown in figure 7.8. At this reduced screen display the 12 point Times type cannot be read and it is shown as 'greeked' text – thick grey lines indicating the overall view of the text on the page. Two alternatives thus present themselves – increasing the length of the text so that it does fill the page, or modifying the design to enable the description to be used largely unchanged. On the

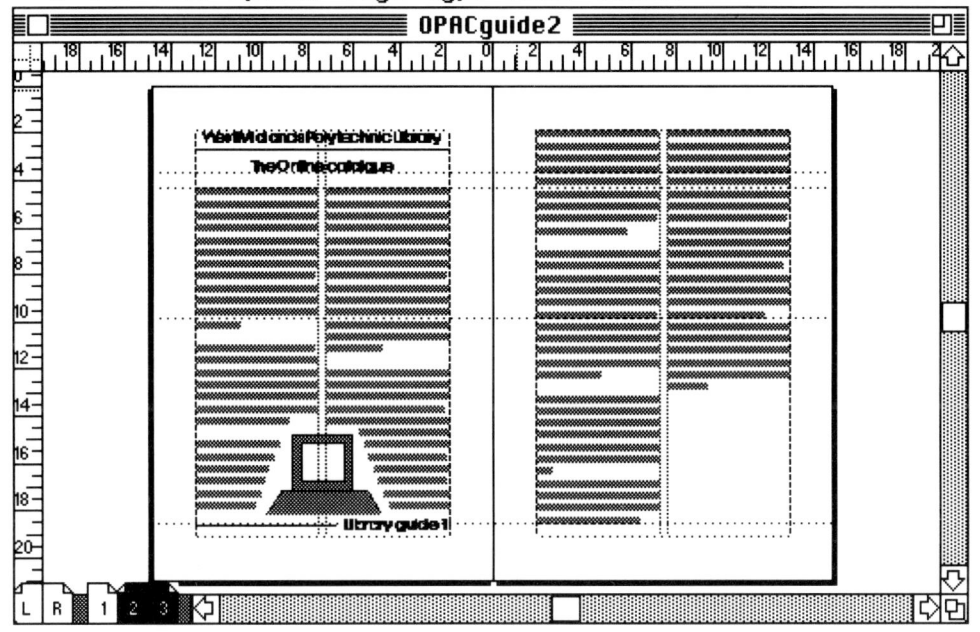

**Figure 7.8 Imported text and graphic before final adjustment**

assumption that in this case the text is adequate (please don't read it too closely!) the latter course has been chosen.

On re-reading the text it was apparent that towards the end a description of the different search possibilities had been included and that this could be separated from the earlier discussion of where to find OPAC in the library and what it was. Accordingly, it was decided to highlight the last few paragraphs to emphasise the difference and, further, to create some interest on the page by enclosing the text in a box and giving it a sub-title.

The first step in this process is to determine how much space can be allocated to the sub-section by aligning the overflow text from the first page at the top of the second. PageMaker allows this to be achieved easily. The search strategies can be separated from the rest of the text and placed on the pasteboard and, by trial and error, the overflow text is evened out so that it occupies the top of the two columns on the page. Some adjustment to the text itself may be required to ensure that the two columns line up accurately. Alternatively, the word spacing can be adjusted in PageMaker to either condense or extend the text block.

The space below this can now be used for the description of search strategies, and to make this stand out it will be enclosed in a box created using the drawing tools from the Toolbox and filled using a light grey pattern from Shades menu. A 10% grey

143

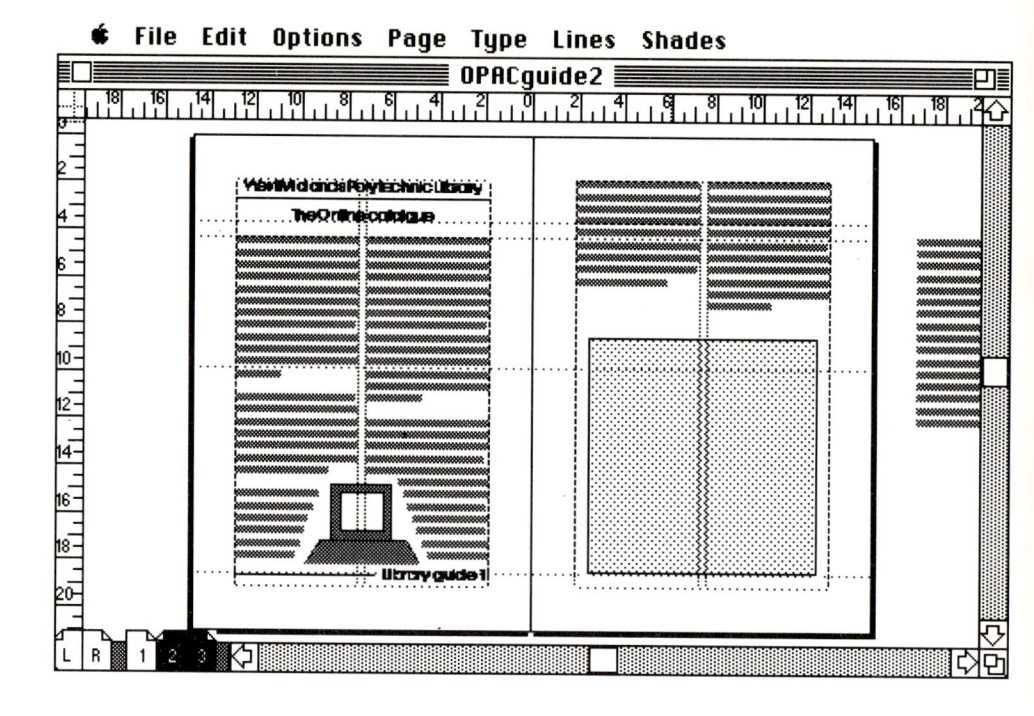

**Figure 7.9 Separation of library guide text into two stories**

fill has been used to make sure that the text can be easily read over the top. This also has the advantage that the text can be made out on the Macintosh screen. Figure 7.9 shows the bulk of the story on page 2 and at the top of page 3 with the box in place and the rest of the text to the right of the guide on the pasteboard. The thickness of the line surrounding the box is adjusted from the Lines menu and in this case a modest thickness of 1 point has been used. By using the 'None' option a shaded box with no line boundary can be created.

Once the box is in position the remaining story can be picked up from the pasteboard and positioned. All that then remains is to create a heading for the boxed section – say, Search Strategies, again in the Avant Garde typeface – and then make any final adjustments to the overall document. This might include modifying small sections of text to balance columns and adjust the size of paragraphs and so produce as polished and professional looking a guide as possible. When the final result is satisfactory, the master copy of the guide can be run off on the laser printer and given to the reprographic unit to produce the requisite number of copies.

The finished two pages of the OPAC guide are presented as figure 7.10. The crop marks referred to earlier in the chapter can be clearly seen at each corner of the A5 page.

# West Midlands Polytechnic Library

## The Online catalogue

The online catalogue is the first place to look if you are trying to find a book in the library. It contains records of most of the books in all five sites and it is easily accessed from the black computer terminals. Some of the older material may only be traced through the card catalogues located on the first floor of the Main Library and at individual sites.

The online catalogue, sometimes referred to as OPAC, can be searched if you know the author and title of a book but it also allows you to carry out searches on subjects and on individual words from titles.

An outline of the different types of search strategy is given over the page but some details are similar for all searches.

If a single book matches the term you have typed in, full details will be given of the author, title, edition, publisher and publication date. You will see that the layout is similar to that provided on the traditional catalogue cards. The number opposite the 'Location' is the subject number and represents the place at which you will find the book on the shelves; this subject number is repeated on the spine label.

To see if you can expect to find the book on the shelves press 'L' and any loans will be indicated against individual copies. If some copies of the book are available on the library shelves the catalogue will indicate 'Not on loan' but remember that the item may be missing for a variety of reasons: it may have just been

## Library guide 1

returned and be awaiting reshelving; someone may be using it in the library; or it may have been stolen! If the book you are looking for is not available you can request it by completing a reservation card available from the Enquiry Desk.

If more than one book matches your search term a range of entries will be displayed in an abbreviated form (author/title/date of publication/subject number) from which individual books can be chosen using the number at the far left. Having selected a number you will be presented with a full entry as described above. If you get lost, pressing 'M' will return you to the main menu when you can start again.

---

### Search strategies

If you know the author and the title the quickest way to find the book is to use **Quick Author/Title Search** by typing in the surname of the author, a comma, and then the first word of the title.

If you only know the title you can still find the book by using **Title Search** and typing in the first four words of the title.

If you only know the author use **Author Search** and, where possible, type in the surname, a comma, and the first name eg Amis, Kingsley.

If more than one author has the same surname a range of entries will be displayed from which you can choose the correct one. If the author has written more than one book the catalogue will tell you how many works it has found.

If you don't know the author or the title but can remember the subject of the book two alternatives are available to you.

**Keyword Search** allows you to search using any word from the title while **Subject Search** uses the subject number that can be found from the alphabetical subject index.

---

**Figure 7.10 Library guide created in PageMaker**

# 8 Library applications

**Introduction**

The applications discussed in the following pages include current awareness bulletins; the writing of books; the preparation of library notices; the production of newsletters; and the combination of DTP and CD-ROM. The chapter concludes with a discussion on the suitability of the different types of packages for particular applications.

**Current awareness bulletins**

One of the main problems with the use of DTP in libraries is not the lack of ideas or applications but the shortage of funds for the purchase of hardware and software coupled with the difficulty of finding the staff time required. As outlined in the next chapter, it will also be discovered that once an easy to use microcomputer and a high quality printer have been installed there is increased demand for their use, and this further aggravates the position. During the writing of this book this situation occurred at Birmingham Polytechnic when, as a result of the implementation of a new staff structure and the creation of an Information Services section, it was decided to reinstate current awareness services for academic departments.

Once the principle of restarting the service had been accepted a decision had to be taken on content and form. It should go without saying that content is by far the most important aspect. The original intention was to produce bulletins for each academic department but due to the vast amount of resources that this would entail work was started on an initial batch of three. For the same reasons it was decided to limit these to the main titles in journals taken by the library, thus excluding – for the time being – new book acquisitions and any scanning of abstracting services. While members of staff were consulted regarding the type of service they would like to see, it was also decided not to target SDI (selective dissemination of information) services at individuals.

Current awareness services come in all sorts of shapes, sizes and forms yet it is too easy for librarians to feel that form is unimportant and that users will be satisfied with any scraps of paper that come into their hands written up with relevant references. The easiest form of bulletin to produce is a list of title pages photocopied from journals and gathered together for regular dispatch to users. This simple (though admittedly effective) practice was immediately rejected but retained in a locked drawer as a fall-back position. The aim was to produce a professional looking set of publications that would create a good and impressive image for the new section and for this reason the first choice was to use DTP techniques.

At the time the library had two Macintosh Pluses connected to an Apple LaserWriter Plus but both computers were occupied virtually full time with administrative and financial work. Fortunately, a TOPS local area network had been installed a few months earlier to enable two Amstrad PCs to 'talk' to each other and to the two Macintoshes, and it was decided to use one of these machines for the basic keyboarding. This was not out of choice but out of necessity and had one advantage in that the staff involved were familiar with WordStar on PC compatibles and so work could begin without much further training.

*TOPS networking*

TOPS is an elegant way of connecting machines working on different operating systems and enabling file transfer between them. It appears to have been developed to connect Macintoshes to other machines – particularly IBM PCs – and it works fine when the need is to transfer files between Macintoshes and Amstrad PCs. When compared with what was available even a few years ago it strikes one as being very elegant although it now appears to be one of several similar products on the market. The hardware requirements are modest and comprise the wiring between machines and a TOPS card for each of the Amstrads – nothing for the Macintoshes. Once the software has been loaded TOPS is available on the Macintosh as a desk accessory and file manipulation can take place at any time, without closing down the current application. On the Amstrad all communications with TOPS must be carried out outside of applications.

In effect, any hard disc on the system can act as a file server to any user on the network but access is controlled from the home machine. Thus, before directories (Amstrad) or folders (Macintosh) can be used by others they must be published by their originator. If sensitive information is held in files that are to be made generally available, then access can be password protected – figure 8.1 – although this is not mandatory. Published folders can then be mounted by any user on the network when they become another volume for access by the

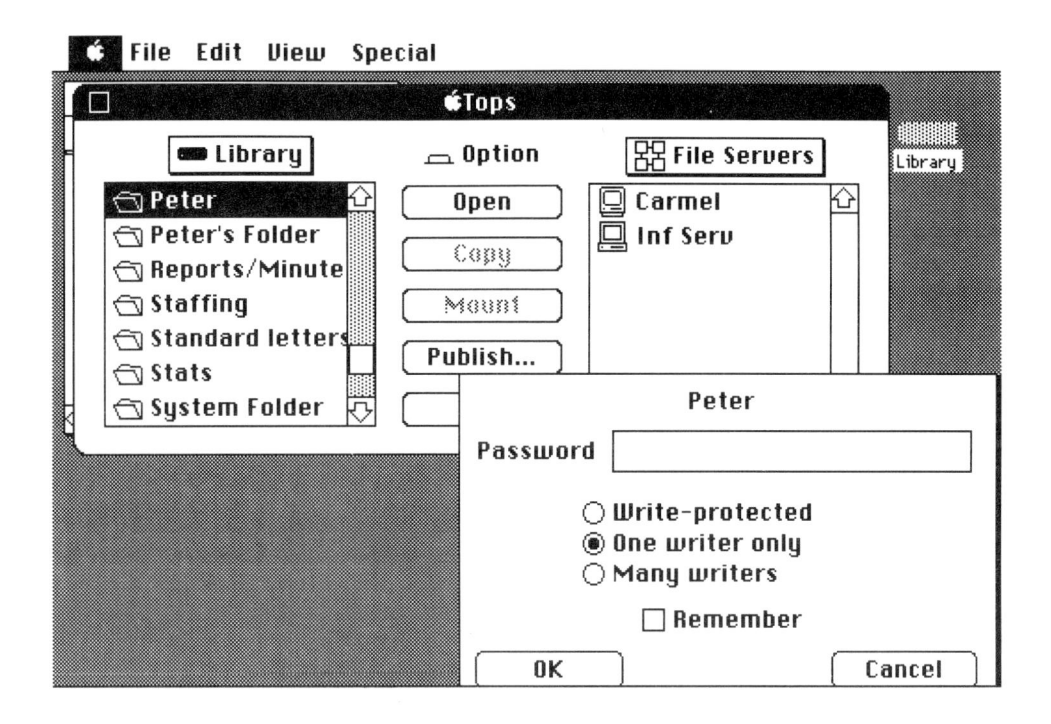

**Figure 8.1 Publishing a folder using TOPS**

host computer – much like another disc. This is particularly useful for transferring information between Macintoshes when the integrity of file formats is retained. The mounted volume can be manipulated in exactly the same way as those on the host computer – opened for the selection of files, closed, copied – the only adverse effect being a slowing down in most disc-based operations. In fact, continued use of a file based on another disc will slow both machines down to unacceptable levels.

An alternative to mounting directories or folders is to simply copy the individual files required, a procedure most suited for transferring files between different machine types. Two ways are provided for achieving this and the choice between them will depend on the job in hand. The most direct method is to use the copy command which enables a PC text file to be converted to a Macintosh text file. However, this function will also work with some files saved directly from PC word processors as long as no formatting information has been incorporated. Thus, to transfer a published WordStar file from an Amstrad to a text only file for use on the Macintosh, TOPS is opened and the file from the Amstrad highlighted on the right hand side of the display (figure 8.2). Pressing the 'Copy...' button brings up a dialogue box when the relevant option can be selected – in this case text only – and the file is copied and appears on the Macintosh desktop. From then on TOPS can be closed down and the file treated as if it had been created in a Macintosh word processor.

149

For most applications copying is the most straightforward method of transferring WordStar files to the Macintosh but as an alternative TOPS also provides a set of translators for distinct file types. The only option for WordStar to Macintosh is to translate into MacWrite format – figure 8.3 – but in practice this has been found to have two disadvantages. The first is that it is more time-consuming than using the copy function because it has to be carried out as a separate operation before invoking TOPS. Secondly, while most word processors profess compatibility with MacWrite format they will not always accurately read the version produced by TOPS. For example, it has been found that MacAuthor II will accept with no problems the MacWrite data produced by the TOPS translator, but Microsoft Word 3.01 discovers unacceptable information in the files. For example, in spite of what it says in the TOPS manual, words with 'bold' formatting in WordStar produce errors when translated in this way and are completely lost from the text. However, translation could prove useful where a single document is to be edited by more than one person on different computers. The original could be translated from a PC format, edited on the Macintosh and translated back for final work to be carried out on the PC.

*Style sheet tags*

As a result of these problems discovered with the compatibility of Word, and because the library was limited in its Macintosh software at the time to MacWrite, Word and PageMaker, it was decided that if the current awareness data was to be entered via the Amstrad it would be manipulated on the Macintosh in PageMaker 3.0. The overriding reason for this was the automatic tagging of style sheet information available in PageMaker, a facility that has since become available in Ready, Set, Go!4.5 and which will no doubt eventually appear in most other Macintosh word processors and DTP programs.

*Tags*

The normal method of applying style sheet information to paragraphs is to place the cursor in the paragraph to be formatted and choose the appropriate style from a pull down menu. However, in a long document or one with a large number of paragraphs such as a current awareness bulletin, this manual operation would be virtually impossible due to the time required. The ideal solution would be a program that recognises style information from other word processors and carries this through unchanged. PageMaker 3.0 and Word 3.01 have such a symbiotic relationship. Alternatively the word processed text could have its formatting indicated – or tagged – so that the styles within the DTP program are applied on importing. This is the approach that was used when creating the contents of the current awareness bulletin in WordStar.

First of all the styles to be used in the bulletin were created in PageMaker. As the bulk of the bulletin was to consist of

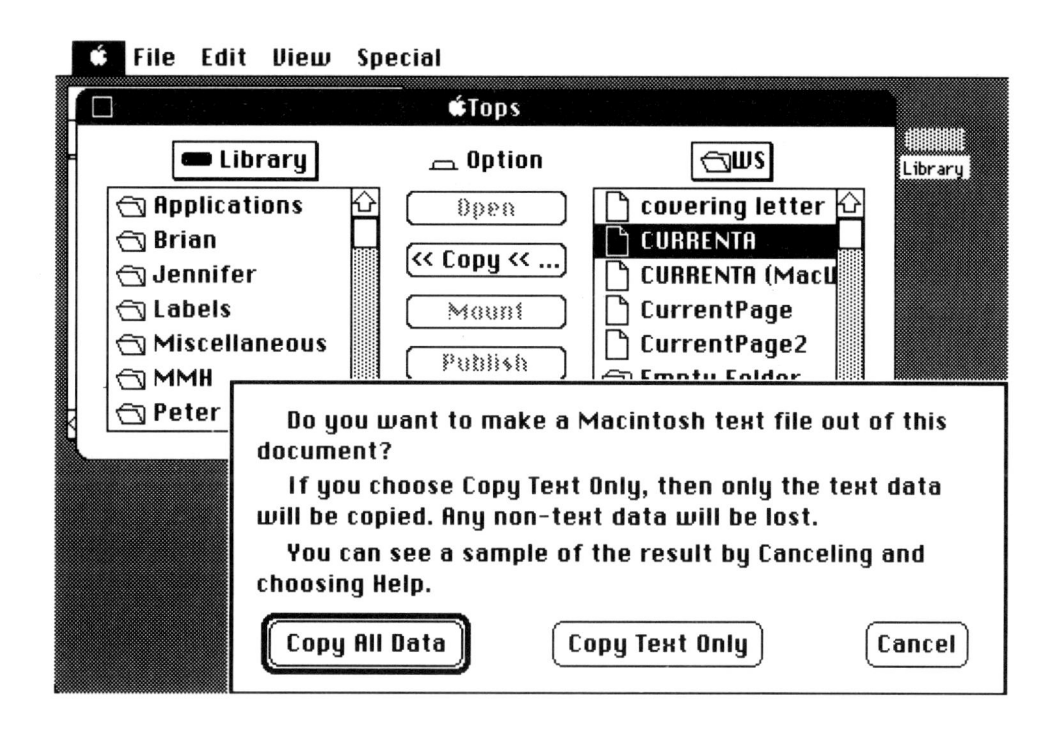

Figure 8.2 Copying a WordStar file to a Macintosh using TOPS

Figure 8.3 Translating WordStar to MacWrite using TOPS

151

bibliographic references separated by broad subject headings only three styles were required and these were named 'p1' for the paragraphs holding author and title, 'p2' for the journal details which were to appear in italics, and 'h1' for the subject headings (details on the creation of styles in PageMaker have already been described in chapter 3). These style names represent the tags that are placed in the WordStar text and they are simply typed in at the start of each paragraph where a change of formatting is required. By keeping the style names short the amount of additional keyboarding is reduced to a minimum, in this case four characters including the opening and closing brackets. No formatting of the WordStar version is necessary and in any case it would not survive the copying operation in TOPS.

As an example, a section heading and the first two references below it would be input into WordStar as shown in figure 8.4. On copying through TOPS and importing into PageMaker the styles are automatically invoked by the tags – as long as the 'Read tags' option in PageMaker's 'Place' dialogue box is checked (figure 7.6) – and the fully formatted text appears on the screen, without the tags. From here any further editing and cleaning up such as the correction of spelling mistakes is carried out in PageMaker. The WordStar file for each bulletin would be imported into a copy of the current awareness template which ensures a consistent format but permits changes to be made to individual bulletin titles, dates and issue numbers, and to the editorial pages. A sample page from one of the bulletins created in this way is included as figure 8.5.

```
<h1>Automation
<p1>Automated systems in Australian libraries: a 1987
perspective
HENTY, Margaret and STEELE, Colin
<p2>Electronic Library 6(2)April 1988, 100
<p1>Book 38: An integrated Library System for the IBM
System 38
STEINSBERG, Graham
<p2>VINE (69) December 1987,25
```

**Figure 8.4 Librarianship current awareness bulletin in WordStar**

# Librarianship
# Current awareness bulletin
# Summer 1988

---

**AUDIOVISUAL MATERIAL**

Use of audiovisual material in prisons
WRIGHT, Bernard C.
*Audiovisual Librarian 14 (2) May 1988, 68*


**AUTOMATION**


Automated systems in Australian libraries: a 1987 perspective
HENTY, Margaret and STEELE, Colin
*Electronic Library 6 (2) April 1988, 100*


Book 38 : An integrated Library System for the IBM System 38
STEINSBERG, Graham
*VINE (69) December 1987, 25*


The electronic library manager's guide to the truth behind installation and getting started
(Editorial)
*Electronic Library 6 (2) April 1988, 67*


The Libertas Acquisitions System
BRITTON, Alan
*VINE (69) December 1987, 4*


Library automation with workstations: using Apple Macintoshes in a special library
VALAUSKAS, Edward J.
*Information Technology and Libraries 7 (1) March 1988, 73*



**Figure 8.5 Librarianship current awareness bulletin in PageMaker**

*Drawbacks*  Using tags in this manner is an extremely easy way of formatting large volumes of text imported from a PC word processor. However, there are a number of drawbacks to the approach, the main one being the dislike of the typists – or in this case the library assistants who were typing – for inputting the tags. There appears to be no rational reason why this should be so, after all they are simply keyboard characters, but this feeling was expressed on more than one occasion.

Another drawback is that variant formatting within paragraphs is not available from the tagging function, but perhaps this is asking too much. Certainly it was the intention to differentiate the journal title from the rest of the reference by using italic style but this was rejected when it was realised that it could not be achieved automatically. As a result, italics were used for the complete line of the journal reference.

Finally, as pointed out elsewhere in the book, there is the lack of anything above the most rudimentary text manipulation tools in PageMaker. The very nature of current awareness bulletins means that the information is received in random order and requires subsequent sorting – in this case alphabetically by title under each alphabetically arranged subject heading. If this sorting operation cannot be automated it must be carried out manually, usually by annotating title pages or, alternatively, transferring the bibliographic details to cards, sorting, and then keyboarding, so transcribing each reference twice. There would appear to be at least two ways round this: the use of a database package or the use of a word processor which incorporates selective sorting i.e. sorting every third line so that complete references are kept together. The database approach has yet to be investigated and, as far as is known, a word processor with this level of sophisticated sorting is not yet available.

*Alternative approach*  Some months after using TOPS in the manner described above another Macintosh was purchased and this enabled other methods of producing the current awareness bulletins to be investigated. The emphasis was on discovering a method of randomly, or part randomly, entering references as they appeared in the scanned journals, and then sorting and formatting to produce the final high quality output. After a number of attempts the most successful utilised a combination of the outliner Acta and the word processor MacAuthor II.

As explained in chapter 6, Acta can be used to sort selected lines of text as long as these exist on the same level of an outline and any associated lines occur at a lower level. In practice, with three-line references made up of title, author, and journal details, this meant the title could be placed on the highest level with the other parts of the citation below it. As an example, the references from the current awareness bulletin of figure 8.5 have been entered into Acta in figure 8.6. In this case the section

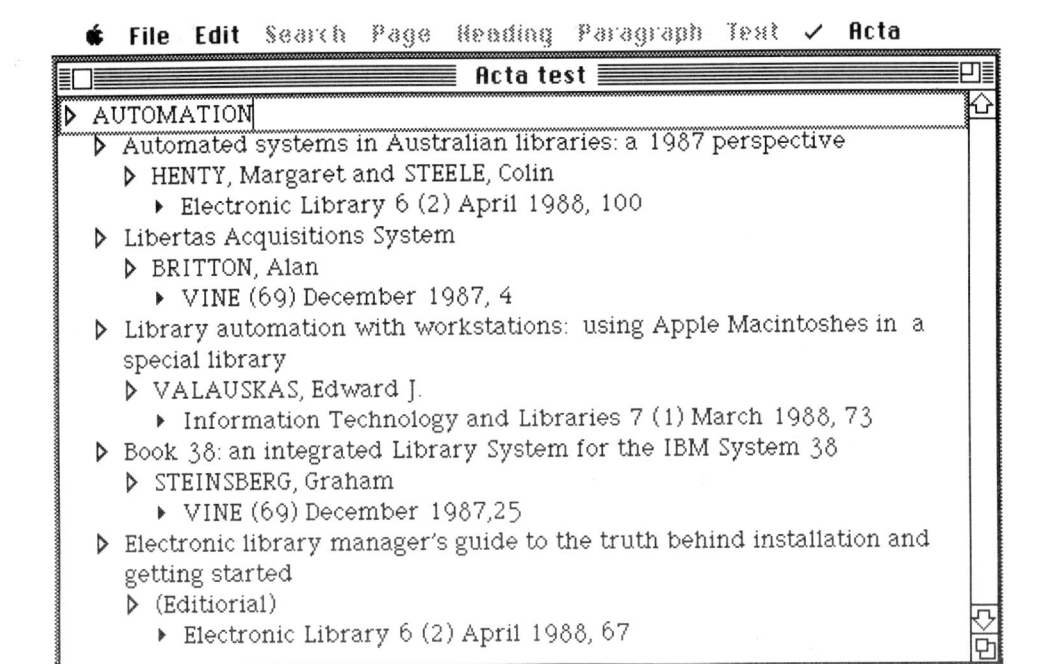

```
  File  Edit  Search  Page  Heading  Paragraph  Text  ✓  Acta
┌─────────────────────════ Acta test ════─────────────────────┐
▷ AUTOMATION
   ▷ Automated systems in Australian libraries: a 1987 perspective
      ▷ HENTY, Margaret and STEELE, Colin
         ▸ Electronic Library 6 (2) April 1988, 100
   ▷ Libertas Acquisitions System
      ▷ BRITTON, Alan
         ▸ VINE (69) December 1987, 4
   ▷ Library automation with workstations: using Apple Macintoshes in a
     special library
      ▷ VALAUSKAS, Edward J.
         ▸ Information Technology and Libraries 7 (1) March 1988, 73
   ▷ Book 38: an integrated Library System for the IBM System 38
      ▷ STEINSBERG, Graham
         ▸ VINE (69) December 1987,25
   ▷ Electronic library manager's guide to the truth behind installation and
     getting started
      ▷ (Editiorial)
         ▸ Electronic Library 6 (2) April 1988, 67
```

**Figure 8.6 Current awareness outline in Acta**

header – Automation – is positioned on the topmost level of the 'outline' with all the automation references below it. The title, author and the journal details have been positioned on subsequent levels so that separate styles can be applied to them when they are transferred to MacAuthor II. When the respective levels have been established the references can be entered in any order under their section header and a final sorting will arrange these alphabetically by the first word of the title. The typeface and style used is also irrelevant as these can be altered as required in MacAuthor II.

When all the references have been added, the Acta file is saved and subsequently opened as a MacAuthor II document. No special formatting is required as MacAuthor II recognises Acta files directly and all the text is imported using the first available paragraph style. In a similar way to the creation of a current awareness template in PageMaker, so a Stationery Pad is built up in MacAuthor II containing all the paragraphs and headings to be used in the bulletins, and the Acta outline is imported into this. As with the PageMaker template, the Stationery Pad can include the headings and text items that are common to all issues of the bulletin.

The second time saver arises from the compatibility between the two programs, for MacAuthor II recognises the different levels of an Acta document and allows different styles to be

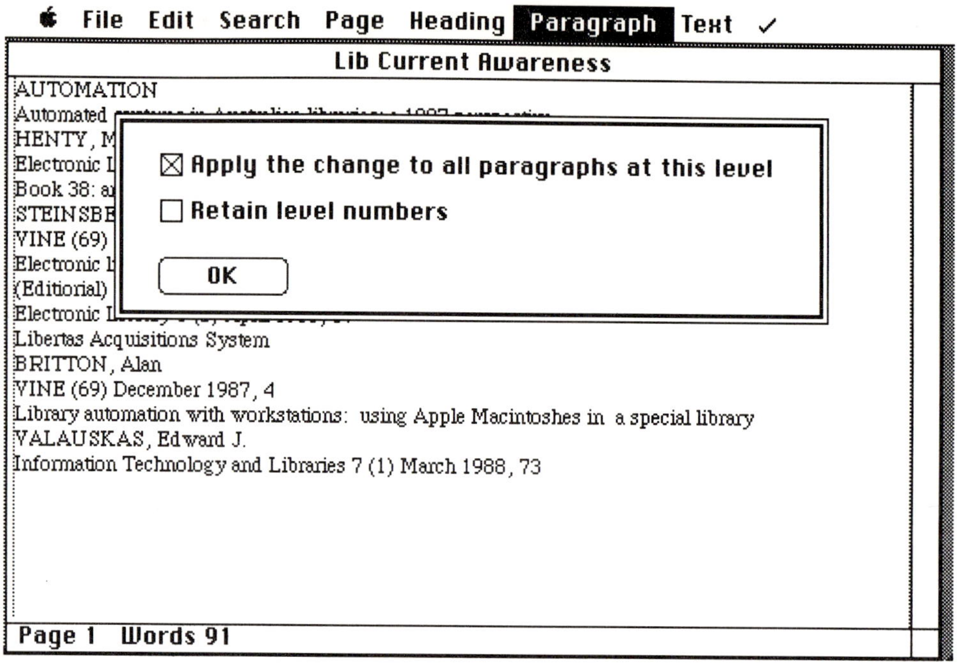

Figure 8.7 Application of MacAuthor II styles to Acta outline

automatically applied to them. As a result, any changes to the style of paragraphs or headings of the imported text need be carried out only at their first occurrence and these are then automatically reflected throughout the whole document. This is achieved from a dialogue box where the style change is applied to all paragraphs at the same level and with only two changes – one for the section headings and one for the line containing the journal details in italics – the document is rapidly reformatted ready for checking and subsequent printing. The formatting dialogue box superimposed on the imported text is shown in figure 8.7. It is also worth pointing out that MacAuthor is a more suitable base than PageMaker from which to carry out any global changes or spell checking, particularly when used in conjunction with Spelling Coach.

**Writing of books**

For librarians writing books any of the packages could prove suitable. The most appropriate will depend on the job in hand and the method of working of individual authors. Some will prefer to write in a word processor and then transfer the text (and any graphics) to a page make-up program such as PageMaker. Others will create the complete formatted document in one of the word processors with page make-up capabilities such as MacAuthor or FullWrite, and then use this for the direct production of output. Another alternative is to compose directly into a page make-up program with word processing facilities like Ready, Set, Go! or XPress.

The limitations of individual packages may rule them out for some jobs but most of these can be worked around even if this involves a fair degree of manual work. Most importantly the librarian author must be happy with the software he or she is using and for the time spent nursing a book into being this will prove more crucial than in any of the other applications. Furthermore, if the book is being written by the librarian at home it is probable that one package – his or her own – will be used exclusively, with all its limitations, on the grounds of cost. Access to a wide range of packages will just not be possible. In the following brief discussion some of the limitations of the packages for this application are pointed out – hopefully not too negative an approach – as well as an indication of the factors that need consideration when writing a book.

However, before starting on that discussion it is worth pointing out one of the main advantages of page make-up programs for book work. In common with other printed publications most parts of a book are viewed as a double page spread and DTP programs permit this display to be active. Thus, if the position of a diagram needs adjusting this can be achieved from any view of the page – in close-up or at any of the reduced views. In comparison, although many word processors have added a 'Preview pages' option, most of the details of the pages remain frozen and can only be adjusted once the full size single page display has been returned. The disadvantage, of course, is that a two page layout cannot easily be aligned on a word processor.

*PageMaker*

To say that PageMaker is unsuitable for books seems an inappropriate comment when so many authors claim to have used it. However, it is decidedly unsuitable for the entering or composing of text, not only because of its limited text editing tools mentioned in chapter 3 but because of the fundamentally different way in which PageMaker treats text when compared to a word processor. This is best demonstrated through the creation of a new page of a document. A word processor does not see this as a particularly difficult operation – the text simply flows and new pages are created and page breaks inserted where appropriate. On the other hand, PageMaker sees text as stories imported from outside its own environment and only through using the 'Autoflow' command can new pages be created automatically. If text is appended to the bottom of a page using the text tool it is added to the column on the displayed page and must then be transferred manually, with new pages being inserted as required.

PageMaker documents are limited to 128 pages but this need not be a disadvantage as sections of a book, or even individual chapters can be created separately and collated as a final job. The lack of a spelling checker and a search and replace facility will be a definite disadvantage if alterations are to be carried out to any extent once the text has been placed in PageMaker. And with a book re-writings, re-phrasings and additions can take place at any time until it is finally surrendered to the publisher. Only those writers who have the self discipline not to change anything once the text has left the word processor should consider using this package although even this is not a hard and fast rule for third party spelling checkers are available. One of these, Spelling Coach, has already been described in chapter 6 but as its operation relies on a search and replace function it is limited in its application to PageMaker documents to the notification of misspellings which then have to be found manually.

It may also be decided that some of the special features are needed for particular sections of a book and one solution is to compose these in PageMaker and integrate the output with that from the other source. For example the whole of Stubley's BLCMP book was written in MacAuthor but when it was decided to incorporate a scanned image from a page of the BLCMP newsletter a package was required that would import a compatible scanned format. PageMaker was the only package available – one of the formats available from the scanner software was TIFF – and so the whole of the chapter was imported as a text only file and integrated with the graphic. The only other work involved the insertion of corresponding page numbers and, more importantly, the adjustment of inter-word spacing to match that created by MacAuthor in the rest of the book.

*Ready, Set, Go!*   For the direct composition of text this program suffers from the same disadvantage as PageMaker: the concept of text as blocks to be moved about at will. However, with its ability to link text blocks from page to page Ready, Set, Go! does move, if only a little way, in the direction of word processors. The chaining process still requires the manual setting up of a definite number of pages and the creation of text blocks on each before any extended writing can begin. The main difficulty is the thought of being faced with such a large number of blank pages already created and waiting to be filled with text. It is enough to generate writer's block. For those who traditionally have difficulty getting started this is one program to leave on the shelf.

For writers still persevering with this method, once the laborious blank pages have been created the word processor of Ready, Set, Go! will be found to operate at a very respectable speed and the built-in features of spell checker and search and replace will be an added bonus for those familiar with PageMaker. The size of a

Ready, Set, Go! document is limited only by the amount of disc space and the available memory.

*XPress*

This is the only DTP program on the Macintosh that operates in a similar way to a word processor when used for direct text entry. Because of the intelligently designed interface described in chapter 3 the writer can set to work almost immediately and, most impressive of all, new pages are inserted automatically as they are required. Just like a word processor! The other features such as the search and replace function and the spell checker have also been mentioned in the earlier chapter.

In spite of these impressive features, the question must still be asked, 'Is XPress the most appropriate package for the process of actually writing a book?'. Certainly using the program on a Macintosh Plus, direct text entry lags somewhat behind the typist and is jerky in its display. This might be acceptable for short documents but most writers would find it irritating in the extreme for a project extending over months. Hewson's 'XPress Companion' was produced with the program but was written using Microsoft Word. In the book he states that (page 4) 'one job for which XPress is not the best program is the initial writing of a book like this. That task was performed using Microsoft Word 3.01 which, as a fast and fully-fledged word processor, is far better suited to it than a page makeup package like XPress. Equally, one would not want to use Word for display page makeup. I have taken the course which I judged to be most suitable one for the job in hand...'.

With this in mind, it is still felt by the author that word processors offer the best means of writing text books containing some diagrams and for submission to publishers as camera-ready copy. Both MacAuthor and FullWrite are by and large suitable for this purpose.

*MacAuthor*

MacAuthor is a competent performer when it comes to writing books, and most of its drawbacks for this purpose have already been pointed out in chapter 4. It is fair to say that the majority of these can be worked around manually or by utilising third party programs like Spelling Coach. In comparison with FullWrite, MacAuthor is short on features such as notes and dynamic links to illustrations but again these can be created manually, if rather laboriously. The main drawback is, as pointed out before, the sluggishness of the program on certain occasions. When ideas come flowing out, the important thing is to be able to get them down (on paper, disc?) as quickly as possible and anything that prevents this just gets in the way. As Levy correctly points out – ironically in a discussion of the slowness of FullWrite on a Macintosh Plus – 'I was unable to concentrate on the task at hand, the one most important task a writer performs when using a word processor: putting text in the damned file!' In spite of all this MacAuthor remains a sound and worthwhile program which has already been used for a number of published works, particularly Douglas Adams' 1987 novel and Stubley's book on BLCMP. All the present work has been written in MacAuthor.

*FullWrite*

FullWrite *feels* as if it was developed to write books. You sometimes have the sensation that if you press the wrong key inadvertently it will even write the damn thing for you: everything else is automated. One or two of the drawbacks have already been pointed out in chapter 4, but in terms of the writing of books there are other shortcomings of the program.

Automated ways are provided of compiling tables of contents and indexes but both suffer from the same drawback. To place headings above the completed sections a header has to be created and there is no way in the program of limiting a header to only the first page of a chapter. The only alternative is to have extra blank space at the top of all subsequent pages but compromises like this are hardly what DTP is all about. The only serious work-round is to compile both of these manually.

In a chapter dedicated to library applications the fact that FullWrite has attempted to compile bibliographies on behalf of authors cannot go unmentioned. Unfortunately, the results are mixed, to say the least, for users are constrained to including references in the manner that FullWrite has ordained.

As explained in chapter 4, a Base style is available to control the formatting of entries in the bibliography. In addition to typographical details, this permits references to be maintained in one of three formats: by name; by name and date (Harvard); and by reference number. Then, when a bibliography note is entered in the text, a window opens into which can be typed the full details of the reference – figure 8.8. On closing this window FullWrite automatically compiles the bibliography in alphabetic or numeric order and, in accordance with the Document Layout dialogue box, places it at the end of the chapter or the end of the document. This all acts very impressively but, perhaps inevitably, there are some real curiosities with this implementation.

The main oddity is that the bibliography note *always* appears in the text of the document surrounded by square brackets and, if that was not enough, for some reason the typeface is reduced in size. There is no way of referring to an author naturally – 'Cisler, in his paper on DTP' – and including this in the automatic bibliography. It always has to be – 'in a recent paper on DTP [Cisler]...'. It is also standard practice to refer to an author by surname only in the text but to include both surname and initials in the bibliography. FullWrite does not allow these two citations to be different and if the bibliography feature is to be used an awkward decision has to be made on the form of name to be used. What will happen, of course, is that no one

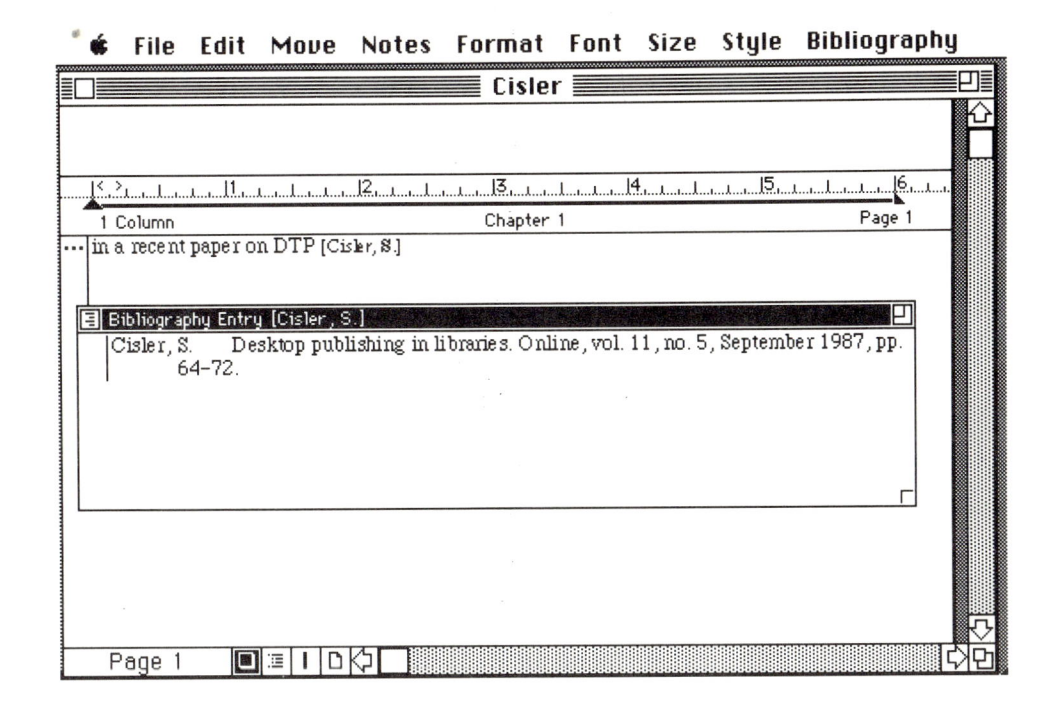

**Figure 8.8 Bibliography note in FullWrite**

who cares about their bibliography will use this aspect of the program until it is improved.

In spite of these criticisms, FullWrite can be used for the writing of books – witness the latest book by Douglas Adams (1988) – and more will no doubt flow out in the future.

**Library notices**

Library notices may come in any number of shapes and sizes but it is this very variety that should both encourage the use of DTP in their production and lead to considerable savings in time. Any program that enables a template to be created and used repeatedly and will print out to a laser printer will be sufficient for this application. The one drawback is the present limitation of most reasonably priced laser printers to produce anything larger than A4 output. But even with this restriction a wide range of notices is possible, from descriptions of the use of various library services to warnings about behaviour, bay-end and other shelving signs, and notifications of meetings. In some cases an A4 master can be blown up to A3 with little loss of quality using an enlarging photocopier.

If the notices are composed of text of varying size and style they can be quite easily created on a word processor and stored as a master file, even if a template facility is not built into the program. Then, as long as a well designed style editor is present, any changes can readily be incorporated. This idea has been used for creating regular notices of meetings such as that in figure 8.9. This was created in MacAuthor but any good word processor would do a similarly adequate job. With DTP there is no longer any excuse for libraries continuing to produce amateurish signs and notices with lettering that is out of alignment.

**Library newsletters**

In many respects the library newsletter is not dissimilar to the library guide: it contains information about the library for circulation to a wide variety of people. Of course, different types of newsletters can have different purposes, some being directed towards library staff and others aimed at users or a specific user group and in general they will be produced much more frequently than the library guide. Whatever, much of what has already been written about the preparation of the library guide in chapter 7 applies equally to newsletters.

The first major concern is that of layout for once this has been fixed there will be little incentive to change and probably not the time to do so. But having said that, the ideal design will not come easily. Templates are provided by all the major DTP software houses but these should be used with care, if at all. Why duplicate the designs created by someone else which could turn up some months later copied by another local amenity or business, when the software is there to let *you* be creative? Throughout this book the pitfalls of a lack of design knowledge have been repeatedly stressed but equally, progress will not be made unless some 'original' work is attempted. Mistakes will doubtless accompany any attempts but gradually the newsletter should metamorphose into the creature that you want it to be.

So, as in the library guide, decide on the page size, work out the optimal number of columns and the width of the margins and then create the features that will invariably appear from issue to issue and so should be part of the master pages. The almost universal use of tabloid size may lure some into following its attractions but this should only be attempted if the printing of it will not cause problems. If a standard LaserWriter is available it will probably be better to stick to A4, in spite of the limitations on layout that this may appear to impose. With A4 a two-column design will be easiest to handle, but in some cases three columns may provide the desired effect. The column size will have a bearing on the white space at the end of lines with unjustified text, on inter-word spacing and rivers with justified columns, and on the level of hyphenation used. In all cases the intent should be to provide a feeling of 'airiness' to encourage people to read the newsletter, rather than to cram all copy into a restricted space.

# LIBRARY ASSOCIATION UC&R

## WEST MIDLANDS BRANCH

*1001 THINGS TO DO WITH*

# ELECTRONIC MAIL

by

Roy Adams

**2.15pm Wednesday December 2nd 1987**

**Seminar Room, Level 2, William Kenrick Library**

**Birmingham Polytechnic**

Roy Adams is Deputy Librarian, Leicester Polytechnic

If you wish to attend please contact:

Margaret Vickery, The Lanchester Library, Coventry Lanchester Polytechnic, Much Park Street, Coventry CV1 2HF

Telephone 0203 24166 ext 448

**Figure 8.9 Notice of meeting created in MacAuthor**

Once the layout of the basic page has been settled other features such as column rules and boxed sections can be applied. And, depending on expected copy and whether some sections will remain the same from issue to issue (staff news; service developments etc.), the master pages can be created so that as much time as possible is saved during the make-up of individual issues. The ideal set of master pages will comprise *everything* from newsletter title and front page design features to section headings and rules on subsequent pages. The main drawback is the potentially variable size of copy, and the unpredictability of receipt of the actual articles from issue to issue, both of which may make this approach at best impractical and at worst unrealistic. An example of master pages set up for a newsletter in PageMaker 2.0 can be found in the article by Neville.

Though the newsletter is a good example of the use of DTP and could even be said to be the seminal application of the technology, it still does not relieve the newsletter editor of some of the traditional chores: badgering contributors for copy; maintaining deadlines; and, in some cases, personally keyboarding the copy. The obvious way to reduce the work of the editor is for each of the contributors to have access to a personal computer and a compatible word processor. Equally obviously this may be impossible due to the lack of resources of libraries. However, as the example of current awareness services shows, 'compatible' can be interpreted broadly to cover WordStar running on an Amstrad PC. In fact there could be an argument for always accepting copy as text only files so that the responsibility of final formatting is seen by everyone as the sole province of the editor.

Consideration, as always, should be given to the method of producing the individual copies for circulation. Production on the laser printer can work out unduly expensive and, if a reprographic unit is close at hand, and they can guarantee speedy turnaround, this may prove the most cost effective way of providing the circulation copies. And the archived copy will always be around (hard disc space permitting) to run off the odd one or two extras if demand of some issues outstrips conventional supply.

## CD-ROM and DTP

In the spring of 1988 SilverPlatter announced that they were going to support the Apple CD-ROM drive and that they would write retrieval software based on the Macintosh interface. Though early versions of the software were demonstrated at computer shows during 1988, the Macintosh-compatible SilverPlatter releases were not scheduled to appear until summer 1989. The transfer of data resulting from the search of a CD-ROM database to a PC word processor has been possible prior to this but the appearance of a Macintosh interface will greatly enhance the link between CD-ROM and DTP.

MacSpirs, the search software for all SilverPlatter databases, uses the WIMPS interface to the full and operates in a very Macintosh-like fashion. Accordingly, it is clear and easy to use and the first-time user can concentrate on defining keywords and creating a search strategy. The thorough help facilities are also aided by the interface and are available as a mixture of pull down menu commands and a context-sensitive feature represented by the question mark in the lower right hand corner of the screen. A window opened from the 'Help' menu and incorporating a section of the information relating to keyword truncation is shown in figure 8.10.

For a search of the ERIC database on the topic of 'hot housing of children' inputting of the keywords is followed by the opening of a search history window and the display of sets in much the same way as for an online search. From here, the full search results can be displayed approximately one record at a time depending on the record length – figure 8.11. It will be seen that the search term is highlighted. In this instance only eleven references were retrieved but the search can be expanded or constrained in the usual way using additional keywords or incorporating other boolean operators. The thoughtful design of

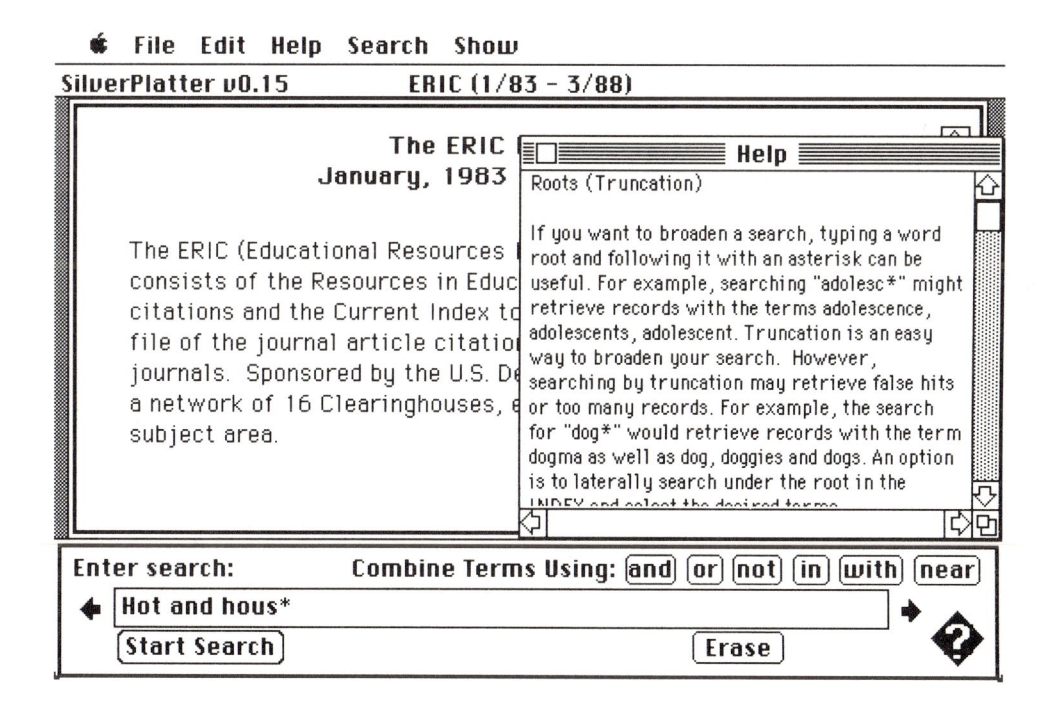

**Figure 8.10 Help screen from MacSpirs**

the CD-ROM interface is particularly shown by the way in which terms appearing anywhere in a citation can be selected with the mouse and automatically incorporated into a search. This is interaction (between the user and the system software) of a high order.

When the user is satisfied with the search results, the retrieved references themselves can be modified to adjust the data actually output. The most obvious way to do this is by controlling the content of the citations. The citations can be as full or as sparse as dictated by the requirement and are fully definable by the user for each search. By this method all the abstruse details that are not important to the end user and do not help in the location of papers can be removed, a feature that should aid in the interpretation of the search data. Figure 8.12 shows the 'Select fields' window opened ready for the choice of citation elements. The second adjustment possible is the manual selection – or highlighting – of the most relevant items. This would be impractical in a search with a large number of retrieved references but it does permit the final tailoring of the results. From here on the results can be printed or saved.

As MacSpirs follows the Macintosh interface to such a great extent, search results can be formatted to a certain degree on screen – by changing the font for example – and these features will be incorporated into any printout, together with the highlighting of search terms. However, printing directly from the search program does not allow the library to take full advantage of the opportunities offered by DTP.

The only way to do this is by saving the search results and transferring them to a page makeup program or word processor. At present, and for the foreseeable future, the only means of saving the citation is as a text only file which must, of course, be subsequently formatted. For any more than a small number of references this would probably prove impractical but even without extensive formatting the method could provide benefits for the library. By transferring the results to a DTP template they can be made to conform to a house style – at least in terms of overall layout and typeface – and a standard header or title page could be included to emphasise this. Furthermore, searches are rarely straightforward and the inclusion of explanatory notes could greatly help in the interpretation of results by the end user. This information could include details of the search strategies and databases used, and any problems or limitations encountered. Certainly for fee-paying customers this packaging of search results will provide the library with a much more high quality and professional face.

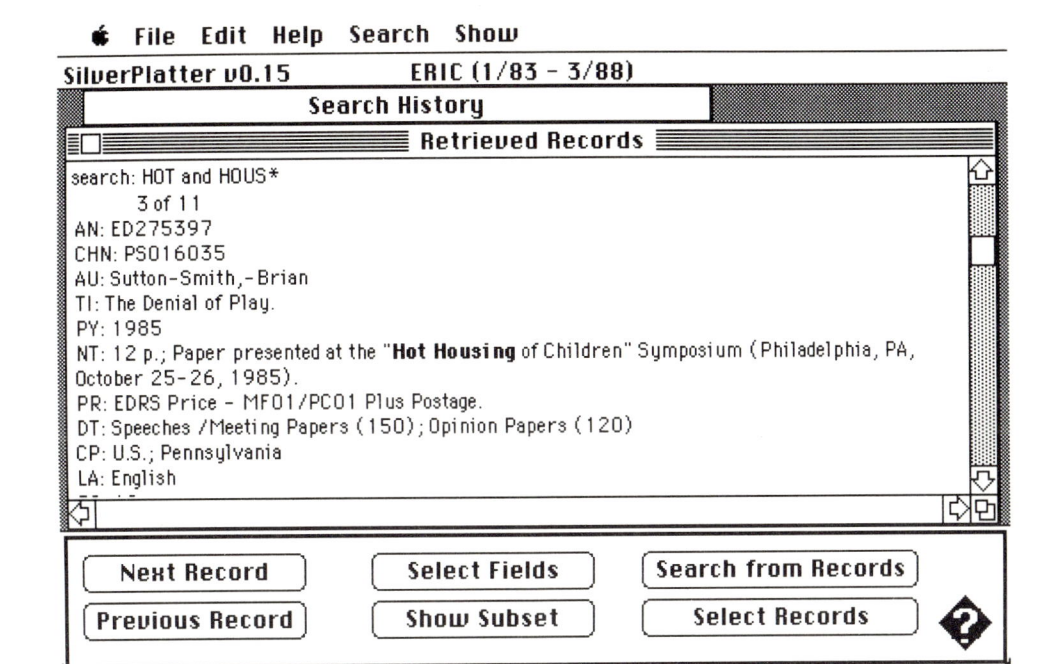

Figure 8.11 Display of record from ERIC search on CD-ROM

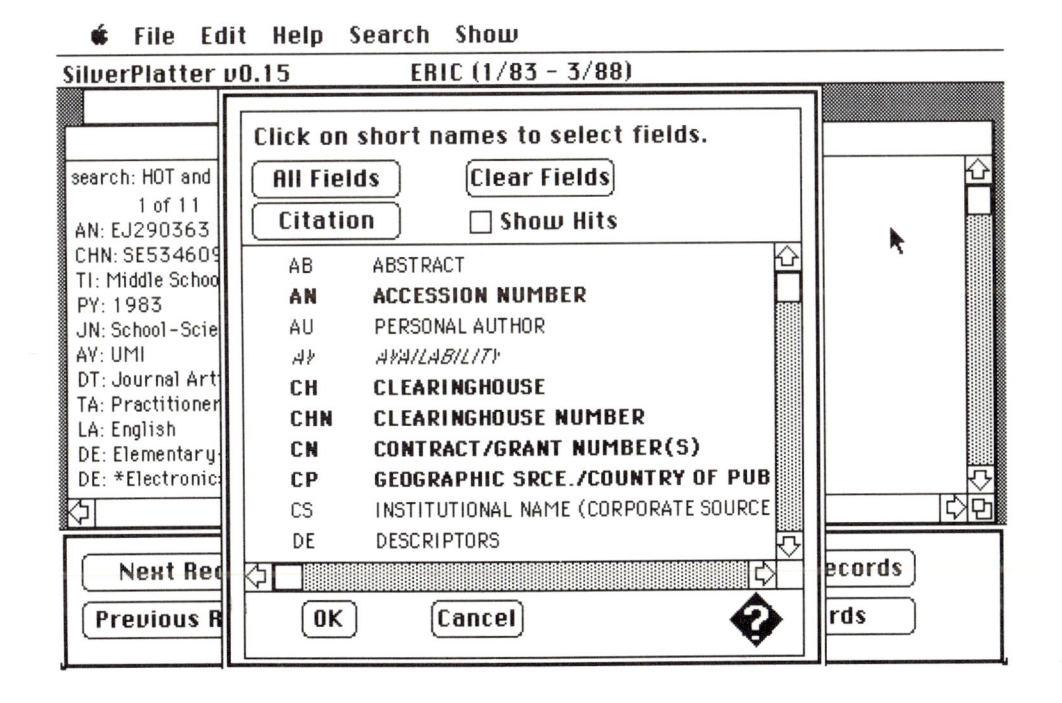

Figure 8.12 Control over citation elements in ERIC on CD-ROM

**The right software for the job**

Desktop publishers will no doubt argue into the night on the choice of the most suitable software package for a particular job. There will probably be a general consensus for some applications but for others plain personal choice will be the deciding factor and this may result in recommendations for some rogue packages away from the mainstream. An example of the type of discussion that might take place can be found in the reference 'Expert opinion' where three users were asked to select their choice of package for a range of applications. The same qualifications should be borne in mind when studying table 8.1, for while an attempt has been made to be objective, personal preferences have crept in from time to time.

The other factor that needs consideration, that is stressed particularly in the next chapter, is the way in which DTP is organised within the library and the level and dedication of the staff involved. In some organisations a package that is easy to get to grips with will be used in preference to one having greater power because of the training implications. This will be satisfactory as long as bottom-of-the-range packages are not purchased which could lead to a compromise in the standards required from the library. Furthermore, some of the publications of the library can take advantage of the high quality output from a laser printer but be written on one of the many other word processors available. Microsoft Word acts as one such general work horse in many institutions and it can be used for DTP in much the same way as MacAuthor and FullWrite, as described by Bayles.

The basic philosophy adopted in compiling table 8.1 is don't use a dedicated DTP package unless it is going to save you time or at least offer other advantages. Wherever you can get by with keyboarding the text only once, use a word processor that is appropriate to the task. Elsewhere, resort to DTP. For some jobs – a poster composed of a drawing and some text – remember that it may even be possible to use a graphics package on its own. There is also the other option, mentioned earlier, of producing a document in more than one package – part in a word processor and part in a DTP program – to get the best of both worlds.

**References**

Adams, D. *Dirk Gently's Holistic Detective Agency*. London, Heinemann, 1987. ISBN 0 434 00900 8.

Adams, D. *The long dark tea-time of the soul*. London, Heinemann, 1988. ISBN 0 434 00921 0.

| Library application | Examples | Software type and program | |
|---|---|---|---|
| Short documents primarily text based, with simple layout throughout | Reports | Word Processor (WP) | Word |
| As above, but importing tagged text from IBM PC word processors | Current awareness | DTP | PageMaker Ready, Set, Go! |
| Documents requiring special soritng capabilities | Current awareness | WP/ outliner | MacAuthor/ Acta |
| Long documents, primarily text based, with simple layout (1 or 2 columns) throughout | Text books | WP<br><br>DTP with direct input | MacAuthor FullWrite XPress |
| Primarily text based but shorter and with greater graphics content – no scanned images | Reports Library guides | WP<br><br>DTP | MacAuthor FullWrite PageMaker XPress |
| Generous mix of text and graphics with text flow around graphics – some scanned images | Illustrated books Brochures | DTP | PageMaker XPress |
| Primarily text based but composed of separate short stories in two or more columns | Newsletters | DTP | PageMaker XPress Ready, Set, Go! |
| Single sheets with text and graphics mix for maximum impact | Notices Bookmarks | WP DTP Graphics | MacAuthor XPress FreeHand |

**Table 8.1 Matching software to library applications**

Bayles, M. and Bayles, M. Publishing with Word. *Macworld*, July 1988, pp. 128–133.

Expert opinion. *MacUser*, no. 26, August 1988, pp. 65.

Hewson, D. *The Quark XPress companion*. London, Heyden & Son, 1988. ISBN 0 86344001 0.

Levy, S. Love and word processors. *Macworld*, vol. 5, no. 10, October 1988, pp. 53–68. (pagination includes several pages of advertisements)

Neville, P. Setting standards. *MacUser*, no. 20, February 1988, pp. 63–67.

Stubley, P. *BLCMP: a guide for librarians and systems managers*. Aldershot, Gower, 1988. ISBN 0 566 05512 0.

# 9    The management of DTP

**Why DTP is different from other IT**

In terms of the quantity of hardware and its physical requirements the introduction of DTP into the library is a little like the coming of the first microcomputers. If this encourages library managers to feel that they have seen it all before and that nothing special need be done then they should think again. The main difference is that DTP is, in general, friendly and flexible software ready to be used whereas many of the early micros gathered dust waiting for suitable library applications to be manifest. The chief outcome is that most staff, when they see what can be achieved with DTP, want a bite at the cherry. Demand from staff in all sectors of the library service will be there and will come even from those who have never been particularly attracted by other programs such as spreadsheets and first generation word processors. Suddenly (and quite rightly) they will want to produce high quality documents to impress their own groups of users.

Thus, to plan for the introduction of DTP the librarian would be advised to carefully and critically evaluate demand from all sections of the library from the start. This is far more easily said than done. In practice it is more likely that DTP will be introduced through the enthusiasm of a small group of staff or a sudden cash windfall, but the potential rising demand from all sides will always be there like an insatiable monster. The handling of this demand is one of the key library management issues regarding DTP, for it directly effects the staffing levels and the costings associated with the technology. And following on from these issues are concerns over staff training and data security.

The one question not dealt with in this section is the one that many librarians will want an answer to: 'Which system should I purchase?'. But this is very much a personal decision depending on individual preferences and local circumstances like the equipment purchasing policy of the parent institution. In the run-up to decision making librarians should do what they have been doing for years when significant new technology purchases are imminent: visit other libraries who have been through the same process. What they might find, of course, is that others have made decisions on the same (irrational?) basis as their own; always encouraging and apt to consolidate that warm feeling on the train journey home. It is hoped that this book provides enough information on the different approaches to DTP software to enable at least informed decisions to be made.

**Staffing considerations**

The main questions facing the manager are similar to those relating to most library services: what qualifications are required and how will the staff be utilised; how much time will it take and how many staff are required; and should the function be centralised or de-centralised. Most, if not all, of these factors will be determined by local circumstances but a few points are presented here for consideration.

*Staff utilisation*

It should not be assumed, because DTP has much in common with word processing, that it can be handled entirely by non-professional staff. Professional librarians have a particular role to play and this is described below but, on the other hand, unless a significant input from library assistants or administrative staff is built into the system from an early stage, professionals will find themselves involved in large amounts of keyboarding as demand increases. This is a procedure not to be discouraged outright but it is a practice that will not necessarily result in the most efficient use of staff resources, particularly if the professionals are two-finger typists. One of the difficulties in defining respective areas of work is that the technology, particularly on the Macintosh, is easy to use and it is entirely reasonable for assistants to wish to be involved in the creative side. In practice a division giving responsibility to professionals for the design of templates for prestige publications such as library guides and current awareness services, and the freedom to senior assistants to modify these in some instances may work. What has to be emphasised at all times is the importance of the publications to the good name and image of the library.

It has been stressed at various places throughout the book that librarians do not necessarily make good designers. Consequently, if a library is contemplating a move into DTP in a big way it may even consider the appointment of a graphics artist or designer. This is not meant as an outlandish suggestion – a number of libraries already have this or a related post – and ultimately it may be the only way for some institutions to maximise their investment in DTP. This is another indication of the way in which the boundaries of traditional library work are breaking down with new technology to incorporate posts such as systems librarians, programmers and technicians.

Even with a graphic designer to hand there will still be a need for the involvement of a number of professional library staff, including some input at a relatively high level. In a large or potentially growing DTP operation there will be a need to create a house style if one does not exist already and the maintenance of this in the face of significant activity and individualism from all library departments will require a professional with, at various times, a great deal of energy, stubbornness, firmness and approachability. Where necessary, contacts must be made with the appropriate departments outside the library to ensure that institutional styles are also being upheld. It is also important, as pointed out by Pyle and Harrington, to determine a strategy for library publications as a coordinated whole and it would be sensible for the professional in charge of DTP to assume this responsibility.

In addition to overseeing the design of all library publications the senior professional would be expected to take responsibility for the current effective operation and future development of the service. Amongst other things this would involve close liaison with local dealers to ensure that a good working relationship was built up and to encourage good service and sound advice. Furthermore, as DTP software is changing so rapidly, with new revisions appearing at least once a year, it will be the job of the person responsible to ensure that the library has registered its purchases and that these updates are obtained. To some extent the person should also endeavour to keep abreast of developments in software generally so that if a new 'super-product' comes on to the market then sound reasons can be presented for its purchase even though the money will not be available.

*Staff time*

In the current staffing difficulties of many libraries it would be totally unrealistic to assume that the staffing requirements described above could be committed full time to DTP. This may be the case in a few organisations but the majority of libraries will treat DTP as they do many other services and administer it from a section with wider responsibilities. The number of staff is also impossible to estimate without some idea of both the quantity and the level of work involved: in terms of design and layout it is not easy to equate one piece of work with another and different publications will be given different emphases in different organisations. Libraries are more likely to specify the approximate amount of time that should be given to publicity and related operations which have a direct link to DTP. The conclusion must be that to provide an adequate DTP service to the library and its users, expertise should ideally be found in four key areas: software and hardware awareness; quality control for house style; graphic design; and keyboarding for speedy text input. This involves a full range of staff from senior through middle management to library assistants.

*Centralised or not?*

The points raised in the previous paragraph would appear to offer a strong, if not insurmountable argument for de-centralising DTP within most libraries. However, de-centralisation in this context does not *necessarily* mean providing lots of DTP stations around the different library departments for staff use but rather the incorporation of the responsibility for DTP into one section with free access to the hardware granted to staff from other sections. The alternative is the creation of a separate publicity or publications unit within the library to handle all DTP jobs.

Working from the premise that one of the key reasons for moving into DTP is to improve the quality of all printed publications and therefore the public face of the library, the natural location for a DTP setup would appear to be in a publicity section. This unit could concentrate on the provision of high grade publications and would quickly build up expertise in design, layout and any keyboarding shortcuts and work towards optimum use of the equipment and the software: the staff would be dedicated in both senses of the word. The main disadvantage *operationally* is that expectations among other library staff would be raised bringing in more work than a unit of limited size could easily handle and so leading to backlogs. The main problem in overall staffing terms would be the difficulty in the justification for such a unit in the face of pressures from elsewhere in the service and in practice it is unlikely that many libraries will proceed with this alternative in the near future. However, with the increasing emphasis on fee income so the importance of high quality publicity will increase and the next few years could see more and more libraries setting up publicity units. These units will have wider responsibilities than just DTP – possibly including a reprographic function – but DTP, if handled correctly, would form an integral and essential part of the operation.

In the immediate future it seems probable that most libraries will allocate the responsibility for DTP to an existing section like Reader Services or Technical Services. Such an arrangement could be administered as either a centralised or de-centralised system. The centralised version would operate in much the same way as that described for the publicity unit with a group of staff within the wider section having responsibility for all the DTP requirements of the library.

In the de-centralised set-up the equipment and software would be made available to library staff from all sections so that it would be the responsibility of section heads to determine their priorities for DTP in accordance with the amount of free time available on the hardware. This type of arrangement almost presupposes the use of a booking system to give all sections equal opportunity of access to the equipment. An alternative arrangement which would provide a more complete de-centralisation would involve the purchase of a workstation for each section networked to a central laser printer.

The adoption of either of these possibilities could be said to strengthen the case for a senior coordinator for DTP, for the reasons already mentioned: the maintenance of a house style for publications; coordination of the publications programme; internal and external liaison; and the look towards future trends.

The main disadvantage with either of the de-centralised arrangements is that DTP expertise does not necessarily reside in a limited number of staff although this will depend on the organisational policy of section heads and in any case may be said to be a positive step. What is likely to happen is that the high degree of expertise possible in a DTP-specific unit will not be met by staff with a range of duties and responsibilities. Similarly, a greater investment in training will be required with the de-centralised system. Another disadvantage is the potential log-jam that could materialise at the networked laser printer in periods of high activity. Lasers are not fast printers at the best of times and a single networked unit in a library with high demand could be an excellent argument for a number of unscheduled coffee breaks. Finally, in a de-centralised arrangement the question should perhaps be asked: what work can be carried out on the DTP system? There will be a tendency to transfer all typing to the new set-up to take advantage of the improved quality and staff must be clear from an early stage whether general and administrative work can be carried out on the equipment.

The type of set-up chosen will also have a bearing on the actual software purchased for as a study of section 2 will show not all packages are equally easy to use. Of the many packages that can tackle library DTP work only a few can be recommended for the de-centralised approach because of the large number of non-specialised staff involved. On the other hand the centralised DTP or publicity section would no doubt welcome the opportunity – and would also find the time – to get to grips with the more complex packages.

## Costings

These break down into hardware, maintenance and consumables.

*Hardware*

There is little point in including hardware prices in a book of this nature for they would be out of date before the publication date. More importantly the figures quoted from dealer to dealer can vary by such a large amount that official list prices can sometimes seem pointless in comparison. Never has the need for the traditional three quotations been so great as when purchasing computer and DTP equipment and software. At the time of writing, and as ball park figures only, a basic Macintosh-based DTP system with microcomputer, integral hard disc, laser printer and some software will cost upwards of £7,500 but discounts can significantly reduce this. Furthermore, if additional equipment such as a scanner, big screen or a high volume laser printer is to be purchased the price can rise dramatically.

*Maintenance*

The cheapest quotation can present problems if all that is eventually delivered is a fascinating range of cardboard boxes containing the ordered goods. One of the main things to remember is that, in spite of the much vaunted ease of use a complex system is being purchased and when problems arise software and hardware support will be required. Librarians are keenly aware of the need for support for their major automation systems because a failure here can have far-reaching effects on the service, but the necessary support for smaller computer systems is sometimes forgotten. In general terms – but this is not always the case – the cheaper the quotation the poorer the after sales service.

Most dealers will provide onsite maintenance for a commercial annual rate of around 8–10% of the capital outlay on hardware and as with hardware costs more competitive rates may be obtained in some situations. Even if maintenance is not taken up at the time of purchase it is worth making preliminary enquiries. The obvious advantage of a maintenance contract is the high cost of replacement parts in the years when the warranty has run out: a main board for an Apple LaserWriter can cost upwards of £1,000 and to this must be added a call-out charge of around £250 per day. It should be stressed that the majority of the equipment is reliable and presents little maintenance problems but the author *has* had the experience of the main printer board failing just within the warranty period. The risk may be worth taking but it could result in a costly bill for the library and an embarrassing period of downtime. Based on these figures and on an annual throughput of 15,000 copies from a £3,500 laser printer, the maintenance cost works out at around 2.0 pence per page.

Finally, it should be remembered that maintenance has a close relationship with the anticipated life span of the hardware and some companies will increase maintenance charges as the equipment ages.

*Consumables*

In the flurry of activity and enthusiasm to introduce DTP the running costs can sometimes be forgotten. While these will not keep librarians awake at nights in comparison to other print costs, they should not be ignored. The main costs involve toner cartridges for the laser printer, and paper.

**Toner cartridges** fall into a category similar to hardware discussed above: there is an official list price and then there is the price you pay. New cartridges can cost between £60 and £100 depending on source but some companies will make arrangements to refill exhausted units and this can work out significantly cheaper: experience will tell if there is any noticeable loss in print quality. It was generally accepted that on the original Apple LaserWriter and LaserWriter Plus a cartridge would last for approximately 2500 copies depending on the type of work: a lot of graphics with shaded backgrounds and shapes would naturally use toner more quickly than continuous typed sheets. From these figures the cost works out at 2.4–4.0 pence per page. With the new LaserWriter series, 3000–5000 copies per cartridge are quoted, giving a figure around 1.5–2.5 pence per page.

**Paper** is an equally important area both in terms of cost and quality. While laser printers can handle most thicknesses up to thin card and transparencies the output will vary with paper quality and it is obviously important that the sharpest image is obtained for masters. For day-to-day printing operations photocopying paper costing say £3.50 for 500 sheets (retail), or anything as low as £1.63 per 500 sheets for bulk purchase, is suitable. For high quality work a heavier (100gm) paper is preferable costing between £12.50 and £25.00 for 500 sheets. 'Everyday' copying can therefore work out at a paper cost of 0.3–0.7 pence per page and high quality copying anything between 2.5 and 5.0 pence per page.

In estimating the throughput of laser printers it is worth remembering that *all* copies of correspondence, including file and private copies, will be produced from this source, and that the previous use of cheaper copy paper for these will probably cease. This will happen because it will be too time consuming to make frequent paper changes between copies and may result in a marginally greater paper bill than in previous systems using typewriters. Alternatively, the cheaper copy paper could be used for all general printing on the laser or some libraries may even have large quantities of scrap A4 which could be used for this purpose.

**Other consumables** include a supply of floppy discs for back-up purposes (see the section 'good computer practice' below), a lockable box in which to keep these, and cleaning materials for screens and floppy disc drives. Dust covers and a 'mouse mat' are further useful – some would say essential – purchases for maintaining the cleanliness of the equipment.

| Component | Low | High |
|---|---|---|
| Toner | 1.5 | 4.0 |
| Paper | 0.3 | 5.0 |
| Total | 1.8 | 9.0 |
| Maintenance | 1.9 | 2.3 |
| Total incl maintenance | 3.7 | 11.3 |

**Table 9.1 Cost per page of output from a laser printer**

*In summary*

The cost of producing copy from an Apple laser printer, covering major consumables and maintenance but excluding hardware depreciation, is presented in table 9.1. The two ends of the spectrum have been chosen deliberately, for they indicate the considerable savings that can be made by judicious purchasing and choice of materials and supplier. However, if true top quality output is required for some jobs, then the savings will not be as great as indicated. This particularly applies to the choice of paper.

For the production of high quality masters there is really no low cost alternative to DTP via a laser printer. The preparation of multiple copies is a different matter and here DTP is in direct competition with photocopying and offset lithography. The cost of these is equally difficult to pin down for it depends on many local factors but particularly on the volume of throughput. Thus, photocopying costs can be anything from 1.25 to 4.5 pence per page and offset lithography varies from <0.5 to 1.5 pence per page. Not that these operations are without their problems. The quality of photocopiers in libraries is notoriously poor and institutional reprographic units have been known to give rise to delays through backlogs. In both cases the impact that is possible with DTP could be dissipated through loss of quality or delays in production.

Unfortunately it is not easy for laser printers to match the throughput of the high volume devices. The life of the Canon engine of the original Apple LaserWriter was quoted as 100,000 copies, or five years at 20,000 copies per year. Though the duty cycle of the LaserWriter II range was increased to 300,000 copies with a new engine, this machine could still have difficulty standing up to the rigours placed on it by a large library publicity department wishing to produce all its copies internally. A printer with a significantly increased engine life – up to 80,000 copies per month – would really be required for these purposes and with this in mind at least one library has chosen a Dataproducts LZR-2665 laser printer. Any library interested in following a similar path must be prepared to pay several times the capital cost of the Apple unit for the advantages of high throughput. The further benefit is that copy cost can be reduced to less than 2.0 pence per page including maintenance, toner and paper.

## Training

In the early days DTP was very much the province of enthusiasts and even in libraries enthusiasts have been responsible for introducing the technology. These are people who are self-starters – at least as far as this technology is concerned – and for who no training is generally required. For the rest of the library staff matters will not be quite so easy and a well-considered training program will be essential to their coming to grips with the technology. However, given the freedom that DTP engenders and the high level of usage anticipated, training must include more than just getting to grips with the available software if the library is to reap the full benefits.

*Computer practice*

When word processing was introduced to most libraries the computers were 8- or 16-bit units and the software and data files were invariably stored on floppy disc. Consequently each member of staff looked after their own data and was able to literally take it away with them and store it in their office or work area. With the onset of DTP operations have become more complex – switching between draw and word processing programs and using various ancillaries – so that the use of a hard disc is virtually essential. At the same time hard disc prices have dropped dramatically so that more computers are being sold with integral hard discs and programs themselves have become larger, taking up more disc space. PageMaker 3.0, for example, occupies more space than is available on a single floppy disc and requires a hard disc for its operation.

The result of the move to hard disc systems is that data from a wide variety of users will be stored in a single place making it essential that the storage and retrieval of files is treated systematically. Sloppy computer practices that may have existed in the past cannot be allowed to persist on a sectional or library-wide machine and all initial training should include an explanation of the importance of hard disc management and the special shut down procedures. The general principles of operation of a WIMPS interface will also be necessary for those staff who have previously been restricted to inputting command line strings. Both of these are especially important on a machine like the Macintosh which is extremely easy to use and accordingly extremely easy to disrupt by inexperienced operators. Some of these aspects are covered in more detail at the end of this chapter.

*Software*

Training in particular software packages must be handled carefully for two main reasons. Firstly, in spite of the ease of use of much DTP and word processing software it must always be remembered that these are, by and large, extremely powerful packages with a wide range of features. Time potentially saved through their use can be wiped out in the wrong or untrained hands. It would be unrealistic to expect all DTP operators in the library to be well versed in all features at their full level of detail and training must accordingly be tailored to specific groups. The important thing is obviously that all staff have a sound knowledge of the basics of DTP. However, once the system is up and running this approach will probably require modification for the staff with an aptitude for the technology will become apparent and higher-level training can be arranged as appropriate. The extent to which this route is acceptable to libraries or to which the alternative egalitarian approach of training all staff is to be pursued will depend on local circumstances.

The second reason for the need for careful training is the very multiplicity of packages. A modest DTP library setup will include DTP software, a word processor, and a graphics package. For good measure a spreadsheet and database may also be purchased and though not strictly DTP, they may be utilised by the same staff. Though these will all be seen by experienced users as distinct packages, each with their own application, there are areas of overlap and for the newcomer it will not always be clear which to use to complete a particular task. Built into the training there must be an awareness of the advantages and limitations of individual packages for carrying out library jobs. And also of the novel and unusual applications to which they may be put.

At all costs, training must ensure that new operators do not become afflicted by a serious addiction to the software brought on by all this new formatting power and encouraged by the easy to use interface. If this happens it is easy to spot for it manifests itself by a (hopefully temporary) loss of productivity as objects are moved into numerous new positions on screen. In some respects DTP really is the new executive toy.

*The trainers*

A decision must be made at an early stage, preferably at the time of purchase, on who will carry out the training. In general terms library staff have been used to providing internal training run by their own enthusiasts and, depending on who provided the incentive for introducing DTP, this might still be possible. By and large libraries do not buy blind and they have very specific reasons for purchasing particular packages. Accordingly, in many cases they will have the expertise to train their own. This is also the most acceptable approach for another reason: that examples specific to librarianship can be developed to increase the pertinence of the technology to any sceptical staff.

Alternatively, training may be available from elsewhere within the institution. In some cases the best solution might be to use the local dealer for computer practice training, and possibly for training on the specific software packages as well. However, before agreeing to any such undertaking the relevance to library applications should be checked so that staff interest is maintained. There is nothing worse than forced attendance at a training session where the trainer is unappreciative (or ill informed) about the special requirements of the audience. Training is a sensitive issue among computer dealers, especially in the education and local authority market, for there is an acknowledgement of the fact that these purchasers are not usually prepared to pay for 'ancillary' services: they either expect them to be provided free of charge or at cost. This comment is not expected to change this status quo, which is obviously on the side of the education sector.

**Security aspects**

Any de-centralised computer system should give rise to questions about data security. This should apply whether the set-up comprises a number of networked machines or a single microcomputer with access granted to staff from different sections. Security should furthermore be maintained to conform to the provisions of the Data Protection Act but also for reasons of basic confidentiality. In a standard library DTP set-up producing documents primarily for public consumption the need for security may in the first instance be considered slight. However, if the machine/s are used for a range of purposes information of a sensitive nature will be available to any other users if precautionary steps are not taken. The most obvious preventative measure is to limit confidential information to a single machine but this may be easier said than done. In any case, really confidential information such as staff details and staff references should never be left on an easily accessible hard disc but always transferred to floppy disc and kept in a secure place immediately on completion of work on the machine.

Maintenance of confidentiality is not the only reason for taking steps to secure data on DTP systems. As stressed in the section on training, it is important that all staff are familiar with the basic operation of the computer so that the integrity of all files held on the hard disc is maintained. Even with the most strenuous training programs the possibility remains that inexperienced staff could inadvertently interfere with important, but not necessarily confidential, files and in extreme instances these could be accidentally destroyed. A security arrangement would thus help to prevent misuse of the system as a whole.

Two methods of software protection are available: password control and encryption. The type of password control used can depend on whether a single computer or a networked system is to be protected. With a single machine some of the password programs require insertion of a special user disc and the keying in of an authorised name and password before access is permitted to the hard disc. From then on all information on the hard disc is available to anyone who cares to look. On a network such as TOPS individual folders have first to be published before they can be accessed by others but these can be further protected by user-defined passwords. TOPS users also have the option of providing read-only access to published files. In this way individuals have control over which of their files are available for general consumption over the network: the measures still do not prevent access to the files directly from the host machine.

Data encryption offers an advantage over password protection in that it permits the protection of individual files. The disadvantages are that encryption and decryption are relatively slow processes and encryption can expand the size of files. Unfortunately, these software products can prove difficult to locate and purchase and some of them apparently utilise algorithms which cannot be shipped outside of the United States. One product that has proved useful and is cheap, but that has also proved difficult to locate, is N'cryptor. Files can be selected singly or as a group, saved under a new filename and then encrypted. At encryption a case sensitive password must be specified which has to be input to decrypt the file to make it available once again. Encrypted files cannot be opened with the package that created them but must first be decrypted. While this is time consuming it does provide a good level of security. Further information on other security products can be found in the brief review article by Stevens.

In the long run, the best form of security for confidential data lies in not leaving it freely available on hard discs for anyone to access. It is the duty of the librarian or at least the senior manager in charge of DTP to define the confidentiality of documents so that secretarial staff are clear of their position and can take the necessary steps. Another alternative, if more than a single microcomputer is involved, is to define some machines as confidential and others for general use, and to strictly enforce this policy. At the same time it should be remembered that this discussion has concentrated on the security of data *from other library staff* and one of the surest ways of ensuring good practice is through careful and considered training.

Many of the points apply equally, if not more so, to security of data – even non-confidential information – from external prying eyes and individual libraries must decide if measures such as bolting equipment to furniture or disabling computers overnight are relevant to their situation.

Another factor to be aware of is the computer virus. While the single Macintosh or network of Macintoshes is operated as a closed system with master copies of program discs there is no risk. However, when files are copied from external computers with an unknown pedigree a virus could be transferred to the library machine from a contaminated application. This is most likely to happen if software is 'pirated' from one machine to another. One method of prevention is through the installation of anti-viral software and a guide to these and a good background to anyone interested in viruses on the Macintosh is provided by Stefanec.

## Good computer practice

*Hard discs*

The fact that hard discs are becoming more reliable and rarely seem to crash should not deter anyone from making regular back-ups of data. For *any* data that is considered valuable – and this must include virtually all work carried out at the keyboard – duplicate copies must be taken so that a restore can be carried out in the event of a hard disc fault. A number of hard disc back-up programs are available but an equally effective method is to ensure that copies of all files are made to floppy disc at the end of each computing session. Added to this, consideration must also be given to the storage of both the master discs of original programs and the back-up copies in safe places.

If a hard disc does crash before a back up has been made programs are available which may be able to recover some, most, or all of the data. Two of these, Symantec Utilities for Macintosh (SUM) and 1$^{st}$ Aid Kit, have been described by Webster, and Shapiro has further extolled the virtues of 1$^{st}$ Aid Kit. In general, hard discs are reliable but this doesn't prevent problems occurring, or even the inadvertent deletion of files when the brain goes on the blink. At times like these, when the accusations start to fly and the tears begin to flow, you will wish you had one of these utilities on your shelf.

The size of the hard disc is now becoming an important consideration for with the present size of software and the files created from them 20 megabytes can no longer be considered large. It is a natural way of working with DTP that a number of different layouts will be attempted before the final one is agreed, and most of the alternative versions will be saved to ensure that useful work is not destroyed. Consequently, the hard disc can easily become filled with rubbish. With a 20 megabyte disc – in fact with any size of hard disc – periodic checks should be made to ensure that all unwanted files are removed so that they are not taking up valuable space. If work involves scanned images cleanups will be needed much more frequently and 40 megabytes may be considered a minimum for this type of activity.

*File organisation*

When work for a wide range of different projects or sections is being carried out on one machine it becomes important that the files are maintained in an order that is logical to all potential users of the information. This could be said to argue against the points made for data security in the earlier section but is essential when attempting to locate files in the absence of their creator. It applies to a certain extent to floppy disc systems but the greatest need, because of the higher potential for disorganisation, is on hard discs.

The Macintosh utilises a method of file organisation known as HFS – the hierarchical file system. For librarians this is an ideal method with which to come to terms for its working closely resembles hierarchical classification schemes. Instead of a numbering system, folders are created with names assigned by the user and a hierarchical set of embedded folders can be built up for any project. In a set-up used by staff from different library sections it would be possible for each section to be assigned a specific number of folders at the top of the hierarchy onto which they would then have to graft their own arrangement of sub-folders. As stressed earlier it is important that the senior professional maintains a watchful eye on this to ensure that the hard disc does not become disorganised and unmanageable. However, within reason, it is possible to give all users responsibility for their own set of folders so that their organisation can represent, as closely as possible, the needs of the sections. In spite of this, in some cases it may be considered appropriate to create folder names according to an agreed master list so that the potential for misplacing files is minimised.

*File management*

When long documents in particular are being produced decisions must be taken on how these are stored: as a single file or split into convenient chunks or chapters. Saving the document as a set of separate files gives two main benefits, the chief of these being that if a file becomes damaged only a section of the complete work is lost. This would be frustrating enough but the loss would be as nothing compared to the virtual destruction of a complete document. The second benefit is that, even with more powerful microcomputers, shorter documents take less time to edit and move around than longer ones. Using the hierarchical file system mentioned above the organisation of a potentially large number of files into a small number of associated folders is a straightforward operation. The main disadvantage with the separate chapter approach is that, at present, few programs maintain active links between the various sections and so a considerable amount of editing work may be necessary to lick the final document into shape.

## Good operational practice

*Environment*  All the arguments that have been marshalled before relating to the physical requirements of microcomputers in libraries (Heathcote and Stubley) can be repeated for the implementation of DTP. It is especially important that adequate work area is provided around the DTP equipment so that working papers can be conveniently positioned; that operator chairs are provided to enable users to make their own adjustments to posture; and that consideration is given to the positioning of equipment in relation to windows and lighting.

## References

Heathcote, D. and Stubley, P. Building services and environmental needs of information technology in academic libraries. *Program*, vol. 20, no. 1, January 1986, pp.26–38.

Pyle, J. and Harrington, S. *Making leaflets work: the librarian's guide to effective publicity.* Sheffield, Publicity and Public Relations Group of the Library Association, 1988. ISBN 095140430X.

Shapiro, E. Crash! *Byte*. vol. 13, no. 13, December 1988, pp. 137–138.

Stefanac. S. Mad Macs. *Macworld*, vol. 5, no. 11, November 1988, pp. 92–101.

Stevens, L. Window shopping. *Macworld*, vol. 5, no. 11, November 1988, pp. 186–188. A review of some products for securing Macintosh data through hardware security, password protection and data encryption.

Webster, B.F. Rescuing a hard disc. *Macworld*, vol. 6, no. 1, January 1989, pp. 144–151.

# Section 4

# Appendices

# Appendix A    Glossary

**A**
**application:** in computing circles generally taken to mean a piece of software used for a particular task e.g. a word processor or spreadsheet. Short for application program
**ASCII:** American Standard Code for Information Interchange. A standard format for transferring text files between different computers

**B**
**big screen:** a large display unit connected to the Macintosh to enable full A4 or A3 pages to be viewed at one time
**boot:** the act of starting up a computer by switching on the power
**bromide:** the photographic paper produced as output from an imagesetter
**bug:** fault in program that stops it working or brings it to a halt, invariably at the most embarrassing time for the user
**bullet:** • solid dot used for emphasis

**C**
**CD-ROM:** compact disc read only memory
**CDEV:** Control Device program with settings that can be varied from the Macintosh Control Panel
**chaining:** *see* linking
**cicero:** French typesetting measure of approximately 4.552 millimetres

**clip art:** pre-drawn graphics distributed on disc that can be used in DTP documents, generally without copyright payment
**Clipboard:** section of Macintosh RAM used for holding information that is to be transferred to another document or elsewhere within the same document
**Cropping:** cutting down or masking an illustration to exclude unwanted sections

**D**
**data encryption:** *see* encryption
**decryption:** rendering a previously encrypted document available for use, generally by keyboarding a password
**default pages:** the name given to master pages in XPress
**desk accessory:** program that can be called up at any time from the Apple menu and used on top of the current application
**desktop:** the grey background screen obtained on switching on the Macintosh
**dithered greys:** greys produced by devices that can only in reality display black and white. The greys are simulated by a controlled mix of black and white dots, in different proportions to give different greys
**downloaded font:** font resident on hard disc rather than in printer ROM and transferred to the printer at the time of printing

**dpi:** dots per inch, generally used to assess or compare printer resolution
**DTP:** desktop publishing, not desktop presentations

## E
**em rule:** — the longest of the rules (em, en, hyphen); used in US to denote ranges e.g. pagination of a bibliography
**embedded code program:** publishing software that uses codes entered in the text which format the document at the time of printing
**en rule:** – longer than the hyphen, shorter than the em rule; used in UK to denote ranges
**encryption:** protection of files by converting them into unintelligible form with password protection
**EPSF:** Encapsulated PostScript Format for graphics which enables printers to use PostScript but which has a PICT component for screen representation
**export:** make a file available for use by another program, possibly by saving in the program's native format

## F
**file:** discrete amount of data held on a disc for a specific task e.g. a single word processed document
**filter :** utility that enables a file in one format to be read by another program with which it would not otherwise be compatible
**folder:** location of several files on related topics held on a disc
**font:** complete set of characters in one style and size including uppercase and lowercase, numbers and punctuation
**fount:** traditional UK spelling of font

## G
**greeking:** the simulation of text by grey lines in a reduced view of the page
**grey scales:** the components of a digitised version of a photograph; dependent on the number of bits per pixel of scanner hardware and display screens

**grid:** a rectangular structure of page layout
**guide:** non-printing marker to aid the positioning of text and graphics on the page
**gutter:** binding margin; also the space between columns

## H
**halftone:** an illustration in which the various shades of grey are simulated by a pattern of black dots of various sizes. The image is photographed through a grid or screen which breaks the picture into dots
**HFS:** Hierarchical File System: the organisation of related files and folders in a hierarchy on a disc
**hyphen:** a short dash (shorter than the en rule) used where the first part of a word qualifies the second

## I
**icon:** graphic representation of an object
**imagesetter:** high resolution printing device for the production of typeset quality copy. Output is to photosensitive paper, film or printing plates
**import:** accept file, generally in a different format, into current document
**INIT:** Initial program that loads itself into RAM on startup

## K
**kerning:** adjustment of the space between letters, especially between specific letter pairs, so that one letter overhangs another

## L
**laser printer:** device using xerographic technology to produce medium resolution printed documents
**leading:** space between lines of text
**linking**: creation of relationship between two or more text boxes so that imported text automatically flows from one to the next

## M

**MacPaint:** the first Macintosh paint program; still used as a common file format for transferring graphics files between different paint programs

**master pages:** pages containing all the details of a publication that will be repeated from issue to issue; term used in PageMaker

**megabyte:** what at one time used to be considered a lot of memory

**MultiFinder:** pseudo multitasking system that permits more than one application to be resident in RAM at the same time

**multitasking:** performing several tasks simultaneously

## N

**network:** a group of computers linked together to permit the sharing of high cost resources such as printers

## O

**optical character recognition:** the conversion of printed text into machine readable form so that it can be recognised by a word processor for subsequent editing

**outline:** an early version of a document giving a broad idea of its content using, say, section headings

**outliner:** *also* **outline processor:** a program used to create an outline, generally with built-in flexibility to allow sections to be moved around as work progresses

## P

**page description language:** language used by a computer to define a complete page of a document – text and graphics – for passing to the printer. A good page description language will allow device independence

**pasteboard:** area used to hold type proofs and illustrations during page make up

**PDL:** *see* page description language

**phototypesetter:** *see* imagesetter

**pica:** unit of typographic measurement equal to 12 points

**PICT:** picture format developed by Apple and recognised by most DTP programs

**point:** basic unit of typographic measurement equal to 0.013837 inches – 72 points to the inch

**pop-up menu:** menu that springs from a dialogue box instead of being pulled down from the menu bar across the top of the document

**posted note:** note that can be attached anywhere within a document as a reminder to self or co-worker

**PostScript:** the primary page description language used in DTP; developed by Adobe Systems Inc.

**printer driver:** software that converts data from an application into a form that can be understood by the printer

## Q

**QuickDraw:** the programs in Macintosh ROM that generate images on screen

## R

**RAM:** random access memory

**raster image processor:** intermediary between computer and imagesetter which receives PostScript code and transmits it as a series of lines

**RIFF:** Raster Image File Format for handling scanned images

**RIP:** *see* raster image processor

**rivers:** white lines appearing to run vertically through a paragraph

**ROM:** read only memory

**runaround:** *see* text wrap

## S

**San Francisco:** sometime home of the Grateful Dead; font you shouldn't use

**scanner:** device for digitising line art, photographs and text

**smart quotes:** real quotation marks – ' and " – instead of misplaced flies legs

**Stationery Pad:** the technique used by MacAuthor for ensuring consistency between related documents; a type of template

**stripping:** process whereby individual components of a page are positioned for subsequent platemaking

**style sheet**: a set of characteristics to ensure consistency of paragraph formats throughout a document

## T

**tagged text:** text file marked up in such a way that style sheet information is automatically applied when imported into a DTP program

**text block:** rectangular area needed by some DTP programs before text can be added to a document

**text only:** a file containing text with no formatting instructions *see also* ASCII

**text wrap:** ability to flow text round the contours of any graphic object

**TIFF:** Tag Image File Format – developed to standardise a format for scanned images. Has not been entirely successful in this

**tool bar:** *see* Toolbox

**Toolbox:** used by PageMaker to denote the main facilities available for page make up. Other programs refer to tool bar and tool palette

**tracking:** adjustment of spacing between characters and words in a selected section of text

**type encoding:** *see* embedded code program

**typeface:** specific style or design of type e.g. Times, Helvetica

**typesetter:** *see* imagesetter

**typestyle:** a variation on a typeface e.g. bold, italic

## V

**virus:** self-replicating code that hides and runs itself when certain operations are carried out

## W

**WIMPS:** windows, icons, mouse, pull down menus: the visual interface of the Apple Macintosh

# Appendix B    Software directory

**Chapter 3**       DTP-specific packages

**PageMaker**

    Aldus UK Ltd..
    39 Palmerston Place
    Edinburgh
    EH12 5AU

    Tel:   031 220 4747
    Fax:  031 220 4789

**Ready, Set, Go!**

    Letraset UK Ltd.
    195–203 Waterloo Road
    London SE1 8XJ

    Tel:   01 928 7551
    Fax:  01 633 9456

**XPress**

| Manufacturer: | UK distributor: |
|---|---|
| Quark, Inc. | Heyden & Son Ltd. |
| 300 South Jackson Street | Spectrum House |
| Suite 100 | Hillview Gardens |
| Denver | London NW4 2JQ |
| CO 80209 | |
| | Tel:   01 203 5171 |
| | Fax:  01 203 1027 |

# Chapter 4    Word processing software for DTP

**FullWrite Professional**

    Ashton-Tate UK Ltd.
    Oaklands
    1 Bath Road
    MAIDENHEAD
    Berkshire
    SL6 4UH

    Tel:  0628 33123
    Fax:  0628 782682

**MacAuthor**

    Icon Technology Ltd.
    9 Jarrom Street
    Leicester
    LE2 7DH

    Tel:  0533 546225
    Fax:  0533 470706

# Chapter 5    Graphics software

**Cricket Graph**

| | |
|---|---|
| Manufacturer:<br>Cricket Software<br>Great Valley Corporate Center<br>40 Valley Stream Parkway<br>Malvern<br>PA 19355 | UK distributor:<br>Principal Distribution<br>Todd Hall Road<br>Carr Industrial Estate<br>Haslingden<br>Rossendale<br>Lancashire BB4 5HU<br><br>Tel:  0706 831831<br>Fax:  0706 211401 |

**Digital Darkroom**

| | |
|---|---|
| Manufacturer:<br>Silicon Beach Software, Inc.<br>9770 Carroll Center Road, Suite J<br>San Diego<br>CA 92126 | UK distributor:<br>TMC<br>Building 4<br>West of Scotland Science Park<br>Kelvin Campus<br>Glasgow<br>G20 0SP<br><br>Tel:  041 332 5622<br>Fax:  041 332 3209 |

**FreeHand**

    Aldus UK Ltd.
    39 Palmerston Place
    Edinburgh
    EH12 5AU

    Tel:  031 220 4747
    Fax:  031 220 4789

**ImageStudio**

    Letraset UK Ltd.
    195–203 Waterloo Road
    London SE1 8XJ

    Tel:  01 928 7551
    Fax:  01 633 9456

**SuperPaint**

| | |
|---|---|
| Manufacturer:<br>Silicon Beach Software, Inc.<br>9770 Carroll Center Road, Suite J<br>San Diego<br>CA 92126 | UK distributor:<br>TMC<br>Building 4<br>West of Scotland Science Park<br>Kelvin Campus<br>Glasgow G20 0SP<br><br>Tel:  041 332 5622<br>Fax:  041 332 3209 |

**The Visual Arts**

    Electronic Pen Ltd..
    Wren House
    Sutton Court Road
    Sutton
    Surrey
    SM1 4TL

    Tel:  01 642 4242
    Fax:  01 643 6453

## Chapter 6    Ancillary programs

**Acta**

| | |
|---|---|
| Manufacturer:<br>Symmetry Corporation<br>761 East University Drive<br>Mesa<br>Arizona 85203 | available from:<br>MacLine<br>Wren House<br>Sutton Court Road<br>Sutton<br>Surrey SM1 4TL |

**Gofer**

Manufacturer:
Microlytics, Inc.
300 Main Street
East Rochester
NY 14445

available from:
MacLine
Wren House
Sutton Court Road
Sutton
Surrey
SM1 4TL

Tel:   01 642 4242
Fax:   01 643 6453

**QuicKeys**

Manufacturer:
CE Software
1854 Fuller Road
PO Box 65580
West Des Moines
Iowa 50265

available from:
MacLine
Wren House
Sutton Court Road
Sutton
Surrey
SM1 4TL

Tel:   01 642 4242
Fax:   01 643 6453

**Spelling Coach Professional**

Manufacturer:
Deneba Software
3305 Northwest 74th Avenue
Miami
Florida 33122

available from:
a good Apple dealer

## Chapter 8          Library applications

**TOPS**

Sun Microsystems
TOPS Division
Sun House
31/41 Pembroke Broadway
Camberley
Surrey
GU15 3XD

Tel:   0276 62111
Fax:   0276 65220

# Chapter 9    The management of DTP

**1st Aid Kit**

Manufacturer:
1st Aid Software
42 Radnor Road
Boston
MA 02135

available from:
The Macintosh User Group
55 Linkside Avenue
Oxford
OX2 8JE

Tel:   0865 58027

**N'cryptor**

Manufacturer:
Mainstay
5311-B Derry Avenue
Agoura Hills
CA 91301

UK distributor:
TMC
Building 4
West of Scotland Science Park
Kelvin Campus
Glasgow
G20 0SP

Tel:   041 332 5622
Fax:  041 332 3209

**Symantec Utilities for Macintosh**

Manufacturer:
Symantec Corporation
10201 Torre Avenue
Cupertino
CA 95014

UK distributor:
TMC
Building 4
West of Scotland Science Park
Kelvin Campus
Glasgow
G20 0SP

Tel:   041 332 5622
Fax:  041 332 3209

# Index

1st Aid Kit 183

**A**
Acta 34, 70, 76, **117–9**, **154–6**, 169
Adobe Illustrator 43, 90, 92, 94, 98, 100, 104
Aldus FreeHand *see* FreeHand
Aldus PageMaker *see* PageMaker
Altsys Corporation 98
Amstrad PC 148–9, 164
Ann Arbor Softworks 77
Apple LaserWriter **5**, **23–4**, 47, 68, 78, 176–179
Apple Macintosh 4, **13–18**
   Macintosh II 16–17, 26, 106, 107
   Macintosh Plus 4, 15, 26, 72, 106, 107, 108, 159
   Macintosh SE/30 17
Ashton-Tate 77
Autoflow command (PageMaker) 39, 50, 139

**B**
Base styles (FullWrite) 81–2, 160
Bezier tool 85, 97
bibliographies 4, 81, 160
big screens **26–7**
book writing **156–61**
borders 64, 85, 104

**C**
case conversion 51, 72
CD-ROM 91, 116, **164–7**
CDEV 21
centralised DTP **174–5**

chaining *see* linking
change function *see* search and replace
Classify command (FullWrite) 83
clear command 20–1
clip art 34, 85, 91, **104–5**
Clipboard 20–1, 75, 85, 124
column rules 85, 164
consumables **176–8**
copy command 20–1, 120, 124, 149–52
costings **175–9**
Cricket Graph 34, 91, **103**
crop marks 132, 144
current awareness bulletins **147–56**
Custom styles (FullWrite) 81–2
cut command 20–1, 70, 76

**D**
dashes *see* em rule, en rule
data encryption 182
Dataproducts LZR-2665 printer 24, 179
data security 181
de-centralised DTP 44, 54, 65, 76, **174–5**
default pages 58, 60
   *see also* templates
default settings 39, 44, 50, 139
Design Grids (Ready, Set, Go!) 48, 49
desk accessories 20–1, 34, 40, 117, 122
desktop 18–19, 20, 45, 149
Digital Darkroom 34, 94, 106, **107–11**
Display PostScript 23
dithered greys 94, 106, 107
Document Manager (MacAuthor) 73
draw programs 19, 33, 34, **89–102**
drawing tools 43, 54, 64, 85–6, 143–4

199

**E**
em rule 9
em space 9
embedded code programs 6
en rule 9
encryption 182
endnotes 81, 84
EPSF 43, 52, 62, 75, 85, 90, 94–95, 100, 104
ERIC 165–6
exporting files from:
   FullWrite 81
   MacAuthor 70
   PageMaker 40
   Ready, Set, Go! 51
   XPress 60

**F**
file management 19, 184
file organisation 184
file transfer 148–52
file translators 150
filters 39, 119
find function *see* search and replace
First Aid Kit 183
flatbed scanners 27
font **8–9**, 15, 17, 24, 25
footnotes 72, 81, 84
format
   FullWrite 78–9
   MacAuthor 68–9
   PageMaker 37–8
   Ready, Set, Go! 46–7
   XPress 57–8
frames 36, 64, 69–70, **73–5**, 79
FreeHand 34, 90, 92, **98–102**, 169
FullWrite Professional 33, 51, **77–87**, 114, 117, **160–1**, 169

**G**
General Computer Personal Laser Printer 24
Get Picture command
   Ready, Set, Go! 52
   XPress 62
Get Text command
   Ready, Set, Go! 50
   XPress 59–60
Global links (Ready, Set, Go!) 50
Gofer 21, 34, **119–21**
graphic design 7, 91–2, 172–3

graphics boxes
   Ready, Set, Go! 52–3
   XPress 56–7, 62
graphics file formats **94**
   FullWrite 85
   MacAuthor 75
   PageMaker 43
   Ready, Set, Go! 52
   XPress 62
graphics handling
   FullWrite 85–6
   MacAuthor 73–5
   PageMaker 43, 141–2
   Ready, Set, Go! 52–4
   XPress 62–4
graphics software 7, 33–4, **89–112**
graphs 91, **103–4**
greeking 136, 142
grey scales 94, 106–7
Grid Setup (Ready, Set, Go!) 48
grids 36, 47, **48**

**H**
hard discs 15, 16, 17, **26**, 179, 182, **183–4**
hardware costs 175–6
HFS 19, 184
house style 166, 173, 174, 175
Hypercard 73

**I**
IBM PC 13, 33, 39, 119, 148, 169
icon bar display (FullWrite) **78**, 84
Icon Technology 67–8, 75
icons 18–19, 54, 55, 78–9, 95, 96, 98
Illustrator *see* Adobe Illustrator
Image control
   PageMaker 43
   Ready, Set, Go! 53
   XPress 62
imagesetters 5, **24–5**, 26, 44, 90, 106, 107
ImageStudio 34, 53, 62, 94, **107–11**
indexing 73
INIT 21
integral graphics
   FullWrite 85
   MacAuthor 75
   PageMaker 43, 141, 143–4
   Ready, Set, Go! 54
   XPress 64

integrated packages 7

**J**
JustText 6

**K**
kerning 9
keyboard enhancers **122–5**

**L**
layer control (FreeHand) 100, 101
layout 8, 162, 164
   FullWrite 79–81
   MacAuthor 69–70
   PageMaker 38–9, **134–8**
   Ready, Set, Go! 48
   XPress 58
Letraset 45, 48, 53, 54, 65, 106
library guide **131–46**, 162, 169, 172
linking 50, 55, 60
Linotronic imagesetters 25
lowercase command 51, 72

**M**
MacAuthor 6, 33, 39, **67–76**, 116, 120, 124, 139, 150, **154–6**, 158, **159**, 162, 169
MacDraw 85, 89, 90, 98
MacLightning 113, 114
MacPaint format 43, 52, 62, 89, 90, 92, 94, 95, 100
MacPaint program 5, 89, 90, 98
macros 122–5
MacSpirs **165–6**
maintenance costs 176
management of DTP **171–85**
Manhattan Graphics 45
markup language 6
master pages 162
   FullWrite 81
   MacAuthor 69–70
   PageMaker 38, **134–9**, 164
   Ready, Set, Go! 48
   XPress 58
   *see also* templates
measurement systems
   FullWrite 78
   MacAuthor 69
   PageMaker 37–8
   Ready, Set, Go! 47
   XPress 57–8

Meta-characters 72
Microsoft Word 39, 41, 50, 59, 61, 70, 81, 150, 159, 168, 169
mouse 18, 19–20, 97, 122–5, 140, 177
mover tool (XPress) 55, 56, 62
MultiFinder 18, 21, 78

**N**
N'cryptor 182
networks (TOPS) **148–52**, 182
newsletters 162–4, 169
notices 161–2, 169

**O**
operational practice 185
outliners 34, 70, **117–9**, 154–6, 169

**P**
page description languages 22–3, 25
Page Setup
   FreeHand 98
   FullWrite 79
   MacAuthor 68–9
   PageMaker 37, 132–3
   Ready, Set, Go! 46–7
   XPress 57
Page view (PageMaker) **136–8**
PageMaker 5, 8, 15, 26, 33, **35–44**, 46, 47, 48, 50, 51, 53, 54, 55, 56, 57, 58, 61, 64, 108, 120, **131–44**, **150–4**, 156, **157–8**, 164, 169
paint programs 89–90, 95–7
paper for printing 177–8
password control 148, 182
paste command 20–1, 76
pasteboard 36, 45, 56–7, 98, 136, 143, 144
PDL 22–3, 25
PICT 43, 52, 62, 75, 85, 90, 92–4, 100, 104, 141
PICT2 52, 94
picture boxes *see* graphics boxes
Picture menu (FullWrite) 85–6
Place command (PageMaker) 39, 43, **139–41**
plug-in paint tools (SuperPaint) 97
pop-up menus 20, 36–7, 56
Posted notes (FullWrite) 84
PostScript 6, 17, **22–5**, 75, 90, 92, 94, 100

201

Preferences
   PageMaker 38
   XPress 58
printers 5, 17, **22–5**, 175, 177–9
printing cost 177–9
pull down menus 18, 20, 21, 68, 135

## Q
QuickDraw 17, 24
QuicKeys 18, 21, 34, **122–5**

## R
Raster Image Processor 25
Ready, Set, Go! 8, 33, 37, 40, 44, **45–54**, 56, 57, 59, 61, 114, **158–9**, 169
replace function *see* search and replace
RIFF 52–3, 62, 94
ruler guides
   PageMaker 137–8
   Ready, Set, Go! 48
   XPress 58
rules 9, 85
runarounds
   FullWrite 86, 87
   PageMaker 43, 141–2
   Ready, Set, Go! 53
   XPress 62–4

## S
scaling 89, 90, **92**, 94, 104
scanned images 16, 91, 94–5, 100, **104–11**, 169, 184
   FullWrite 85
   MacAuthor 75
   PageMaker 43, 158
   Ready, Set, Go! 52–3
   XPress 62
scanners **27–8**, 91–2, 106, 107
search and replace 116, 158, 159
   FullWrite 82
   MacAuthor 72, 76
   PageMaker 40
   Ready, Set, Go! 51–2, 54
   XPress 61
security aspects 181
selective sorting 119, 154–5
sheetfeed scanners 27
sidebars (FullWrite) 78, **79–80**, 85, 86
Silicon Beach Software 95, 106
SilverPlatter 164–6

software selection 168–9
software training 180
sort facility 118–9, 154–5
spelling checkers **113–7**, 158
   FullWrite 82
   MacAuthor 73
   PageMaker 40
   Ready, Set, Go! 51, 54
   XPress 61
Spelling Coach 21, 34, 73, **113–7**, 158, 159
staff time for DTP 65, 132, 147, 173–4
staff utilisation 172–3
stationery (FullWrite) 81
Stationery Pad (MacAuthor) 68, 69–70, 155
Style Editor (MacAuthor) 71, 76
style sheets **40–1**, 150
   FullWrite 81–2, 87
   MacAuthor 68, 69, 70–2
   PageMaker 40–1, 139
   Ready, Set, Go! 51, 52
   XPress 61–2
style sheet tags *see* tags
SuperPaint 34, 85, 90, **95–7**, 141
Symantec Utilities for Macintosh 183

## T
tags 41, 50, 51, 150–4
templates 8, 152, 155, 162, 172
   FullWrite 81
   MacAuthor 68, 69–70
   PageMaker 38–9
   QuarkStyle 55
   SuperPaint 97
Tempo 124–5
text blocks (Ready, Set, Go!) 46, 48–51, 158
text boxes (XPress) 57, 59–61, 64
text editing
   FullWrite 82–4
   MacAuthor 72–3
   PageMaker 40, 157
   Ready, Set, Go! 51
   XPress 61
text entry 132
   Cricket Graph 103
   FullWrite 81
   MacAuthor 70
   PageMaker 39–40, **138–41**
   Ready, Set, Go! 48–50

text entry [cont.]
   XPress 59–60, 159
Text Specifications (XPress) 58–59, 61–62
text wrap
   FullWrite 86, 87
   PageMaker 43, 141–2
   Ready, Set, Go! 53
   XPress 62–4
thesaurus 82, 114, 116
TIFF 43, 52–3, 62, 75, 85, 94, 95, 107, 108, 158
Title command (MacAuthor) 72
toner cartridges 177
tool bar (Ready, Set, Go!) 45–6
tool palette (SuperPaint) 97
Toolbox (PageMaker) 36, 43, 135, 137, 141, 143
tools (XPress) 55–6
TOPS networking **148–52**, 182
tracking 9, 76
training 7, 36, 44, 65, 87, 92, 111, 148, 168, **179–81**, 182
translators (TOPS) 150
type encoding programs 6
Type specifications (PageMaker) 36, 41, 135–6
typography 8

**U**
Uppercase (MacAuthor) 72
user interface 13, 122
   FreeHand 98, 99
   FullWrite 77–8
   MacAuthor 68
   PageMaker 36–7
   Ready, Set, Go! 45–6
   XPress 55–7, 64

**V**
Visual Arts 14, 34, 91, **104–5**

**W**
wild cards 61, 72
WIMPS **18–22**, 165, 179–80
windows 18–9, 97
word count 61, 67, 68
Word *see* Microsoft Word
WordStar files 39, 148–54, 164
writing of books **156–61**

**X**
XPress 6, 33, 37, 40, 50, 54, **55–65**, 113, **159**, 169

DATE DUE